# FACING EAST

A PILGRIM'S

JOURNEY

INTO THE

MYSTERIES OF

ORTHODOXY

*Frederica Mathewes-Green*

HarperSanFrancisco
*A Division of* HarperCollins*Publishers*

Portions of material in chapters 13, 27, and 35 originally appeared in the following columns for Religion News Service: "Loving a Daughter and Letting Her Go"; "When There Is Faith, Death Can Also Be a Victory"; "Lives of the Saints, Lifestyles of the Stars." Copyright © 1996 by Religion News Service. All rights reserved. Reprinted with permission.

The Prologue first appeared as "In the Passenger Seat" in *Regeneration Quarterly*, Spring 1995.

Chapter entries for February 11, 17, 18, and 26 and March 5 first appeared as "A Year in Orthodoxy: Preparing for Lent" in *Image*, Spring 1995.

A portion of the chapter entry for March 12 first appeared in "Through a Glass More Clearly" in the September/October 1995 issue of *Books and Culture*.

A portion of the chapter entry for April 22 first appeared in "The Kissing Part" in *The Christian Century*, April 13, 1994.

A portion of the chapter entry for February 2 first appeared in "The Subject Was Noses" in the January/February 1997 issue of *Books and Culture*.

HarperCollins Web Site: http://www.harpercollins.com
HarperCollins®, ☗ ®, and HarperSanFrancisco™ are trademarks of HarperCollins Publishers.

Book design by Claudia Smelser
Set in Minion and Runic

FIRST HARPERCOLLINS PAPERBACK EDITION PUBLISHED IN 2006

*Library of Congress Cataloging-in-Publication Data*
Mathewes-Green, Frederica.
Facing east : a pilgrim's journey into the mysteries of Orthodoxy / Frederica Mathewes-Green.—1st ed.
ISBN 13: 978–0–06–085000–5
ISBN 10: 0–06–085000–0
1. Mathewes-Green, Frederica. 2. Orthodox Eastern converts—United States—Biography. 3. Antiochian Orthodox Christian Archdiocese of North America—Biography. 4. Orthodox Eastern Church—United States—Biography. 5. Spiritual biography—United States. 6. Spouses of clergy—United States—Biography. 7. Orthodox Eastern Church—Apologetic works. I. Title.
BX738.A759M385   1997   281.9'73—dc21   96-36700

06 07 08 09 10 RRD(H) 10 9 8 7 6 5 4 3 2 1

*With love*

*to my brothers and sisters*

*at Holy Cross Orthodox Mission.*

*Many years!*

# CONTENTS

PART III
**HOLY WEEK**

PART IV
**PASCHA**

PART V
**PENTECOST**

PART VI
## NATIVITY & THEOPHANY

## PART VII
## PREPARING FOR LENT

# PREFACE

## Full Disclosure

In offering this little book I realize that I am in danger of being mistaken for someone who knows what I'm talking about. Already I find acquaintances presuming I'm an expert on Orthodoxy. No, I'm only an expert on my own experience: what it's like to be a recent convert figuring my way along in a small mission church. It's a journey I'm enjoying very much, but that doesn't make me a church historian, theologian, or liturgical whiz. I have just enough education in theology to know that a little knowledge is a dangerous thing, and I urge those interested in loftier theory to consult others wiser than I.

My other, greater fear is that in my eagerness to celebrate this Church I love so much I have failed to convey its most constant feature, its majesty and dignity. The very act of writing an affectionate and somewhat humorous account like this is in itself a distinctively Western thing to do, and something of the essential Orthodox experience is likely to have been lost in the translation. If this is the case, I need the forgiveness of many, not least the reader. The best antidote is to come and see for yourself what I so clumsily try to portray. Come and learn firsthand what Orthodoxy is.

# PROLOGUE

## In the Passenger Seat

*Saturday, December 21, 1991*

---

# Vespers

He was an Episcopal priest, but he was standing in an Orthodox church on this Saturday night and thinking about Truth. At the altar a gold-robed priest strode back and forth swinging incense, moving in and out the doors of the iconostasis according to rubrics that were as yet unfamiliar. Golden bells chimed against the censer, and the light was smoky and dim. Over to the left a small choir was singing in haunting harmony, voices twining in a capella simplicity. The truth part was this: the ancient words of this vesperal service had been chanted for more than a millennium. *Lex orandi, lex credendi;* what people pray shapes what they believe. This was a church that had never, could never, apostatize.

She was his wife, and she was standing next to him thinking about her feet. They hurt. She wondered why they had pews if you had to stand up all the time. The struggling choir was weak and singing in an unintelligible language that may have been English. The few other worshipers weren't participating in the service in any visible way. Why did they hide the altar behind a wall? It was annoying how the priest kept popping in and out of the doors like a figure on a Swiss clock. The service dragged on following no discernible pattern, and it was interminable. Once the priest said, "Let us conclude our evening prayer to the Lord." She checked her watch again; that was ten minutes ago, and still no end in sight.

It was a long journey from that evening to my present life as an Orthodox priest's wife. For many, converting to Christianity or changing denominational allegiance is the result of a solitary conviction. As I ponder my pilgrim's progress to Orthodoxy, however, I realize that I didn't make the trip alone but in a two-seater. And I wasn't the one driving.

This is more relevant than may initially appear. Something about Orthodoxy has immense appeal to men, and it's something that their wives—especially those used to worshiping in the softer evangelical style—are generally slower to get. The appeal of joining this vast, ancient, rock-solid communion must be something like the appeal of joining the marines. It's going to demand a hell of a lot out of you, and it's not going to cater to your individual whims, but when it's through with you you're going to be more than you ever knew you could be. It's going to demand, not death on the battlefield, but death to self in a million painful ways, and God is going to be sovereign. It's a guy thing. You wouldn't understand.

When I asked members of our little mission, "Why did you become a member?," two women (both enthusiastic converts now) used the same words: "My husband dragged me here kicking and screaming." Several others echoed that it had been their husband's idea—he'd been swept off his feet and had brought them along willy-nilly. Another woman told how she left Inquirer's Class each week vowing never to go again, only to have her husband wheedle her into giving it one more try; this lasted right up to the day of her chrismation. I can imagine how her husband looked, because that's how my Gary looked: blissful, cautious, eager, and with a certain cat-who-ate-the-canary, you'll-find-out smile.

That night at Vespers a few years ago I was one of those balky wives. Gary and I stood side by side feeling radically different things, but the pattern could have been predicted from the beginning. When we first met over twenty years ago, he was a political animal who just didn't think much about God; I was a passionate agnostic, angry at God for not existing, eagerly attacking the faith of Christian friends.

Gary's shell began to crack when a professor required his philosophy class to read a Gospel. As he read the words of Jesus, he became convinced that here was one who "speaks with authority." Since Jesus said there was a God, Gary began to doubt his doubting.

This reasoning left me unconvinced. By the time of our wedding I was going through my Hindu phase, but I didn't object to visiting cathedrals on our honeymoon hitchhiking through Europe. One day in Dublin I looked at a statue of Jesus and was struck to my knees, hearing an interior voice say, "I am your life." I knew it was the One I had rejected and ridiculed, come at last to seize me forever. It was a shattering experience from which I emerged blinking like a newborn, and decades later I still feel overwhelming awe and gratitude for that rescue, that vast and undeserved gift. It's like the story of the farmer who had to whap his donkey with a two-by-four to get its attention. I imagine that when God needs a two-by-four this big, he must be dealing with a pretty big donkey.

True to form, Gary needed Truth, while I needed a personal, mystical experience. In the years that followed we went to Episcopal seminary together, were baptized in the Holy Spirit together, and spent several years in the early charismatic movement. He was ordained a priest, and we moved to a new church every few years, having babies along the way. When the charismatic experience grew stale, he rediscovered the high liturgical tradition of his childhood, while I went into spiritual direction and centering prayer. Though there are pitfalls along each of these paths—high-churchiness can devolve into form-but-not-substance, mysticism can float into goo-goo-eyed self-centeredness—neither of us lost our central commitment to Jesus as Lord. Wherever we went, God kept us near himself and each other.

As I shifted my aching feet on the floor of that dim church I wondered whether Gary's new direction would ever make sense to me. What had pushed him in the door of this church in the first place was growing unease with changes in the Episcopal Church, changes both moral and theological.

For example, in July of 1991 I was present for a vote of the Episcopal House of Bishops, a resolution requiring ordained clergy to abstain from sex outside of marriage. When the ballots were counted, the resolution had failed. I remember thinking, "This isn't a church anymore; it has no intention of following its Lord."

Meanwhile, it became fashionable to doubt Jesus' miracles, the Virgin Birth, even the bodily Resurrection. Before his consecration as England's fourth-highest ranking cleric, David Jenkins claimed that miracles were in the eye of the beholder. Of Jesus' physical resurrection he sniffed, "I'm bothered about what I call 'God and conjuring tricks.'" He was consecrated Bishop of Durham in Yorkminster Cathedral on July 6, 1984; two nights later, lightning struck from a cloudless sky and burned down a wing of the building. Beholders thought they might have seen a miracle.

Home in Baltimore such shenanigans were wearing on my husband. He banded together with five other "troublesome priests" and wrote a document asserting seven points of theological orthodoxy; they called it the Baltimore Declaration. It prompted a minor dust storm, but the national church lumbered on its way as undisturbed as a water buffalo by a mosquito.

Gary at last decided that he could no longer be under the authority of apostate bishops; he had to be in the line of Truth. But where to go? He briefly considered the "continuing" Anglican churches but felt he couldn't climb further out from the branch to a twig; if anything, he had to return to the trunk. Also, he began to believe that the compromising flaw lay at the very heart of Anglicanism. The beloved doctrine of "comprehensiveness" suggested, "Let's share the same prayers, the same words about the faith, but they can mean different things to you than to me." Not a common faith, but common words about the faith—mere flimsy words. A church at peace can survive this way; a church attacked by wheedling heresies must tumble into accommodation, reducing orthodoxy to shreds.

Roman Catholicism was the next obvious choice, and we looked into the Pastoral Provision whereby married Episcopal priests can become married Catholic priests. But, ironically, pro-Provision literature gave us serious doubts. One book by a priest's wife painted an unintentionally grim picture; would we have to sell our furniture and live in a furnished apartment, never be allowed to retire, be ordered to teach high school instead of pastor, and be fourth on a huge staff under supervision of people whose views were uncomfortably similar to those of the Episcopal bishops he was fleeing? Despite that author's cheery "it was worth it all," it sounded to me like jumping from the frying pan into the fire.

Then there was the matter of theology. We remained worried by traces of salvation-by-works theology in Catholic practice and a habitual tendency to frame human relations with God more as business transaction than as love affair. Catholic theology seemed in general too overdone, compelled to parse every sentience and split every infinitude.

Gary was invited to join a small group of Protestant clergy for an evening with Orthodox evangelist Father Peter Gillquist, and he went carrying some hard questions; Father Peter later said he thought Gary was the one present that night who would never convert. But the questions were evidence of urgent wrestling. Gary particularly needed assurance that the Orthodox cling to salvation given by God's loving grace, not earned by human effort. Father Peter directed Gary to the fourth-century commentaries of St. John Chrysostom. In a sermon on 1 Timothy, for example, Chrysostom says that the best purpose of the law is to reveal that it cannot save us; it then "remits us to Him who can do so."

Then I reencountered a history lesson that had eluded me in seminary but now took on vital importance. For the first thousand years, the thread of Christian unity was preserved worldwide through battering waves of heresies. The method was collegial, not authoritarian; disputes were settled in church councils, whose decisions were not valid unless "received" by the whole community. The Faith was indeed common: what was believed by all people, in all times, in all places. The degree of unity won this way was amazing. Though there was some local liturgical variation, the Church was strikingly uniform in faith and practice across vast distances, and at a time when communication was far from easy. This unity was so consistent that I could attribute it to nothing but the Holy Spirit.

Then a developing split between East and West broke open. The Church had five centers: Jerusalem, Antioch, Alexandria, Constantinople, and Rome. The bishop of Rome was accorded special honorary status but no unilateral power to determine doctrine or to command the other bishops. However, by the eleventh century the concord between the four Eastern centers and Rome was disintegrating. The East believed the papacy was seeking expanded power over the worldwide Church and balked particularly at Rome's insistence on adding the word *filioque* ("and the Son") to the Nicene Creed, a statement of faith that had been in common use since 325 A.D. So serious a change as rewording a creed would have to be won by consensus in church council, not imposed by command.

While the *filioque* controversy sounds at first picayune, it had theological reverberations that are significant, as disputants at the time realized. In an effort to elevate the second person of the Trinity, it dilutes the singular authority of the Father and changes the Trinity from—visually speaking—a triangle with God the Father at the top to one tipped over, both Father and Son above the Spirit. Orthodoxy is indeed "patri-archal," that is, the Father (the *pater*) is the *arche*, the source and font of all.

In Orthodoxy the all-male priesthood is not based on the idea that women can't represent Jesus; if replication of the specifics of the Incarnation is the goal, only a first-century Jew could come near that. In Orthodoxy, it's not Jesus but the Father whom those serving at the altar represent, and whatever else a woman can be (and in Orthodoxy she can be anything else: choir director, lector, teacher, head of the parish council), she cannot be a Father. She can be a Mother, of course, and so there is a recognized and honored role for the priest's wife, with a title: *Khouria* (Arabic), *Matushka* (Russian), or *Presbytera* (Greek).

The *filioque* controversy, then, had implications that reach further than initially appear. The bishops of Antioch, Constantinople, Alexandria, and Jerusalem objected that the Holy Spirit would not have waited a thousand years to clarify the role of the bishop of Rome and that a church council would be necessary to amend the creed. The conflict grew worse, and the legate of the pope excommunicated the patriarch of Constantinople on Christmas Day of 1054 A.D. The patriarch returned the favor, and the split was on.

When West severed from East in this four-to-one split, the Orthodox churches continued united, as they have to the present day (Russian Orthodox, Greek Orthodox, and so forth being just national expressions of the same worldwide church). Unlike the Western church, the church of the East went through Christianity's second millennium without being shattered into fragments by theological disputes. This is despite horrific persecution and martyrdom: twenty million Russian Orthodox are estimated to have been martyred in this century alone.

Once unchained from the need for consensus with other bishops, the Western church continued freely developing Christian doctrine, while the East had laid the task to rest with the end of the seventh Ecumenical ("worldwide") Council in the eighth century. As Western Christian theology grew more elaborately defined, it offered more fodder for protest and eventually for Protestantism. Five hundred years after the East-West split, the Reformation emerged, spurred by a desire to whittle back to the simpler original. But though some Reformers read the Church Fathers and made an effort to learn from Orthodox leaders, barriers of geography, culture, and language made cross-fertilization difficult. For the most part, the Reformers relied on the Bible as their only guide, and it's a book that sincere people can interpret in wildly different ways, as shown by the existence of nearly twenty-five thousand different Protestant "Bible-based" denominations. Subsequent generations continued the split from ancient practice. Like untrained gardeners going into an overgrown garden, successors to the Reformers hacked about with machetes, slashing unknowingly through material that had been affirmed for the first thousand years: the sacraments, the honoring of Mary, the eucharistic Real Presence. Protestants were trying to rediscover the ancient Church, but instead they created a dancing array of sorcerer's apprentice brooms, all trying to sweep one another clean.

The constant experience of doctrinal disagreements contributed to a Western tendency to make the Christian experience more about ideas than about heart-driven living faith, more what you think than what you do; more *assensus* than *fiducia*, more ideas about God than surrender to him. The Orthodox Church, escaping this sort of discord, could admire a butterfly without having to pin its head to a board. Orthodoxy has had many failings and controversies, but they are most often about use and abuse of earthly power; they are not about theology. It's not yet perfection on earth, but there is to a refugee Westerner a certain bliss in bypassing theological arm wrestling about things too big for our puny understanding. For example, rather than overdefining Jesus' presence in the Eucharist or tossing out the concept entirely, Orthodox are content to say that the bread and wine become his body and blood simply because they "change." In Orthodox theology there is a humility, a willingness to let mystery remain beyond comprehension.

The stance of an Orthodox believer is similarly humble and childlike: we are sinners, receiving the overwhelming love of God, and we stand before him in gratitude. This is, I think, one of the reasons we kiss so much; we kiss icons, the Gospel book, the cross, and one another. Most Sundays we use the Divine Liturgy of St. John Chrysostom, and we thank God for sending his Son "into the world to save sinners, of whom I am chief." Grateful repentance is such a constant in Orthodox worship that mystic surfers, looking for smells, bells, and thrills, rather than submission to Jesus as Lord, find they can't take more than a couple of weeks—not without conversion.

I paint here in hindsight a rushing tide of conviction about the truth of Orthodoxy, which swept my husband away. At the time, I was having none of it. Orthodoxy was too foreign, too old, too fancy. I didn't care what they said, I just couldn't believe that this was what the worship of the early church looked like—all the cluttered doodads of gold, incense, and fancy vestments.

My vague assumption was that early Christians just sat around on the floor, probably in their blue jeans, talking about what a great guy Jesus was. It was embarrassing to review Scripture and realize that from Exodus to Revelation worship is clothed in gold, silver, precious stones, embroidery, robes of gorgeous fabric, bells, and candles; I don't know of an instance of scriptural worship that doesn't include incense. God ordered beauty, even extravagant beauty, in worship even while his people were still wandering the desert in tents. Beauty must mean something that no-nonsense, head-driven Christians fail to grasp.

Gary was rarin' to go, but I put on the brakes. Oddly, I wasn't concerned about finances, even though becoming Orthodox meant throwing away a fifteen-year career when our three kids were entering their teens. Nor did I feel loyal affection for the Episcopal Church, either nationally or in our little parish (where, as a cultural conservative, I often felt like the odd man out). But I was afraid we would be leaving for the wrong reason: because we weren't happy. Too many people break up marriages, shirk obligations, and betray commitments because they feel insufficiently fulfilled. Besides, even if the Episcopal Church was lost to apostasy, didn't God need chaplains on the *Titanic?* Hadn't we better stay where he planted us?

But Gary's dedication to Truth was stronger than my hesitation, and I finally agreed to go along. On January 30, 1993, I found myself standing before Bishop Antoun as he anointed me with holy oil, calling out, "The seal of the gift of the Holy Spirit!" "Seal!" the congregation shouted. Five other families came with us from our Episcopal parish that day, and two weeks later we celebrated our first liturgy, at a homemade altar, in a borrowed space, with borrowed appointments. Three years later, Holy Cross Mission numbers forty families—nearly every one a convert.

A continent away someone I've met only by mail is writing me a letter. She's a multigeneration evangelical, descended from missionaries and professors at Christian colleges. Now her husband has begun looking into Orthodoxy and shows the signs, so familiar to me, of beginning that plummeting dive. Her words, too, are familiar:

> This is a church whose disciplines and life, I feel, appeal initially more to men. To me it all seems so . . . hard. In my spiritual walk up to this point my heart has led my head. I might go to church

mad and unrepentant, but with a worship chorus in a lilting tune or a heartfelt spontaneous prayer, my heart would begin to soften. I'd come out ready to live the obedient life.

Orthodoxy makes sense in my head, but I yearn for something to grab my gut and help me over the hump labeled "self." All the "soft" music, and so forth, that used to draw me is missing, and I'm left in this massive struggle with my will. Does that make sense? Doesn't a spoonful of sugar help the medicine go down, and all that?

And how do women eventually come to terms with this somewhat austere church?

How did I? Now I can't imagine ever not being Orthodox. Here is my home, my joy, my fulfillment; I tasted and saw, and nothing can compare. But how did I get past the bare truth part, the aching feet part, to discover the rich, mystical beauty of Orthodoxy?

A kaleidoscope of images flashes through my mind. The textures, the scents, the music of the liturgy, a continuous song of worship that lifts me every week. The Great Fast of Lent, a discipline far more demanding than I'd ever faced in my Christian walk. Kneeling on Holy and Great Thursday and listening to the hammer blows resound as my husband nailed the icon of Jesus' corpus to the cross; seeing my daughter's shoulders shake with sobbing. Easter morning giddiness and champagne at sunrise. Hearing my son say that after a year of the Divine Liturgy, he didn't like the sentimental hymns of the last three hundred years anymore: "They make me feel further from God." Seeing icons change from looking grim and forbidding to looking challenging, strong, and true. True.

Truth turns into Beauty in unexpected ways. What was strange and perplexing has become my sweetest home. As I look over my shoulder, I can see this friend not far behind me on the road, on the cloverleaf of conversion, and it's by now a familiar sight. Her husband is driving, and she's in the passenger seat.

# 1

*February 11, 1995*
*St. Blaise the Martyr*

WEEK OF THE PUBLICAN AND THE PHARISEE

## How to Make a Church

How to Make a Church: My husband, Gary, was an Episcopal priest for fifteen years. Believing that that great hulk of a denomination was about to shipwreck in apostasy, repealing the creed and condoning immorality, he led us out—myself, our daughter, and our two sons. A handful of others came with us from our Episcopal parish: a widow; a young woman whose husband doesn't attend church; a pair of newlyweds; a couple with four young children, the oldest son autistic; a couple with two teens, the dad in a wheelchair with multiple sclerosis.

At the end of January 1993, we were chrismated together into the Orthodox Church, and my husband was ordained a priest. (Chrismation is the initiation rite that brings previously baptized Christians into the Orthodox Church; it's analogous to confirmation in the West.) Two weeks later—Valentine's Day—we celebrated our first Divine Liturgy in the echoing front parlor of an empty old house. We were Holy Cross Antiochian Orthodox Mission of Catonsville, Maryland. There were more letters in our name than there were of us.

How to Make a Church: Basil sized up the room and began pointing. A massive, scarred oak library table stood in the middle of the floor, ringed with bulky crate-built wooden chairs. Residue from the room's weekday tenants—adults with psychiatric disabilities—still littered the tabletop: dried glue, glitter, smears of red elementary school paint, spattered coffee stains. Another table, a long folding contraption with a ruined top, had been set up toward the back and surrounded by orange plastic chairs with tubular chrome legs. A jumble of other chairs and boxes dotted the floor.

"Okay," Basil said, waving a hand. "All of this hasta go."

Holy Cross Mission had quickly outgrown our parlor and subsequently had moved to this space, the home of ReVisions, an adult day care program. The building itself is lovely, an 1878 red brick schoolhouse with a high white vaulted ceiling, beam braced, here in the assembly room. High in the arch of the wall behind the altar-place is a large window made of eighty square mullioned panes. The view through the old glass is wavery, though a few crisp replacement panes interrupt almost rudely. Through the seasons I can see the heights of the spreading tree next door change colors, shed leaves, then burst with the "sticky little leaves" of spring (I think of my tormented co-religionist, Ivan Karamazov). Birds shoot past without warning, softly distorted by the old glass as if swimming underwater, then snapped into focus by a new pane.

The upper twelve feet of the room are lovely, but at eye level it is cluttered with bulletin boards, mismatched shelves, Valentine's Day decor, cubbyholes, and a defunct aquarium. There is a strong scent of industrial cleaner. I stand on the left with the choir every Sunday and look across the room at a Parcheesi game and a sewing machine on the top of a tinny metal cabinet. They never move.

The visual story of this room, descending from the airy ceiling and window, through the jumble, ends with the floor: rubber linoleum squares in bright streaky green. The only eye-level touches with any charm are the aged slate blackboards, devouring large sections of wall and framed in wood. Some of these are set with what must have been the controller for a primitive central-heat-and-air device: a big black disk of iron, topped with a big black lever. The lever swings from left to right, allowing two alternatives: "WARM AIR" or "COLD AIR."

All of this hasta go, or at least as much as is portable. Basil heads the Temple Set-Up/Take-Down team, and he's a natural take-charge guy: about sixty, with sharp black eyes, a Greek nose, and the pear-shaped figure that must inevitably come to a short-order cook. His team today includes Frank, a retired hotel exec who was chrismated with his wife Jeanne just a few months ago. Frank is a small mountain of a guy, with the feigned gruffness of a city-beat cop; simultaneously large and compact, he looks like somebody pushed him together with a snow plow. Jeanne is fluffy and good-natured, and I call her Smiling Jeanne to differentiate from Hard-working Jeannie, the parish workhorse.

The other guy on the team, Jay, is one of the original band of converts and came with Heidi and the four kids. It is his son, Jared, who is autistic. Jay looks worn lately. Jared at nine is getting big and pretty strong, and though he's usually quiet he still sometimes interrupts the liturgy with a scream or sudden lunge. I try to take those moments as gifts; they serve to remind me of how little I comprehend of the things of God. The distance from Jared's understanding to mine is short compared to the distance from me to the mind of our Holy God. I take communion as lost in incomprehension as Jared; all I can do is receive.

While Jay and Basil shift the tables and chairs, my husband and Frank pull out from the corner a wooden cube, about a yard on each side, and turn it around. This is our altar. "You want to empty all this out first," Gary tells Frank, "and then when it's unloaded and light we can put it in place." Inside the back of the altar the shelves are stocked with a brass blessing cross, brass candlesticks, glass cruets, tall candles, votive candles, and a silver-covered Gospel book. This new one replaced our original Gospel book, which had been given to us secondhand by another parish when we first started out. "I'm afraid it looks pretty worn," the priest had apologized, "because it's been kissed so much." Orthodox kiss a lot.

I don't know what to call my husband. New converts usually take saints' names when they're chrismated, and when we became Orthodox he went from "Father Gary" to "Father Gregory." But when I tried calling him "Gregory" around the house he frowned. I had said "Gary" for over twenty years; now, he said, it sounded like I was talking about another man. At church I fumble for the right appellation; once I called out a default "Oh, Sweetie," but that didn't seem right, either. In public I try to remember his official name and say "Father Gregory," but at home he's just plain ever-was Gary to me.

He brings out next the incense supplies in a brimming cardboard box: charcoal disks, plastic bags of the fragrant nuggets of resin, and a brass censer, worn by polishing, with round bells on its chains. When the clients return on Monday, the place won't smell of industrial cleaner.

Still more comes out of the back of the altar, like clowns pouring out of a circus car: the pieces of three metal music stands and two large wooden easels; an old red Oriental rug I bought at a thrift shop; two large icons and about twenty smaller ones; altar cloths and vestments, a processional cross and segmented pole, and a stand for the censer. I recognize with a pang of nostalgia the squat four-legged stool that sits under the processional cross: my fifteen-year-old son, David, made it a decade ago while going through a fit of hammering the scrap wood in the garage. He painted the square top chartreuse, which contrasts interestingly with the green floor. Last, Frank peels back the movers' quilt that covers the altar all week. The golden altar boy robes are folded on top, and my David's is very, very long.

While Jay sweeps, Basil drags chairs and arranges them at the edges of the room. Orthodox traditionally stand for worship, so we don't have pews or rows of chairs; the center of the room is empty, and the faithful will cluster there (though never as close to the altar as my husband prefers). A few chairs are left at the edges of the room for those who need to sit from time to time; standing is not rigidly enforced. Most of us sit during the sermon, many simply sinking cross-legged to the linoleum.

In this, as in many things, variation abounds. While we avoid sitting, some Orthodox churches, especially those that bought their building from another denomination, will have pews and use them. Liturgical music should be sung without instruments, but those who acquired an organ with their building often use it, too. Some congregations worship in English and some in other languages or a mix; those who use English use different translations. When someone is chrismated, does the congregation respond "Seal!" or "Amen!"? Depends; are they Antiochian Orthodox or Russian?

Some things, like that last item, vary among jurisdictions (those organizational bodies of believers identified by their ethnic roots); some, like the strictness with which the fasts are observed, vary among parishes and even among individual church members. Some practices, like the requirement that communion be received following a strict fast from food and drink, are uniformly honored everywhere. Discovering what may change and what is immutable took up much of my confusing first years as Orthodox, and I have much more to learn.

Basil notices my scribbling. "Ya taking inventory?" he asks. "That's a gal after my own heart." Then, a little louder, "Keep an eye on that Jay. He's sumpn' else." Basil continues muttering as he shuffles chairs. "That Jay, he's a trip. I tell ya. Keep an eye on him."

Time for Vespers is drawing near. My daughter, Megan, almost eighteen, arrives with David and Stephen, the youngest. Stephen turned thirteen just a couple of days ago, making me officially the mom of three teenagers. I was wary about this landmark, but so far I appear to have retained any marbles I had. Right behind them is Rose, who has just taken over the volunteer position of church secretary and is suitably laden. She's fresh from the office supply shop and is burdened with paper: the new church directory (pink), the monthly newsletter (blue), and tomorrow's service bulletin (green). "I think every church in town has people in there copying on Saturday afternoons," she tells Gary. "I also made copies of that flier for the theological conference, and I gave one to an A.M.E. pastor I met at the shop. He says he's going to come visit our church." Rose is also carrying three homemade loaves of communion bread, or prosphora, for tomorrow; it was her turn on the roster to bake.

Rose and Tom had met in a Bible study back at our last Episcopal church, and their wedding was one of the last my husband performed there. They didn't come over in the first wave of converts but have joined us more recently, and Rose is a hard worker who has quickly made herself indispensable. Not long ago she miscarried her first pregnancy, and it hit her pretty hard. It's good to see her looking chipper today.

The altar is set in place about five feet from the back wall of the room, with the processional cross behind it and the small Oriental rug in front. "If you pull the rug up close," Gary tells Frank, "it conceals the little plastic things the altar slides on." There needs to be room on all sides of the altar because the priest will circle it, swinging incense, during the liturgy. Another five feet in front of the altar, Frank sets up the two wooden easels, to the left and right of the rug. Onto the right one he hefts a large icon of Jesus, looking very stern in judgment; onto the left goes another icon, this one of an almost-smiling Virgin Mary and infant Jesus nuzzling cheek-to-cheek. The baby's little bare foot is turned up toward the viewer. Icons are of certain standard designs, and one like this is called "Sweet-Kissing Jesus."

Before every Orthodox altar there is an iconostasis or icon stand. In some churches it is a virtual wall, blocking view of the altar, with doors through which clergy and altar boys appear and disappear. At the other, minimal, end is an arrangement like ours: Jesus on the right, Virgin on the left (though we call her "Theotokos," God bearer, in stubborn refutation of an ancient heresy that claimed Mary bore only Jesus' humanity). Most Orthodox churches are as full of icons as they can be, a visible reminder of the heavenly community surrounding us in worship. Once Frank has the big icons in place, he begins setting votive candles and smaller icons all along the windowsills, top and bottom, and across the top of the blackboard. It is like opening a family scrapbook and seeing beloved faces of friends.

Meanwhile, Gary is hammering a loose corner of the altar back into place. "Several people have offered to make us a new altar," he says. It is getting a little shabby. "But I hope we'll be in our own place before long, and I'd hate somebody to build one till we're in. I'd hate to have it done now and not fit." It's not wise to construct a cube-shaped altar until you've measured the doorways; you can't just turn it on its side and angle it in. Cubes are stubbornly cubes, no matter which side is up.

The last pieces are falling into place. In the entryway there are several icons, which worshipers will kiss hello on the way in, plus a box of sand in which to set taper candles, with prayers for special needs or for the departed. The altar is set with two large brass candlesticks, the brass blessing cross, and the Gospel book. A side table, the table of preparation, holds two candles, the priest's belt and lace-on cuffs, Rose's prosphora loaves, an icon of the Nativity, the red napkin the altar boys hold under the communicant's chin, and a small thermos (during the Eucharistic Prayer the wine is mixed with hot water, as the priest says, "The warmth of faith, full of the Holy Spirit"). Gary also puts out a flashlight-shaped water sprinkler and the order of blessing for an icon, in case someone shows up with a new one to be blessed.

It is forty minutes since they started, and the room is complete. Gary looks around and says, "Okay. Now it's a temple." Once he makes this pronouncement, no one is to go past the two large icons without a liturgical reason. He turns to me and says, "We should have become Quakers. Then we'd just come in here and take stuff down."

Basil is my husband's stoutest supporter, a pillar of Holy Cross. He is one of our only "cradle Orthodox"; apart from Basil, his eighty-six-year-old mother, Lillian, and his son, Michael, we are almost all converts.

When experienced converts hear the term *cradle Orthodox* a set of images flashes to mind, not all complimentary. Eager converts, aflame for the faith, sometimes complain that cradle-Os are stodgy and lacking in a deep commitment to the Lord—the vocal evangelical-style commitment they favor.

The collision is not unpredictable. Cradle-Os are immigrants (or are their children and grandchildren), and the immigrant's impulse is to submerge in the dominant culture and be accepted. This runs headlong into the conservative Christian's penchant for challenging the status quo. Likewise, the Orthodox faith emphasizes receiving: mysteries, mercy, forgiveness. It doesn't naturally emphasize showing off an individualized, emotional response to those mysteries. Cradle-O believers may not easily put into words faith that can run very deep.

Basil grew up Greek Orthodox. He spent his life flipping burgers over a hot stove at Pete's Grill, the family business begun in the nineteen-teens; son Michael grew up there, standing on a crate to wash dishes at the age of eight. Pete's Grill stood around the corner from our church on Frederick Road, the main road through Catonsville, sandwiched between a fire station and a hair salon.

To the east Frederick Road slips inside Baltimore city limits and winds through blue-collar neighborhoods, past brick rowhouses with marble steps; west, it rolls for forty country miles toward the city of Frederick. But here in Catonsville it is narrow and cluttered, lined with shop buildings a hundred years old. It has not been gentrified. Seedy bars alternate with a military recruiting station, a thrift shop, an upholsterer's, a Realtor's. There is little new construction, but most of the old has been improved with large plastic signs. Bill's Music beguiles customers with one displaying a giant portrait of Bill, circa 1970; he looks like the early Sonny Bono. The street is a scrapbook of Catonsville history, ancient and modern. Just a few doors from the grill is a large, wordy wooden sign proclaiming "Village Park, 1967" and thanking its founders; it stands on a patch of dirt and shrubs twelve feet on a side, surrounded by parking lot. I like to picture all the folks out in bell bottoms on dedication day.

Six miles west on Frederick Road, people are driving through quaint 'n' charming Ellicott City and exclaiming, "Oh, isn't it adorable!" Ellicott City has been redone within an inch of its life, the old shops filled with forty-year-old "antiques," astrology books, crafts, crystals, and health food.

But no one drives through Catonsville's main drag thinking it's adorable. They're too busy cursing the lack of parking.

Until Pete's Grill closed last year, my sons and I could stop in for a late lunch after school. Up three steps from the street, through a narrow screen door lay a tiny space with four well-used tables and creaky brown bentwood chairs. A high counter separated customers from the work area: jumbled ledges, giant condiment bottles, and a furnacelike industrial stove. There Basil stood in a spattered apron, sweating furiously (the place was not air conditioned), slapping burgers on the grill barehanded. The fastidious would not be pleased, but for the kids it was an adventure.

The burgers were huge and overladen with stewed onions and chili. They came as close as any could to meriting the claim painted six feet high on Basil's windows: "Praise Jesus! World's Number One Cheeseburger!" and "Praise Jesus! World's Number One Chili Dog!" On each window the artist had lovingly portrayed the celebrated meals, brilliantly colored and Olympian in size.

Basil had had a somewhat wayward life and had been divorced twice. Then, a few years ago, he had undergone a conversion experience and came through it fired with zeal. When the windows were improved, so was the shop's interior: the name of Jesus was written on just about every notice, menu, or bit of wall decor available. The side wall was decorated with an assortment of icons, a glossy da Vinci *Last Supper* made more useful with the addition of a gold-toned clock, and ancient grammar school religious art by Basil's nephew. On the counter stood a blunt painted-plaster version of the Lourdes Grotto, with Bernadette admiring a rocket-shaped Virgin. Above this jumble of devotion the pinky-tan walls grew ever more brown as they ascended, shellacked with the grease smoke of a million Number One Burgers.

When converts hear *cradle Orthodox,* they don't think of someone like Basil. His exuberance was such that my husband had to ask him not to holler out "Amen!" during the sermon (he said it threw him off; Gary, after all, used to be Episcopalian). He also asked him to refrain from shouting "Axios!" at other points of the service. In an Orthodox ordination service the bishop proclaims the ordinand worthy, and the people respond "He is worthy!" in English, Greek ("Axios!"), or Arabic ("Moustahiq!"—though my untutored ear at first heard "Moosehead!"). Basil is emphatic about my husband's worthiness, but he was persuaded to refrain from voicing it. Basil is emphatic about most things; his characteristic line is, one finger held high, "I tell you *one* thing."

I tell you *one* thing. When Basil is in charge of setting up the temple, it gets done. Axios!

WEEK OF THE PUBLICAN AND PHARISEE

## Beef Stew on Friday

I feel a little twinge of guilt as I open the can of beef stew. It's a Friday, when Orthodox are usually fasting from meat, but this is the week of the Prodigal Son, and there's no fasting. There's a reason to grab advantage of this dispensation: Lent is coming, just ten days away. After the Sunday of the Prodigal Son comes the Sunday of the Last Judgment, also known as Meatfare Sunday. After feasting that day, we'll have no more meat for the eight weeks until Pascha (a.k.a. Easter). Not even breaks on Sundays.

That's the least of it. The Sunday after Meatfare is Cheesefare. From that day for the following seven weeks, Orthodox will eat no meat, cheese, milk, eggs, or any dairy products and no fish with backbones (shellfish is allowed, but not tuna). We'll also use no olive oil, wine, or alcoholic beverages. We'll read a lot of labels: do they use milk solids in these crackers? Are there eggs in the tube of cookie dough? We'll feel, sometimes, grumpy and deprived. Television ads for burgers will strike with an almost hallucinatory force.

We'll share discoveries on Sunday: there are no dairy products in guacamole; here's a recipe for eggless chocolate cake; yes, you really *can* get used to tofu. Christians of many denominations fast, but few do it all together and few at such rigorous length. Here at Holy Cross Mission we'll join Orthodox around the world in a united fast as we prepare for Pascha.

We don't even get to feel self-righteous about this discipline. Orthodoxy is clear that salvation can't be bought; any good deeds we do are just tools to bring us into deeper yieldedness, repentance, and gratitude. A hymn appointed for mid-Lent warns,

> In vain do you rejoice in not eating, O soul!
> For you abstain from food,

But from passions you are not purified.
If you persevere in sin, you will perform a useless fast.

Aw, shucks.

Gary said the other day that he could feel Lent coming "like a freight train." There is no way to prepare for a discipline like this. This is our third Lent, and I know from the past two the bottomless well of deprivation that opens in the midst of that time. I want to devour as many goodies as I can now, while I have the freedom to do so. I bought a bag of chocolate peanuts and a box of chocolate mints, plus a couple of candy bars, and hid them in my desk; milk chocolate, after all, will be forbidden because of the milk. By the time I finished it all I felt pretty crummy. At one point I found myself thinking, I'll be glad when it's Lent and I don't have to eat all this chocolate anymore.

WEEK OF THE PUBLICAN AND PHARISEE

# Vespers Before Lent

The church was darkened except for the altar and a few lights illuminating our service books. We had gathered for Vespers, the Saturday evening service that marks the beginning of Sunday observance; at our mission Vespers attendance is not as large as Sunday morning's, and so there were about a dozen of us standing here and there in front of the altar.

In the middle of the floor David had set up his music stand. David's wife, Margo, is our usual choir leader, but this night she was home preparing a teaching on Orthodox music for the church women's group. They are both converts: her dad pastored a nondenominational church in Michigan that gradually studied its way into Orthodoxy, and David was American Baptist. Because we've got two Davids—this one and my teenaged son—I'll call the choir director's husband "M. David." *M* is for Musical.

Both Margo and M. David are gifted musicians with beautiful voices, which is fortunate because Orthodox music is intended to be all a capella. Two years ago they took our congregation, an assortment of folks who had never sung without an organ, and gradually built up our courage in singing without that handrail. They taught us to feel at home with the Byzantine and Russian chants that strike the Western ear as so haunting and profound. Eventually a choir of six or eight emerged; depending on who shows up, we have two-, three-, or four-part harmony, leading the rest of the congregation. Thanks to Margo's genius and firm leadership, we sound pretty good. Father Peter Gillquist, the Antiochian jurisdiction's overseer of missions, called us "the best small choir in America."

This night M. David stands before his open worship book, rocking slightly on his heels and waiting for my husband to begin. M. David waits well. His whole manner suggests suspended time, patient anticipation, a languid, quiet joy. He is attenuated in form as in presence, tall and graceful, and from the height he observes with a mild, fond detachment. The first time I met them was a year before we converted, at the crowded coffee hour at another Orthodox church. Pretty, bright Margo engaged me in chatter right away, while M. David stood far above us, turning his face left and right like a periscope. Then I thought he was aloof; now I know he's just quietly observing, waiting. My sons, altar boys, remark on how blissful he looks as he takes communion.

The Saturday Vespers service, like the Divine Liturgy, changes very little from week to week. In about forty minutes we sing psalms, intercessory litanies, and the ancient Phos Hilaron, one of the oldest hymns of the church. St. Basil the Great, writing in the fourth century, noted that it was already so old no one remembered who had written it:

> O gladsome Light of the holy glory
> of the immortal, heavenly, holy, blessed Father:
> Jesus Christ.
> Now that we have come to the setting of the sun

and behold the light of evening,
we praise God: the Father,
Son and Holy Spirit.
For meet it is at all times to worship thee
With voices of praise, O Son of God and Giver of life;
Therefore all the world doth glorify thee.

Year round all these pieces are mostly the same, but one set of verses (*stichera*) changes every week. M. David sings these alone. His voice is golden colored, dropping with liquid weight through the lines appointed for this week, the Lenten-preparation week of the Prodigal Son:

> I was entrusted with a sinless and living land, but I sowed the ground with sin and reaped with a sickle the ears of slothfulness; in thick sheaves I garnered my actions, but winnowed them not on the threshing floor of repentance. But I beg Thee, my God, the pre-eternal husbandman, with the wind of Thy loving-kindness winnow the chaff of my works, and grant to my soul the wheat of forgiveness; shut me in Thy heavenly storehouse and save me.

Such a typically Orthodox hymn: just-as-I-am abjection but with a flourish of elegant rhetoric, doffing one's plumed hat with a gallant bow. It is also a disarmingly intimate prayer—that, too, is very Orthodox—and M. David prayed it tonight for all of us, his honey voice falling through the still, dark air. Candles flickered, and we looked down at the green linoleum floor. Lent is coming.

*Sunday, February 26*
*Meatfare Sunday*

SUNDAY OF THE LAST JUDGMENT

# Busy Sunday

Gary once read a study of businessmen who had been asked to describe a typical week. They listed the meetings and appointments peculiar to each workday, then were asked if their current week matched that schedule. "No," most responded. "This week is an exception." The typical week doesn't exist.

This Sunday is an exception. Last week we drove south to visit family and returned late Saturday, so everything was backed up. This morning I left Megan to bring her brothers to church and dashed to the grocery store because it was my team's week to bring refreshments for coffee hour. I grabbed the easy thing, a big tray of Danishes, and bought a second one for my afternoon meeting. Orthodox fast before Divine Liturgy, so when it's over we're ready for real food. I hoped that Smiling Jeanne and Hardworking Jeannie, the other people on my team, were bringing food realer than this, but I didn't have time to simmer meatballs and cube cheese.

I dashed to the church late and ran to place the pastries in the cafeteria room we use for coffee hour. Two more large trays of sweet rolls were already in place. I slipped into the choir in time for the hymn that comes before the Epistle. I was pretty late.

Like Vespers, the Divine Liturgy changes little from week to week. I had just missed one of the few variables, the hymn (*kontakion*) appointed for the day. It was another stinger:

> When thou comest, O God, to earth with glory, and all creatures tremble before thee, and the river of fire floweth before the Altar, and the books are opened and sins revealed, deliver me then from that unquenchable fire, and make me worthy to stand at Thy right hand, O righteous Judge.

An hour later I swept through the coffee-hour room, piled a paper plate with pastries, grabbed a cup of coffee, and ran to the car. My afternoon meeting was an hour away, by a diagonal route that wound down narrow roads, past woods and farms. I don't work on Sundays, but this week is an exception. I'm a freelance writer, which makes for an ideal work-at-home, flexible-hours life, provided making a living is not one of your priorities. Writing leads to speaking engagements, which has me traveling once or twice a month; speaking leads to more writing. Writing means I interview people, and writing and speaking means other people interview me. Truth be told, this whole business is a small-town square dance, and the mere ability to stand behind a podium or sit under television lights can get you treated as an instant expert on a surprising number of topics.

The topic I've most concentrated on is pregnancy and abortion prevention, representing a pro-life approach sometimes termed "seamless garment" (opposing war, abortion, euthanasia, and the death penalty). The meeting I'm heading for is a Common Ground session, bringing together pro-life and pro-choice advocates in dialogue. I was a pro-choice feminist in college, so increasing understanding between the two sides is important to me. Last fall a pro-choice friend and I organized a daylong workshop with the help of Mary, a conflict-resolution mediator. We have been meeting on Sunday afternoons every six weeks or so ever since, continuing to talk.

The last meeting was only a few days after the Brookline abortion clinic shooting, and the resulting conversation was vivid and deep. I was especially touched by an articulate pro-choicer, a gay rights lawyer with an AIDS lapel pin who consistently referred to "violence outside abortion clinics."

"I know some of the shooting has been inside clinics," he said, "but I want to differentiate between these shootings and abortion itself. I know you pro-lifers believe that what goes on inside abortion clinics every day is violence." Moments like that are the reason for Common Ground.

When I arrived today, late, the group of fifteen turned my way. Mary the mediator said, "We'll forgive you if you brought pastries again." I held up the plate and was greeted by laughter and applause. "Pro-life, pro-choice," I said, "but everybody's pro-Danish."

Four hours later I am driving back down the darkening roads, feeling more subdued. My friend with the AIDS pin has just lost his job; we'll meet for lunch next week to discuss the group's purpose statement. I wonder how I can help him. He is a lanky, dry-tempered man, Jewish, detached, and quietly ironic. A chasm deeper than the abortion debate, a chasm of faith, divides us; I don't know how to bring encouragement to anyone without bringing them to Christ. On the car stereo the singer is unreeling a sonorously deep voice, intimate songs about his wrestling with God. Leonard Cohen is

Jewish, with a lanky and dry-tempered voice, murmuring quietly ironic lyrics. "Complain, complain, that's all you've done, ever since we lost," he sang. "If it's not the Crucifixion, then it's the Holocaust."

The sprawling shopping center has a health club at one end and an all-you-can-eat buffet at the other, and I do them in the right order. After lifting weights, riding a bike, and swimming laps, I scoot down—still running late—to meet my family at the restaurant for a last-day-before-fasting meal. But all I have had to eat all day is pastries, and I want lighter fare than the slabs of beef on my kids' plates. After wolfing down salad and fruit, I realize I don't have much room for the prime rib, ham, chopped steak, and fried chicken. This makes me sad.

Gary and the boys are up making repeat trips to the carving bar. "Go ahead, Mom," Megan says. "It's your last chance. Just eat as much as you can. That's what I'm planning to do." This is probably not the correct Orthodox attitude, but I do my best to follow her advice.

When I walk in the house, my office phone is ringing; it is my friend Connie, another pro-family activist, calling to describe a population control conference she'd just attended. When I ask a pro-forma "How are you?" she responds, "My quadriceps are killing me." Connie is Byzantine-rite Catholic; her church is under the authority of the pope but uses the same liturgical and devotional practices we do. She has just finished the evening service for Cheesefare Sunday, which we will do next week. The Catholics, and the rest of Christendom, are a week ahead of us this year on the Paschal schedule. The Cheesefare evening service, Forgiveness Vespers, requires a lot of bowing, and Connie thinks she pulled something in the process.

This whirlwind Sunday is barely over, but Connie reminds me of the next one looming up ahead, when Lent will officially begin. Complain, complain.

# 2

## LENT

*Sunday, March 5*
*Cheesefare Sunday*

FORGIVENESS SUNDAY

---

## Forgiveness Vespers

"Lent begins on page fifteen," M. David is fond of saying. On the evening of Cheesefare Sunday, about thirty of us are standing here and there on the green linoleum floor, holding the little purple service booklets that will bring us to that moment. We are surrounded by evidence of the current concern of the building's daytime tenants, and it isn't Lent; as at schools and shopping centers, the decor here plunges manically from one holiday to the next. As soon as the St. Valentine's red came down the St. Patrick's green went up, and handmade versions of leprechauns and pots of gold adorned the walls. Pinned up behind the choir is a shamrock cut out of cardboard and painted with a thin wash of green, with a border of silver glitter. Upside-down letters still command through the paint: "EEP REFRIGERA." Holy Cross Mission is honoring St. Patrick, too, in our own way—his icon is on the windowsill above the table of preparation—but tonight we are thinking more about the journey through Lent to Pascha.

The Vespers of Cheesefare Sunday evening begins like any Vespers, with litanies and psalms. The variable verses or stichera appointed for this evening begin with abasement and move to jubilation: "Let us begin the fast with joy! Let us cleanse our soul and cleanse our flesh! . . . That we all may see the passion of Christ our God, and rejoice at the holy Pascha!" As we follow along in the purple booklets I watch the page numbers count down.

At page fifteen my husband moves toward the table of preparation. There's a silent pause as he changes from gold vestments to purple-black brocade, a sweep of fabric that seems to blot the light. When he returns to the altar we sing the next "Lord, have mercy" to a new tune, the minor melody used in Lent. The moment is grave yet exciting, something like the first lurching ascent of a roller coaster. No turning back now.

We sing through the litany, say the Prayer with Heads Bowed, and sing the Song of St. Simeon, as recorded in the Gospel of Luke: "Lord, now lettest thou thy servant depart in peace." Basil's son, Michael, then leads us in chanting forty "Lord, have mercys," running the words together Byzantine style: "Lord have mercyLordhavemercyLordhavemercyLordhavemercy," he intones. Michael is a slender man in his late thirties, and when he sings he opens his Greek-black eyes very wide but holds his mouth nearly closed. I believe this is the opposite of what voice coaches usually recommend; nevertheless, it lends the song an effective dark and cavelike tone. The forty-fold "Lord have mercy" is a distinctively Orthodox practice; it's rumored there's a bumper sticker that says, "Honk 40 times if you're Orthodox."

We come at last to the fourth-century Prayer of St. Ephrem the Syrian, a prayer used frequently during Lent:

O Lord and Master of my life! Take from me the spirit of sloth, despair, lust of power, and idle talk.

At this point the booklet instructs the worshipers to make a prostration. We fold where we are standing, dropping to our knees, a process that takes longer for some than others. We place our palms on the floor, then lean forward to touch the floor with our foreheads, then stand up again. A prostration is a shuffly process. Seeing prostration was one of the first things that moved Gary toward Orthodoxy; he said, "That's how we should be before God."

The Prayer of St. Ephrem goes on:

But give rather the spirit of chastity, humility, patience, and love to Thy servant.

Another prostration here. More shuffling.

Yea, O Lord and King! Grant me to see my own transgressions and not to judge my brother, for blessed art Thou, unto ages of ages.

A third prostration.

This is followed by saying twelve times, "O God, cleanse me, a sinner." With each one we make a deep bow and sweep our right hands to the floor, a movement called a *metania*. Orthodox worship is a full-body event.

We sing through the dismissal, but no one moves to go. My husband turns from the altar to stand before the gathered worshipers. "Now we are going to do something the devil hates," he says. "Any time brothers and sisters in Christ stand face-to-face and ask for one another's forgiveness and give forgiveness, the demons shudder. We intend here," he goes on, "to build an outpost of the Kingdom of God. These outposts are built brick by brick, person by person. With every act of forgiveness, we extend the Kingdom of God in our midst."

He gives directions for all the worshipers to form a long line, extending to his left; they move into place, standing along the side wall and facing the center of the room. Then he says, "The first person in line—in this case, my son, David—will stand in front of me. He'll make a prostration or a metania—you can do whichever you want—and ask for my forgiveness. And you can say this however you want: 'Forgive me for all my sins against you,' or 'Brother, please forgive any way I have offended you,' or any variation, whatever comes naturally. I'll offer forgiveness, then I'll bow to him and ask him to forgive me as well. Then we'll embrace.

"After that, David, you'll move over here to my right. The next person in line will go through the same forgiveness process with me, then with David, then stand on David's right. And so forth; we'll continue until everyone has moved over to my right side, and every person here has exchanged forgiveness with every other one."

The six of us in the choir begin singing quietly the song that we will trumpet on Pascha morning: "Let God arise! Let his enemies be scattered!" Gary and David stand face-to-face, or as nearly so as they can; David at fifteen is several inches taller than his dad. David's dark blond hair curls on his shoulders, and his blue eyes behind wire-framed glasses are wide and peaceful; this son is a quiet, centered sort. I watch father and son bow to each other and murmur unheard words. The rest of the congregation watches quietly, and David looks a little awkward; he hates being the center of attention. David and Gary embrace, and tears sting my eyes. I look quickly back to the music.

A moment later I look up to see David embracing his younger brother, Stephen. Where David is a cool stream, Stephen at thirteen is a geyser, full of passionate opinion, deep sentimentality, wide-flinging love, and, not infrequently, anger. There were things to be forgiven there. The brothers embrace, David bending stiffly over; powerhouse Stephen is compact, nearly nine inches shorter.

By the time the choir finishes the anthem and joins the end of the line, about half the worshipers have moved to my husband's right. One at a time I bow to people I worship with every week, looking each one in the eye, men and women, children and aged. Each interchange is an intimate moment, and I feel on the wobbly border between embarrassment, laughter, and tears. Just to pause and look at each fellow worshiper for a moment, to see the individual there, is itself a startling exercise.

Individuals respond to the ritual in individual ways. When I ask twelve-year-old Melanie to forgive me, she says, "Not that you've *done* anything, but okay." Basil is giving out enveloping bear hugs with exclamations of "Praise Jesus! Praise Jesus!" His son, Michael, offers a courtly, "I forgive, as God forgives." Choir director Margo is teary-eyed as she hugs me and bursts out in a whisper, "I love you!" Down the line, as worshipers dip and bend, embrace and move aside, it looks like a dance, a dream-paced country dance laced with dreamy smiles.

I come to my daughter, Megan, who will be eighteen in a few days. She has made it safely to adulthood past an adolescence that had its rocky places; yes, there are things to forgive here, too. I bow to her and manage to say, past the lump in my throat, "Megan, please forgive me for any way that I have offended you." I could think of a million mistakes I had made. She looks at me, her lashes wet, and says, "I forgive you, Mom." Then she bends to touch the floor and stands again and says to me, "Please forgive me, Mom, for everything."

Can a mother do such a thing? You bet. A moment later we are in a marshmallowy embrace.

Back in the cafeteria Rose is packing away the book table, putting everything in boxes until next week. Her husband, Tom, is sitting nearby at one of the dining tables; Rose doesn't permit help with this careful process. Tom is wearing a happy, somewhat surprised expression.

"That wasn't so bad!" he says as I come in the room. "You know, I'm not one of those people that's big on hugging. I don't like to hug a lot. But that wasn't so bad!" He throws his arms around his own shoulders and gives a squeeze to demonstrate. "That was okay!"

Tom and Rose make a contrast in several ways: she's Dutch-blond with thick, cascading locks, while a fair proportion of Tom's locks has departed completely. She has a dry, droll wit and a sub-dued manner, but Tom is habitually as bright and bouncy as a boy on Christmas morning. When we started home-schooling the kids for the first time this year, we called on Tom for help; Gary teaches David, and I teach Stephen, but we send Megan to Tom's house for physics. There are some things even I can't be an instant expert on.

Rose is stacking small icons face-to-face and placing them by layers in a cardboard box. Book tables are a staple of Orthodox churches; there are few Orthodox bookstores where our peculiar goods can be bought, and these packable shops fill the need. On the spread table there remain copies of about thirty books, mostly about Orthodoxy, saints, and prayer; incense, charcoal, and small censers, for home use; Orthodox magazines; and the seal used to press an imprint in altar bread as it rises. There are stacks of church calendars, which are usually funded by the local funeral parlor. I was amused by these calendars when I first saw them, because they demonstrate so clearly the Orthodox passion for displaying icons in every feasible way and even in some unfeasible ones. My leaning, as a calendar designer, would be to decree that the tiny squares allotted for each day are too small to stuff with icons; the written notes needed for the day would have to be absurdly abbreviated, or even turned sideways, to fit, and the icon itself would be too small to appreciate. Obviously the designers of Orthodox calendars do not agree.

There are also icons, or iconic images, on a stack of T-shirts and sweatshirts printed by our home-grown iconographer, Carolyn. Carolyn owns a silk-screening shop, and when she began painting icons it felt natural to put some on her T-shirts. But not long ago when I was wearing one an Orthodox monk teased me, "How are we supposed to venerate that icon?" The Orthodox custom is to kiss icons, an awkward prospect when one appears on the front of a lady's shirt. I went back to Carolyn with this jest, and she said, "But they're not really icons. I left the names off, on purpose." On a real icon, she explained, the name of the subject floats near his or her head; the T-shirts bear no such "Hi, My Name Is" labels. (Another priest tells me, with a smile, "But when you really love a saint, you don't have to see his name to want to kiss him.")

There are pro-life bumper stickers, and others reading "Orthodoxy: Proclaiming the Truth since 33 A.D." We all use this, though it doesn't quite hit the mark; still, it improves on the previous version, which read ". . . Telling the Truth . . ." That one seemed to imply we were telling something else before the year 33.

Larger stretches of table are becoming visible as Rose fills her boxes. "This is great," she says. "It looks like I'm going to have a whole empty box left over. I guess that shows I did sell some stuff this weekend." The last thing to go in are the prayer ropes, or *chotkis;* these are analogous to a Roman Catholic rosary but are loops of knotted black yarn. For each knot, the user recites the brief "Jesus Prayer": "Lord Jesus Christ, son of God, have mercy on me, a sinner." This prayer discipline has spread far beyond the bounds of Orthodoxy, thanks to a popular Russian book of the last century, *The Way of the Pilgrim* (and J. D. Salinger's reference to that book in his novel *Franny and Zooey*). Prayer ropes come in a variety of sizes, from thirty-three knots to three hundred; many Orthodox, like my husband, habitually wear a small rope around a wrist.

My sons, divested of their acolyte robes, come in, and I set them carrying boxes to Rose's trunk. As my husband follows them in, Tom tells him happily, "Hey, that was okay!" He put his arms across his chest again, hands on shoulders. "I'm not used to hugging so much. But once I got into it, I really didn't mind." He hugs himself once more. "That was okay!"

It takes an hour or so to take down the icons, blow out the candles, and pack everything back into the altar. Though there are more helpers, the mood is relaxed and chatty, and no one is in a hurry to leave. At last the altar is shrouded under its gray blanket in the corner, and the old oak table once more commands the center of the room.

As we step out the front door my two boys break into a run, shouting, "I get the front seat!" Megan puts her arm around me as we amble along. I look up at a black sky spattered with stars.

In a few weeks we'll be standing here again, under the gray dawn sky, preparing to enter to begin the Easter service. My husband will pound on the door, as we all stand clustered behind him, trembling a little with the chill and anticipation. He will shout, "Lift up your heads, O ye gates, and be lifted up, O ye everlasting doors, that the King of Glory may enter!" Someone from inside will respond with the line, "Who is the King of Glory?" We'll all know the answer to that.

A desert stretches between that night and this, but it is a desert that will disclose sudden, startling blooms. I wait to see them.

Lent has begun. Pascha is coming.

FIRST WEEK OF GREAT LENT

# Icons

Jesus is lying on his side on my dining room floor, leaning against the radiator, balanced up on one finger and one toe like a gymnast. He is flattened, just a sheet of painted wood, and from pointed toe to the tip of his halo he is about four and a half feet tall. For protection, for storage, Jesus is swathed in a blue tablecloth that has been knotted around his ankles and pulled up over his head. When I push it aside I can see his form, a crucified body without a cross. His extended arms are like the wings of a bird; he floats in sorrow, head sunk toward one shoulder, eyes shut, face washed with death.

His arms are spread like gull wings; he flies like Superman to save us. But Superman flew twinkle-bright with punchy fists out front, and our Jesus floats, wide armed, fistless, hands open and drilled useless with holes. He comes to save us broken, hobbled, and swathed here on my dining room floor. It is the only way he can save us; it is the only way we can be saved.

For many, many years, I didn't like icons. I kept this a secret. People I respected loved icons dearly, so I knew there was something I just didn't get. I didn't admit this because I didn't want to look dumb. My kids have a saying: "I played it off." It's what you do when (how familiar!) you want to pretend you understand something: laughing at an obscure joke, nodding at an opaque reference, all in the name of saving face. A friend would pause before an icon, and I would hear that sharp intake of breath and her words, "Oh! Isn't it *beautiful.*" "Yes," I'd agree, "how marvelous." I searched the image, trying to find something other than a wizened, severe, and apparently angry Christ. I was thinking, What's beautiful about this? But I played it off.

I can see, in retrospect, that my problem wasn't with the role of icons, just with the style of them. When Megan was a toddler we spent many a bedtime story with a little yellow cloth book titled *The Little Lost Lamb*. The shepherd climbed over rocks in search of his lamb; he would not let it go. The last page showed Jesus surrounded by children, and the text read: "Jesus is our Good Shepherd. He loves us and will always take care of us."

"This is Jesus," I told little Megan. "He loves you. We *love* Jesus," I said and kissed the picture. "I love Jesus, too," she repeated and gave it a noisy smack.

When David came along I went in search of something sturdier for permanent display. I bought a small laminated plaque of a gentle, smiling Jesus and wrote on the back the date and this inscription: "So that David can know Jesus." Again, we kissed this picture good-night. I knew this was only the thinnest glimmer of who Jesus was, that it omitted a great deal of what Christianity entails, but I urgently wanted to establish this beachhead: Jesus is real, he loves you, you can love him, too.

My problem, then, was not with using images of Jesus or depictions of Bible stories or heroes of the faith. I knew our love wasn't being lavished on a laminated plaque but was being offered through the picture to the Lord himself. The image was like a window, a seen object opening us to things unseen.

I had a dim idea that Orthodox icons were something different from this; I thought they were end-in-themselves objects of worship, idols. I was wrong. Orthodox often use the same analogy I did, calling icons "windows into heaven." St. Basil the Great explained, "Honor shown to the icon passes to the prototype it represents." It's not the wood and paint that matter but the Lord pictured there.

So why did the Lord pictured there have to look so scary? A dozen years ago Gary and I were at the cresting wave of the Episcopal renewal movement; every Wednesday night I played guitar at the Prayer 'n' Praise service, and we sang happy songs about a Jesus who loved much and demanded little. Everything about renewal was bouncy and bright; icons looked then like the manifestation of a sad faith, a faith that was cramped and sour.

But eventually the renewal movement began to taste stale; it seemed forced and even a bit desperate. There had to be something deeper. I had been in spiritual direction for about three years, keeping a brief version of daily hours and spending nightly time in wordless adoring prayer, when I read about a show coming to Baltimore's Walters Art Gallery: icons, as early as the tenth century, that had never before been seen outside Greece. Gary wanted very much to go. Yes, that would be wonderful, I said—playing it off.

The Walters, to its credit, had endeavored to present the icons as something more than merely "good art." Gary Vikan, the guest curator of the show (which was titled "Holy Image, Holy Space"), wrote, "We had a second, more ambitious aim. Namely, we hoped to present the icon on its own terms, not simply as art, but as sacred art . . . born of equal measures of art and spirit." To that end, the show began with carved wooden church doors, then led to a reconstructed chapel of icon frescos. Byzantine liturgical music, haunting and strange, drifted through the air. I began to understand the mood of solemn awe that inspired these paintings.

Directly in my path stood a towering icon of Jesus holding an open book, right hand raised in blessing. Red letters floated on the gold background on either side of his head: *IC XC, H Sophia Tou Theou;* Jesus Christ, the Wisdom of God. His face was a subtle mix of emotions: though the brows were knit, the brown eyes were wide and kind. Light wrinkles radiated from the corners under his eyes, even suggesting a smile. The text on the book was in Greek too advanced for me, but I could make out the root for "forgive."

Moving closer, I realized that the sheet of Plexiglas covering the icon was smeared. No, I saw with surprise, that was lipstick. In fact, there were a dozen kiss marks scattered over the face of the Plexiglas. Kisses! Who would kiss a painting in an art museum? And who would feel moved to kiss this painting in particular? This icon wasn't as harsh as some I'd seen, but it was still a far cry from Megan's Good Shepherd.

The path led on to another standing icon, this one two-sided, scarred at the bottom where a pole had been attached for procession. The side facing me had the familiar outlines of a Madonna and Child, but this Madonna was different from any I'd seen. Her heart was clearly broken. The Virgin's eyes stared wide with shock and sorrow, dark pooled and seared with pain; they darted sideways, away from us, away from her child, resting unfocused in midair. Her head was ducked forward, held low in an attitude of helpless imploring; her halo had turned a dull brown-green. One hand was lifted to gesture toward the child, not a gesture of pride but of helpless resignation. The watery fingers were transparent, ripples in her robe showing through.

I thought about "a sword will pierce your heart also," and I wondered what she could see that we couldn't. When I walked around to view the other side I got my answer. A brutal image filled the panel: Jesus dead, head sunk to one shoulder, magnificent and broken.

The sight arrested me; I felt pinned to the spot. The image was badly damaged, with large areas of paint peeled away and exposing the pitted raw wood. Jesus' head filled the center of the panel, tipped to one side, as round as his tilted halo and capped with streaming black hair. His eyes were closed with eyebrows lifted peacefully. His mouth was relaxed, drawn down, with only a touch of red on the lip as a reminder of life. All over the surface of that beautiful face ran the scars and scratches of eight hundred years, and all over the Plexiglas were dotted the kisses of the faithful.

The magnificent head was set on an inadequate body: arms thin and useless, held pinched against the torso; shoulders round as wheels; an unnatural, wide-ribbed breastbone. He had no neck; the head was not joined to the body but lay awkwardly over the upper chest like a coin. This broken body was set before a wooden cross, and behind it the background was not gold but a somber dark blue. The border was a brilliant crimson.

I don't know how many minutes I stood there transfixed by the searing beauty of this silent image. I felt that there was something here I had not met before in religious art, indeed in conventional Western devotion. So much of my journey to that point had been focused on me, whether it was the giddy fun of renewal or the more recent self-improvement project of spiritual direction and centering prayer (a kind of soul aerobics). But looking at this icon, I felt aware of nothing but him. I was flooded with love for his sacrifice. How could it be that he would do this for me, who had once spent years in anger and rebellion, ridiculing him and even trying to undermine the faith of Christian friends? Yet he had come to claim and rescue me when I was lost, endangered as a lost lamb on a rocky cliff. For me he had suffered this ultimate humiliation, abandoning all his power. I read the plaque on the cross above his ruined head: Jesus Christ, the King of Glory.

That was enough for me. When we reached the end of the exhibit, Gary and I picked up a handful of brochures; they included photos of several of the icons, including, fortunately, the King of Glory. At home we set up shop in the garage, sawing boards to size, spray-painting them red, and sticking the cut-out icons on with decoupage glue. I wanted this King of Glory with me everywhere. I put one over my desk, one on the bedside table, one over the kitchen sink, one over the washing machine, even one on the dash panel of my car. Gary, meanwhile, had bought some full-sized icon posters and was applying them to larger stretches of lumber. The garage fed out a strong scent of spray aerosol every time the door was opened, and a fine red mist was settling on all the stacked boxes. Spare minutes after dinner found us rushing back in to saw another board or smooth wrinkles from the damp paper faces. We thought we were making icons.

Today after liturgy we're sipping coffee while waiting for Carolyn to begin her Sunday school lesson on the painting (properly, the "writing") of icons. She lays out one at a time the ones she's currently working on, images of the Virgin and saints at various points of materialization. This lesson in icons was scheduled for today because this first Sunday in Great Lent is called "Sunday of Orthodoxy" or sometimes "Triumph of Orthodoxy." The triumph has to do with icons.

When a Christian bows before an icon and kisses it, why isn't this idolatry? A fervent battle raged over this in the eighth and ninth centuries; when the iconoclasts (icon smashers) were in the ascendance they did such a thorough job that few icons from before the tenth century now remain. But the concern had simmered intermittently in Christendom for many previous centuries.

One defense, which strikes me as sweetly childlike, was "How could they be idols? They're pictures of Jesus. If it was a picture of Baal, that would be an idol. But Jesus is God!" The icon of a holy person or scene could not be unholy.

At the same time, the pro-icon party, the iconodules, were clear that the icon's tangible substance did not capture or imprison divine reality. St. Theodore the Studite (died 826) suggested that it was like the impression left by a signet ring. Whether pressed into wax, clay, or any other material, it leaves the same seal; these materials can faithfully convey something they do not intrinsically possess. "The same applies to the likeness of Christ," St. Theodore wrote, "irrespective of the material upon which it is represented."

A frequent defense of icons is that it is not the image that receives the honor but the Lord whom it depicts. The icon is a focal point, an open window through which we offer devotion, not an end in itself. Leontius of Neapolis (died ca. 650) said, perhaps testily, "When the two beams of the cross are joined together I adore the figure because of Christ who was crucified on the cross, but if the beams are separated I throw them away and burn them." Of course, we treasure the physical icon just as we might a photo of a distant loved one, and the more ancient and beautiful an icon is the more precious it seems. But Orthodox have no illusion that an icon itself is a god. They distinguish between worship—given only to God—and veneration, the honor that may be accorded an icon, a saint, or the Theotokos.

Still, there seems something shocking about using representations of Jesus in our worship. It is the same shock that is sometimes called "the scandal of particularity"—that God who is ineffable and invisible, who commanded that no image of him be made, took flesh and became a baby. He became visible, concrete, with shocking specificity: a man of a certain height, build, and eye color, eating a real roast fish on a Sunday afternoon. Because God chose to become visible, we can represent him, the iconodules insisted; we can represent any person or event in his story because these are manifestations of God's will to invade earthly life, to make himself concrete and visible. What he chose to make visible, we should reproduce in visible fashion; "What God has cleansed you must not call common," the overly scrupulous apostle Peter was warned.

The iconodules grasped that to diminish the role of icons was to undermine the Incarnation. If it were conceded that matter was shameful or evil or merely inconsequential, all of orthodox

Christology would begin to totter. The countless battles over the full humanity of God the Son had taken centuries to resolve, and iconoclasm, they saw, was a last infiltration of the anti-Incarnation spirit. Just as Jesus come-in-the-flesh was a sign of God's intention to restore his whole earthly creation, icons are a foreshadowing of that restoration: a holy seal impressed on humble wood and paint.

The use of icons was vindicated at a church council meeting in Nicea in 787; this was the seventh and last ecumenical church council, the first having also met in Nicea (to write the Nicene Creed) in 325. I say "the last," but in theory there could always be another, if the Holy Spirit so moved. These seven councils, where the whole church met to come to consensus on theological disputes, constitute the foundation of the Orthodox faith.

This morning at the end of Liturgy we recite a portion of the proclamation written at the seventh council, and it is triumphant indeed. The instructions say we are to read this "in a loud voice"; one of the pleasures of Orthodoxy is the opportunity to be emphatic all together!

> As the prophets beheld, as the Apostles have taught,
> as the Church has received, as the teachers have dogmatized,
> as the Universe has agreed, as Grace has shown forth,
> as Truth has revealed, as falsehood has been dissolved,
> as Wisdom has presented, as Christ awarded,
> Thus we declare, thus we assent,
> thus we preach Christ our true God,
> and honor his saints in words, in writings, in thoughts,
> in sacrifices, in churches, in Holy Icons;
> on the one hand worshipping and reverencing Christ as God
>    and Lord;
> and on the other honoring as true servants of the same Lord
>    of all
> and accordingly offering them veneration.

Louder! the instructions read.

> This is the Faith of the Apostles,
> this is the Faith of the Fathers,

this is the Faith of the Orthodox,
    this is the Faith which has established the Universe.

By the end we are thundering. That settles that.

I watch Carolyn's hands as she lays out the icons. They are artist's hands, strong hands with short nails, and they are nervous hands. Carolyn is the other soprano, and she stands next to me in the choir, kneading her hands together, especially when a difficult passage comes up. She is younger than me and a good bit slimmer. Where my voice is, how you say, full-bodied, hers is delicate, with a birdlike tremor.

Carolyn's shiny brown hair swings at her shoulders, and her eyes are wide and turquoise green. They often look startled. She is the hippest dresser in the parish; where most of the rest of us do some variant on Church Lady, Carolyn wears black leather stomper boots, khaki and black dresses, and a red bumpy-leather jacket that I envy. She runs a T-shirt print shop a little farther up Frederick Road and is one of our original pioneer band. Her husband, Keith, travels; he's road manager of a perennial on the soul music stage, and we rarely see him at church.

Carolyn clears her throat and begins reading her notes in a formal voice. "Traditionally, icons are painted by monks and nuns, in a monastery dedicated to painting icons. With fear and trembling I attempt to do this." When we chuckle, she goes on, "Not too much trembling, because then I couldn't paint a straight line. Icons are painted with prayer and fasting—I struggle with both of those!—so Lent is a perfect time to be painting icons."

A while ago, Carolyn had told me that it was icons that originally drew her to Orthodoxy. She had always been an artist and noticed that in art class they just skipped over Byzantine art: "It was treated like 'This is what they did before the Renaissance, before they knew how to *paint.*'" Icons gave her a new freedom. "Now I can paint Christ and Mary and not feel intimidated—I was always intimidated that I couldn't paint the Madonna and Child like Raphael. Now I can do it, I can copy icons. And I just love it." Thus far she has painted a large crucifixion scene and many smaller icons as well;

parishioners regularly commission eight-by-tens of their name-saints.

The corpus lying on my dining room floor is also one of her offerings. On the Thursday night before Pascha, Holy and Great Thursday, my husband will carry a large wooden cross around the church, then lay it on the floor and hammer this corpus to it. Carolyn, when she finished painting it, had to create those holes for the nails to pass through; she laid the icon down and drove through Jesus' hands and feet with an electric drill.

The first icon she displays is a Virgin and Child. These are usually one of two basic styles. The Virgin Hodegetria ("of the Way"), portrays a dignified Mary gesturing toward her son with an open hand, showing the way; the icon that so impressed me at the Walters show was a variation of this type. The other is the Glykophilousa, the Virgin of Tenderness or "Sweet-Kissing Jesus" that shows mother and child cuddling cheek-to-cheek. Variations on these two types abound. Carolyn explains that icon painting moves from darkness to light, so on this Theotokos she has laid down the darkest colors and has just begun to highlight the robes. The faces of the mother and child are blank silhouettes of a surprising dark greenish brown.

"That color's called 'first flesh,'" Carolyn explains. The next icon, of St. Mary of Egypt, has acquired "second flesh," a shade lighter and more red. Mary of Egypt was a fifth-century courtesan who fled to the desert in repentance; she is depicted as she was found by a monk fifty years later, withered and dark, with wild gray hair. The third icon, of St. Helena, has gained "third flesh," and with it facial detail and expression. Helena was the mother of the fourth-century Emperor Constantine and discovered the relics of the Cross in Jerusalem. She wears an elaborate robe and a fan-shaped crown studded with jewels, which looks interesting next to Mary of Egypt, who's wrapped in only a scrap of green robe.

Next, Carolyn reads some "Rules for the icon painter":

Before starting work, make the sign of the cross, pray, fast, and pardon your enemies.

During work pray in order to strengthen yourself, physically and spiritually.

Avoid above all useless words, and keep silent.

When you have chosen a color, stretch out your hands interiorly to the Lord and ask his counsel.

Do not be jealous of your neighbor's work, his success is yours also.

When your icon is finished, thank God that his mercy granted you grace to paint the holy image.

Carolyn explains that icons are to be of historical incidents, not speculative. "We can show Jesus, and the Holy Spirit as a dove, but not God the Father." Occasionally you'll see God the Father depicted as an old man with a beard—Michelangelo did this on the Sistine Chapel ceiling—but the church frowns on such conjectures. "What about the 'Old Testament Trinity'?" someone asks. This familiar icon was painted by the Russian iconographer Andrei Rublev about 1411 and shows the three "angels" who came to tell Abraham and Sarah they would have a son; they are sitting down to the meal Abraham prepared. Popular devotion holds that the angels actually represent the Trinity. "We can't just paint our idea of the Trinity, but that dinner was an actual, historical occurrence," Carolyn explains. "We can paint that."

When Carolyn says that icons are usually flat, though they may have a raised border, I ask if they are ever more three-dimensional than that; it strikes me that I've never seen Orthodox statues. No, Carolyn says, they're flat because they're supposed to be like windows; you're supposed to have the sense of looking *through* them, not at them. Three-dimensional representations have a tempting way of taking on a life of their own.

Smiling Jeanne, Frank's wife, breaks in. Their conversion from an evangelical Episcopal parish is still recent, and old friends and family are still somewhat baffled. "I have difficulty explaining to my evangelical family why I have icons. They raise their eyebrows and . . ." she shakes her head and laughs. "So I had been asking the Lord to give me the words to share with them. This week I was keeping my little three-year-old grandson, and he wanted to phone his mom. They had a nice little conversation and he said, 'Bye-bye, Mommy,' and he *kissed* the *phone*." The group begins to chuckle; we can see what's coming.

"When my daughter came to pick him up, I asked, 'Did you get your kiss?' She said, 'Yes!' and just beamed. I asked, 'Do you think he was kissing the telephone?'" This brings on a wave of appreciative laughter.

As Carolyn carefully layers her icons and puts them away, Sheila prepares to spread out her project, our epitaphion. On the Friday before Easter, Holy and Great Friday, Orthodox process around the outside of the church carrying a wooden bier on which is laid a sizable fabric icon representing Jesus' dead body; creating a needle-pointed epitaphion is an enormous undertaking.

Like Carolyn, Sheila is an artist, and her personal style is artistic; today she is wearing a long brown cotton sweater over a long purple cotton dress, brown socks and sandals, and abalone-shell purple earrings. Her gray-brown hair escapes from bobby pins and flies out like electricity. Unlike Carolyn's wide, watercolor eyes, Sheila's are dark and intense behind red-framed glasses.

"I was asked to develop an epitaphion for use during Holy Week," Sheila begins. "It depicts the death of Christ—what, in the West, we call the deposition from the Cross." Sheila began by assembling several examples of epitaphion, then chose a border and a center image. The border is borrowed from a modern piece and runs around the four sides of the image; it is inscribed with the words: "Noble Joseph, taking down thy most pure body from the tree, did wrap it in clean linen with sweet spices and he laid it in a new tomb." The center is based on a more ancient icon and shows the long, pale body of Jesus lying very straight on a terra-cotta patterned platform. His little bent feet bear dots of shocking crimson. Mary is sitting on an inlaid wooden stool and cradling his head, and she is bent so nearly double that they are almost face-to-face. It is a sad echo of the "Sweet-Kissing Virgin"; her face is pink, but Jesus' is a mix of pearl gray and yellow.

St. Joseph of Arimathea and St. John also hover over the body, similarly bent double. St. Joseph clutches the edge of the white shroud in both hands and stares at the body in sorrow; St. John has characteristically cradled his cheek in his palm and looks on with a distracted gaze.

Sheila had sketched the design full-size on white paper, then, laying sixteen-squares-to-the-inch needlepoint fabric on top of it, carefully daubed the color on dot by dot. From there the project had gone to Joan, our champion needlepointer. Joan is a stylish, trim woman with silver hair and unerring classic taste; today she wears a toast-yellow wool suit, black sweater, and gold jewelry. She and Sheila demonstrate vivid fashion alternatives. So far, Joan has worked the figure of Mary and the face of Jesus; "I had a terrible time doing this," she says, "because I was so drawn up in the pain and agony." She shows us how she taped the church's intercessory prayer list to the edge of the canvas as a constant reminder. She handles the project with evident awe.

"Jesus looks so *dead,*" Rose blurts.

"Yes, isn't it marvelous?" Joan responds.

We invite anyone who knows how to needlepoint, or would like to learn, to take part in the project. Sheila had initially projected three years of work, but perhaps it could be ready by next Lent; this year we will once again borrow a spare epitaphion from another church. Sheila begins rolling up the work; I see that her hands, like Carolyn's, are strong, and she grips the piece firmly. "My heart is in this," she says.


Sunday of Orthodoxy concludes each year with a Vespers service that brings together all the Orthodox parishes in the area. Greek, Antiochian, Russian, and other Orthodox jurisdictions are not separate denominations but different geographical expressions of the same worldwide church. They hold the same beliefs and use the same liturgy; the chief difference, as far as I can tell, is the kind of pastries served at coffee hour. Logically, all Orthodox living in America should constitute an American Orthodox Church, and Russian missionaries came across the Bering Strait to Alaska in 1793, intending to evangelize and provide just such structure. The Russian Revolution eventually disrupted that, at a time when a flood of Orthodox immigrants from many lands was arriving and seeking services in their different languages. Parallel church structures were then set up, almost as an emergency measure. The multiplicity of hyphenated-Orthodox churches in America is something of an anomaly, and there is a movement to unite them.

Tonight we gather at St. Demetrios Greek Orthodox Church, a beautiful new complex of buildings on a wooded hilltop just north of Baltimore. The members of Holy Cross who attend look around a little enviously. But the airy, spacious church doesn't quite please; it has pews and even an organ. Too Western for us. When we get our building, we want it to look like an *Orthodox* church.

This phenomenon might fall under the heading, "No zealot like a convert." But a more subtle dynamic is also at play. I keep finding that those Orthodox still close to their immigrant roots are most inclined to want to look like ordinary Americans. A woman raised in the Greek church of immigrant parents explained to me that as a child she found it embarrassing when people noticed she was fasting; she wished she could pass as Episcopalian. On the other hand, fed-up American converts (many of whom used to be Episcopalian) gladly embrace Orthodox distinctives as a way of challenging the status quo. Born and bred in the culture, we're eager to look countercultural. While the members of Holy Cross are dazzled by St. Demetrios' size and grandeur, more than one fellow parishioner whispers to me, "But in *our* church, we aren't going to have pews!"

The nine priests line up for the procession, each one holding the icon that represents his church. As they pass by, I can recognize them: there's St. Matthew, with his best-selling book; St. Andrew, with his X-shaped cross; and two churches named after the Theotokos, or Virgin Mary: Annunciation and Nativity of the Virgin. My husband holds the icon of the elevation of the Holy Cross and walks at the head of the line, as the priest most recently ordained. As the last he goes first.

This year only the priests process, but at my first Sunday of Orthodoxy all worshipers were invited to join. Everyone had brought the icon of his or her name-saint, and we shuffled in a long procession around the interior of the dark church. I saw near me a little boy of three, waiting to join the line. He held in one drooping hand his icon and in the other gripped a small figure of Batman. He had brought both of his personal action figures, the main one and a spare. I'm glad no one asked him which was which.

---

# The Akathist Service

You might sometimes wonder what your neighbors are up to behind those closed doors on Friday night, but it's not likely to be this. I drive down the gracious, leafy lanes on the high-priced side of Catonsville and find nestled among the wide old colonials a little brick rancher. This is Basil's house. The countertop Lourdes shrine and a plastic "Praise the Lord!" sign are displayed on the front porch near the door, an indication that you are not entering an ordinary Fine Catonsville home.

A typical Orthodox home will include an "icon corner," a corner of the living or dining room where a few icons and a vigil lamp hang. Basil's icon corner has been slowly spreading, taking over the whole living room. On the wall opposite the front door are hanging Carolyn's corpus of Jesus (moved here, to more fitting storage, from my dining room floor), three icons of Mary, two of Jesus, a Resurrection and a Last Supper, and a panorama photo of Jerusalem. Basil went with my husband and a dozen others on a tour of the Holy Land last December and enjoyed it tremendously. He purchased a flowing Arab headdress, a *keffiyah*, and wore it continuously for the last several days of the trip. The other pilgrims think this, combined with his Mediterranean appearance, had something to do with Basil's being the only one of the party to have his luggage vigorously explored at the customs exit.

This laden wall is not part of the icon corner proper. On the adjoining wall, above a small altar, are twenty-four icons and two crucifixes. Just to the left of this, above the mantelpiece, are another fourteen icons, some decked with plastic flowers. From this concentration point more icons flow around the walls of the room in a stream. I count twenty-four lit candles and leave uncounted the many other crosses, angel figures, and silk and plastic flowers.

There's a framed photo of my husband at his ordination. On a table, ivy is growing out of a planter shaped like a hot dog.

Michael and David are standing behind a music stand, facing the altar. It's a small crowd tonight: besides them and my husband, only Jay, me, and my son, Stephen. Basil's mother, Lillian, sits in a corner of the couch, looking a little crumpled; she has a bad cold and sore throat. She is small anyway; when she is stretched to full height the top tufts of her white hair almost reach my ear. I'm five-feet-one.

We have come together tonight for the Akathist service, which is offered on the first five Friday nights of Lent. The service centers around the Akathist hymn, which was written by St. Romanos the Melodist in the sixth century; it is an acrostic hymn, twenty-four verses of varying lengths, in honor of the Theotokos. The Akathist hymn has been called the greatest achievement in Byzantine religious poetry.

I have to admit, I'm not as close to the Theotokos as most Orthodox I know. I like her and everything. I respect her. She's his *Mom.* Scripture said all generations would call her blessed, so we do.

But I don't have the heartfelt devotion to her that I see other people have. Some people, my husband included, have a special, tender appreciation, a love that drinks her in. I look at this from the outside, puzzled. I feel a formal distance, like we're still at the pleased-to-meetcha stage. Is this like with icons—one day I'll suddenly catch on?

One thing I have noticed is that people with a devotion to Mary understand purity and modesty better than I do. I pretty well jettisoned these with both hands during my wayward college years and still am more coarse, self-centered, and vain than I ought to be. Tenderness of soul is not something that grows back naturally, apparently, and it looks to me as if people with devotion to Mary have more of this than I do. Sometimes I ask her, "Mary, teach me about modesty," and I try to keep my ears open for instruction.

The service opens with the Trisagion prayers, a set of short prayers that Orthodox use routinely; they constitute our all-purpose basic prayer set. In addition to the Trisagion itself—the threefold repetition of "Holy God, Holy Mighty, Holy Immortal, Have mercy on us"—there are prayers for God's indwelling and for forgiveness, Lord have mercys, and Glory to the Fathers, winding up with the Lord's Prayer. I use the Trisagion prayers four times a day—rising, noon, sunset, bedtime—followed by short prayers that match the time of day.

My favorite experience with the Trisagion prayers occurred when I was invited to speak at a pro-life rally in a large Southern city. I had suggested the organizers invite the local Orthodox priest to give the benediction, but by the end of the evening when he came to the podium, he had figured out that the crowd was 90 percent charismatic. So he prayed the Trisagion prayers, just as any Orthodox would do, but in a heartfelt way with pauses, as if the phrases were just coming to him:

"Holy God," he said.

"Holy! Holy! Our God is holy!" all the charismatics around me murmured.

"Holy! Mighty!" the priest went on.

"Mighty! He is a mighty God!" the charismatics echoed.

"Holy! Immortal!" said the priest.

"Immortal God! Yes, Lord!"

"Have mercy on us," the priest concluded in a deep rumble.

"Mercy, Lord! Mercy! Yes, Lord!"

I don't know when I've enjoyed anything so much. I sat in the front row with my arms in the air, just rejoicing in the mercy of the Lord, buoyed on the bosom of all those good, good people.

Tonight we finish the Trisagion prayers, chant several psalms, and begin a series of hymns to Mary. These praise her not for her own sake but for her being the bearer of God: she is a seashell, a field, a table, a throne. One image that doesn't quite make it over the culture barrier is "Hail, O mystic heifer that didst bear the spotless Calf." There are about ten pages of these praises, but not till they are finished do we come to the Akathist hymn itself.

The hymn is divided into twenty-four verses, called *oikoi*, a long one followed by a short; the oikoi, in turn, are grouped into four *stases*. The first stasis (the first six oikoi) is used on the first Friday of Lent, the second on the second, and so forth; on the fifth Friday, the entire hymn is chanted as one.

The Akathist hymn traces the birth narrative in the Gospel of Luke, from the Annunciation through Simeon's prayer, and concludes with several more oikoi of praise. It takes a lengthy quotation to communicate its graceful elegance of form and expression:

First Stasis, Oikos 1

PRIEST: An angel chieftain was sent from heaven to say "Hail!" unto the Theotokos. And beholding thee, O Lord, taking bodily form, he stood rapt in wonder, and with bodiless voice cried aloud to her in this wise:

Hail, thou, through whom joy shall shine forth; Hail, thou, through whom the curse shall be destroyed.

Hail, thou restoration of the fallen Adam; Hail, thou, redemption of the tears of Eve.

Hail, thou that art a kingly throne; Hail, thou that holdest the Upholder of all.

Hail, thou star that showed the Sun; Hail, Womb of the divine incarnation.

Hail, thou through whom Creation is renewed; Hail, thou through whom the Creator becomes a babe.

Hail, O Bride without bridegroom!

CHOIR: Hail, O Bride without bridegroom!

Oikos 2

PRIEST: Boldly spake the holy maiden unto Gabriel, conscious of her chastity: To my soul thy strange message seems hard to grasp; how speakest thou of a virgin conception, crying aloud, Alleluia.

CHOIR: Alleluia.

Oikos 3

PRIEST: Craving to knowledge unknowable, the Virgin cried out unto him who ministered unto her: From a maiden body, how may a Son be born; tell thou me! To her he spake in fear, and thus only cried aloud:

Hail, thou initiate of the ineffable counsel; Hail O faith of those who pray in silence.

Hail, thou beginning of the miracles of Christ; Hail, thou crown of his decrees. . . .

Hail thou who ineffably didst bear the light; Hail, thou who told none how 'twas done.

The Akathist hymn is as lovely as its reputation promises. A favorite line is the one in Oikos 10, about the Magi departing to preach the birth of Christ, "and they left Herod as a trifler who knew not how to sing: Alleluia."

At the end of the Akathist hymn we return to the Trisagion prayers, a few more hymns to Mary, including the familiar one that hails her as "More honorable than the Cherubim, and more glorious beyond compare than the Seraphim." Except in this booklet she is compared to the "Cherumbim" and "Serphim." Western Christians used to orderly worship books produced by businesslike denominational headquarters are continually tripped by the typos and inconsistencies of translation found in Orthodox prayer books. The engine of bureaucracy to regiment this is simply not in place, so we sing of "our God and Savious Jesus Christ" or hear about the healing of "the man who was impotent for thirty-eight years."

There is a pause in the service, and I look up to realize that everyone is looking at me; my husband gestures toward the book I'm holding. Yes, someone has written in pencil above the next prayer *Woman,* and I'm the only woman available; Lillian is coughing softly on the sofa.

It's a long prayer, and I start in and almost immediately wish I could stop.

> O Sovereign Lady, Bride of God, spotless, blameless, pure and immaculate Virgin . . . despise me not, an accursed sinner, though I have rendered myself unworthy by my shameful thoughts, words, and deeds, and through indolence have become a slave to the pleasures of life. . . .

Everyone is standing still, listening. I know I asked her to teach me about modesty, but I wish it weren't so public.

> Mercifully have compassion upon me a sinner and a prodigal, and receive my prayer, though it be offered unto thee by unworthy lips; and using thy boldness as a mother, entreat thy Son, our Lord and Master, that He may extend to me His goodness and mercy, so as to overlook my numberless transgressions, and turn me to repentance, and show me forth as a zealous doer of his commandments. . . .

I think, desperately, that I wish I had chanted it instead of reading it. Chanting allows a little distance. "I'm not really saying this *personally*," it says, "I'm just taking my turn for all of us." Chanting is the royal *we* of prayer.

At last the prayer is over, and Michael reads the shorter one that follows, over which someone has penciled *Man*.

> And grant to us, O Master, when we depart to sleep, repose of body and soul; and protect us from the murky sleep of sin and from all the dark pleasures of the night. . . .

With a final round of intercessions for everybody, including "For those who love us and for those who hate us," the Akathist service comes to a close. I walk over to the icon corner to make some notes, and soon Lillian comes to stand at my elbow. She leans against the doorway.

"I'm feeling weak," she says in answer to my question. "I don't like sitting so much. I'm okay as long as I can lean up against something." Lillian always speaks in a quiet, slightly hoarse voice; her eyes are bright and her manner somewhat conspiratorial. There is amazing strength in her bony arms. You can't stop her from serving; a lifetime of restaurant work doesn't stop when they close the shop. During coffee hour, while the rest of us are listening to the Sunday school lesson, she's hauling the coffee pot to the kitchen, rearranging the dishes, and sweeping.

I tell her that it must be a blessing to have church services here; we use their home every time we can't get use of the ReVisions building.

"My mother ought to have been living to see this," Lillian says. "I'll miss having it here, but we need a church of our own so we can grow."

I have mixed feelings about getting a church building. I like the humility of meeting in a borrowed space, but then I don't have responsibility for the setting up and taking down every week. Something gets solidified when you get your own building, though, and I treasure these limitless-possibility days. The first generation is lit with a flame, but its task is to box that flame. The second generation is the curator of the museum-exhibit of its parents' passion. The third generation wonders where the fire went and longs for revival. So it goes, inevitably I suppose, and I don't see any way to prevent it. We have to box the flame; we have to build a church.

Lillian says, "I have a ceramic plaque downstairs of the Last Supper that I'm antiquing. When we get a church I'm gonna donate it." I picture Holy Cross's beautiful someday home, frescoed with icons and carved wood. I hope Lillian's plaque has a place right up front.

<br>

*Sunday, March 19*
*Gregory Palamas Sunday*

SECOND WEEK OF GREAT LENT

## Rose Is Pregnant

At the end of the Divine Liturgy my husband says, "I think Rose has an announcement." Some people are smiling; they already know her news.

Rose comes to stand at the front of the church; she is wearing a blue jumper and sandals with socks. Her voice is characteristically flat and ironic and her style direct and unadorned.

"Well, a lot of you have been praying for this, so I wanted to tell you that I am pregnant." Sounds of happy surprise break forth, and Rose tucks a smile in her cheek, looking at the floor. "So don't stop praying now. Because I don't want to have a miscarriage again, like last time." She moves back into the congregation, interrupted by many hugs.

When Holy Cross first began, I was struck by how many childless women we had; several had been trying to conceive for years. Then, about a year ago, the miscarriages started. Jan and Rose and Barbet each had miscarriages; Margo had two. I thought of how an old car might rattle and cough when it first tries to start. At least there were conceptions, where before there had been only empty wombs; the Holy Spirit was at work, doing something. We began praying that every woman in the church who wanted a baby would have one by Pascha.

Barbet's baby, Mattison Marie, was born a few weeks ago, and Jan is due a few weeks from now. Rose is pregnant. But Margo is not.

After today's service Hardworking Jeannie comes up to me. "Three down, one to go," she says. "I'm still praying that Margo will be pregnant, too, by Pascha. There's still time!" She tilts up and wiggles her right foot. "I have terrible foot problems. But I told the Lord, I'll keep my foot problems if you'll just make Margo pregnant!"

Every parish, if it's lucky, has a Hardworking Jeannie. I recall standing with her one Sunday after church and listening to our lovely Mary, in her seventies, tell of upcoming surgery. I commiserated and said, "Oh, I'll pray for you." But Jeannie, the strapping, vigorous mother of four young girls, was fixing Mary with her hawk-eyes. "You tell me what day it is, and I'll drive down to Annapolis and pick you up, and I'll take you to the hospital and wait while you have surgery. And then I can bring you home afterward. We don't want your husband, John, having to worry about all that."

Right, that's Jeannie. She was instantly willing to rearrange her life, make a seventy-mile round trip, and sacrifice a day or so, and there I was, saying I'd *pray*.

But, in Margo's case, I'd like to think my prayers could be useful. Some people have prayer specialties; mine is pregnancy and birth. From the first time a friend showed me photos of fetal development, nearly twenty years ago, I have been fascinated by the process. I taught childbirth classes for eight years and devised my own method of pain relief, preparing about four hundred women for their birth experiences. I had three healthy pregnancies, two "take out" deliveries (out of the hospital in a couple of hours) and the last one at home. Much of my work in recent years has been speaking and writing about preventing abortion with supportive care for women in tough pregnancies.

I have a special prayer connection for infertility, too. Once I got a Christmas card from an old friend saying she and her husband wanted to have a baby; I knelt and prayed right then that God would give them a son before the following Christmas, an uncharacteristic audacity. The next Christmas her card contained a photo of her infant boy. Another time I took the opportunity of getting my coat from upstairs at a party to pray over the bed of an infertile couple. It was only when we returned for the christening party a year later that I learned I had prayed not over their bed, but over the one in the guest room. "Listen," I said, "don't let *anybody* sleep in this bed." If those prayers were strong enough to slip down the hall and turn left, who knows what direct exposure might do?

Ever since I met Margo I have had a very strong mental image of her with two daughters. I see two little girls, close together in age, with long brown hair; very pretty girls, like their mother. This image is so strong, I once told Margo, that when I see her I want to ask, "Where are your children?"

Margo has endured miserable fertility treatments and has lost two children to miscarriage. She is the last of the four women we were trying to pray into motherhood and the only one for whom our prayers have not yet been rewarded. I wonder how she feels about Rose's announcement and seek her out at coffee hour.

She looks serene. It's different now, she says; before, she had no children at all, and now she knows she has two children in heaven. That tie to eternity is enough to comfort her.

"I often think," Margo says, "about how you wanted to say to me, 'Where are your children?' Now there's an answer that comes to me right away. When I think of that question I want to say, 'Why, they're upstairs. Sleeping.'"

*Wednesday, March 22*
*Holy Martyr Basil, Bishop of Ankara*

THIRD WEEK OF GREAT LENT

# The Baze-Man

In the wee hours of the morning I was awakened by barking; it was Sparky, our very watchful black Lab-dalmation watchdog, objecting to the presence of a human outdoors somewhere in the neighborhood. I came to consciousness aware of lingering, uneasy dreams. How dare I write about the members of Holy Cross? People will be offended at what I say about them. They won't say anything to me, but bitterness will spring up. A spirit of resentment and mistrust will begin to bloom in the church. People will drop out and begin attending elsewhere. The church will collapse, and it will be all my fault. The barking died to a few indignant ruffs, but I was still awake.

When morning came I ran off copies of what I had written so far and gave it to Gary to take to Matins. We'll start with Basil; he's profiled pretty thoroughly, and he's a man of strong opinions.

A few days later I see Basil at church. "I read what you wrote," he says. "Pretty good."

"You don't mind?" I ask, relieved. "What I said about you, it's okay?"

"Hey! It's true, isn't it?" he retorts. Then he goes on, "You know what they're calling me now? The Baze-man. Can you believe it?" He shakes his head in a those-kids-today manner. "The Baze-man!"

*Sunday, March 26*
*Adoration of the Holy Cross*

THIRD WEEK OF GREAT LENT

# Adoration of the Cross

Today we're supposed to be adoring the Holy Cross, but at the beginning of the service everyone prefers to adore Mattison Marie. It is her first visit to church, and she's propped up pretty and bright-eyed in her daddy's arms. I keep thinking, if she lived at my house, I'd never get anything done. I'd just look at her all the time.

Carolyn's corpus is set up on a large wooden cross behind the altar. We sing repeatedly, slowly and in a minor key, "Before thy Cross we bow down and worship, and thy holy Resurrection we glorify." Most of us bow, but in the choir behind the music stands, room is a little tight. I lean over to touch the floor, and Michael makes a prostration. I wonder if everybody else knows a trick I don't—how to sing and bend over at the same time and not drool.

We are bowing before an image. In Protestant eyes, this is dangerous stuff. A few years ago I read Shusaku Endo's novel of the persecution of Christians in seventeenth-century Japan, *The Silence*. I described to my Calvinist friend, Sally, the hub of the plot: an imprisoned priest is tormented by the moaning of his parishioners as they undergo hideous torture. He is told: if you will only put your foot on this image of Jesus' face, we will set them free. It's only a formality; you don't have to mean it. In desperate prayer, the priest hears only silence. The agony of his decision pervades the book.

When at last the priest is confronted with the worn copper medal affixed to a dirty plank, he sees the face of Christ for the first time since coming to Japan. In this climactic scene, the passionate love of God that icons can inspire, the hunger to touch the image of Christ, is powerfully expressed. Years of pain and persecution flood the priest's memory as he gazes at the face he loves most in the world: "This face is deeply ingrained in my soul—the most beautiful, most precious thing in the world has been living in my heart. And now with this foot I am going to trample on it." For me, this was a heartrending scene.

But not for everyone, I guess. "Well, so what?" Sally asked. "Why not step on it? It's only a picture."

I didn't know what to say. I fumbled that, even if it was only a picture, it was the act the persecutors had chosen to demonstrate rejection of the faith; to go through those motions was to accept their terms. Sally understood this. Later, I wished I'd said, "Well, what if he had been told to put his foot on a Bible?"

At the end of the service my husband processes through the church carrying a silverplate tray on which is laid a brass cross, heaped around with flowers. He holds the tray high above his head, and through the gap I see momentarily framed the faces of parishioners, old and young, even baby Mattie. He sets the tray on a small table—an end table I remember from my parents' den, now topped with my grandmother's embroidered tablecloth—and circles it with incense, while we sing "Holy God, Holy Mighty."

Before we venerate the cross, Gary asks for announcements. Pascha is drawing nearer, and we have sign-up sheets for the feast, for flowers, and for cleanup. Temple setup will be particularly trying, because ReVisions is having a dance Saturday evening. In order to be ready for the Pascha service at 6:00 Sunday morning, the team will have to come in after the dance, at midnight or 1:00 A.M.

Gary says, "Lance, why don't you bring Mattie up here for a better look." Dad and daughter come forward to applause, and Basil shouts, "Axios!"

Gary then goes on to say a few words about confession. All Orthodox are required to make their confession in Lent, before taking communion on Pascha. "Does that sound legalistic?" Gary asks. "The church believes that, for the whole body to be healthy, every part must be healthy." He reminds us that confession is not for punishment but for healing. Confession is made to Jesus, with the priest as witness; priest and penitent stand together before the icon of Jesus, and the priest lays his stole over the confessor's head. As sins are confessed, the priest offers counsel and advice for overcoming future temptation and pronounces absolution.

A Russian Orthodox prayer book suggests the priest use these words of instruction:

> Behold, my child, Christ stands here invisibly and receives your confession. Wherefore be not ashamed, neither be afraid, and conceal nothing from me; but tell me without hesitation all things which you have done, and so shall you have pardon from our Lord Jesus Christ. Lo, his holy image is before us, and I am but a witness, bearing testimony before him of all things which you have to say to me.

Gary describes a friend's reaction to confession, and it strikes a familiar chord. On the way in: "I hate confession!" On the way out: "I love confession!"

With announcements ended, the process of venerating the cross begins: we line up to take turns kneeling before the table and, leaning into the profusion of flowers, leave a kiss at the base of the cross. Some people make three prostrations as their place in line draws closer to the front. Jay's youngest daughter, Greta, age three, has to stand to reach the Cross; she gives it a smack and then turns to skip away.

*Friday, March 31*
*Holy Martyr Hypatius*

FOURTH WEEK OF GREAT LENT

# Lillian's Sister at the Akathist Service

"A nice thing happened at the Akathist service tonight," Gary says at dinner. While he was at the service at Basil's house, I was caught in a phone call and missed it; David was at work, waiting tables at the retirement home.

"The phone rang during the service, and—"

"Michael went to answer it and didn't come back to sing for the rest of the service?" David asks. I give him a kick under the table. David, future famous singer and rock star, has an opinion about Michael's hollow-chant voice.

"No, at first they couldn't figure out which line was ringing," Gary goes on. "They were running into the kitchen and back to the bedroom. I was getting really irritated. I tried to keep my mind on worship, but I was really annoyed."

He helps himself to another ladle of soup. "Then Lillian got the phone from the back room and stretched the cord out as far as it would go and stood in the doorway of the living room! She stood there for the rest of the service just holding the phone up toward the room. I really resented all the disruption.

"At the end of the service she told me what it was. Her sister had happened to call at just that moment, her sister who's disabled and has been in bed for twenty years. She called right in the middle of the service, so Lillian held up the phone and let her hear it. When she got back on the line, her sister was crying. She said it was the most beautiful thing that could have happened to her and that it was just what she needed, to be there at worship with us."

Gary looks down at his soup bowl. "I felt really ashamed of myself. Here I was all irritated, when it was the Lord making a way for this lonely old woman to join us in worship." Looking up, he says, "Wasn't that a beautiful thing?"

*Wednesday, April 5*
*Martyrs Claudius and Diodorus*

FIFTH WEEK OF LENT

# Wide World of Fasting

Sunday evening Vespers included this exhortation: "Having passed beyond the middle point in this holy season of the Fast, let us go forward to the part that still remains. . . ."

It's hard to believe that the fast is actually half over. This third time around feels very different from the first two.

The first Lent was utterly bewildering. We had been chrismated only a month before and did not realize until we were on the doorstep of the fast what it actually entailed. Practical instruction extended only to a couple of pages in the front of a book titled *The Lenten Triodion,* and trying to understand the fast by reading them was like trying to appreciate a new symphony played over the telephone. Some things just can't be comprehended with hints and pieces from the outside; you have to actually be there. When there is no there there, when everyone is a first-timer just sorting things out, it's confusing.

So we were shocked to read that in the first five days of Lent "only two meals are eaten, one on Wednesday and the other on Friday," but after a few more instructions we were told, "It should be added at once that in practice today these rules are commonly relaxed." How relaxed, and to what extent, was not specified. Lenten eating confines itself to *xerophagy* ("dry-eating"), but the term confused me; it didn't mean only dried foods, but fresh, juicy fruits, and foods cooked in water or even oil. On some days, the book said, some Orthodox go beyond xerophagy and fast completely or eat only one meal or eat only uncooked foods; the guidelines for this escaped me. However, "in present-day practice . . . the full strictness of the fast is usually mitigated."

While the general rule is no meat, no dairy products, no fish with backbones, and no olive oil or wine, on weekends wine and olive oil were permitted. On the feast of the Annunciation, March 25, fish is allowed along with wine and olive oil. Unless it falls on the first four days of Holy Week, when you can't have fish. Or the last two days of Holy Week, when you can't have olive oil, either, though you can have wine on Holy Saturday. But the *Triodion* says, "At all times it is essential to remember that 'you are not under the law but under grace' (Rom. 6:14) and that 'the letter kills, but the spirit gives life' (2 Cor. 3:6)."

Confused yet?

The first Lent felt to me like an obstacle course, one scattered with weird, unidentifiable obstacles. Obviously this was something you had to learn by doing, so I consulted those who had been doing it for years and got widely differing advice. Some advised careful reading of labels to make sure, for example, that there was no whey in bakery products; whey is the watery substance that collects on the top of yogurt. We were advised that gelatin was actually a form of meat, made as it was with cow's hooves. I stood in the grocery store comparing the cheaper cinnamon rolls with the more expensive ones; yes, but the cheaper ones were made with lard. What to do?

One priest advised me to go with the cheaper ones and not worry so much about labels: "If you can't see it, it isn't there," he said. This made sense on one level; it wasn't as if I ate cinnamon rolls to get a lard rush. But, on the other hand, weren't the transitory inconveniences and disruptions part of the fast?

Then I made the mistake of mentioning to this priest that we were using margarine. He was shocked, because butter was forbidden on the fast. I said no, margarine, just vegetable oil; we're not using olive oil, of course. No, he said, margarine is just a substitute for butter. It breaks the spirit of the fast to use it.

This sense of how the fast works out in practice, in an ordinary Orthodox home, is something that you must learn by doing, by growing up in an Orthodox family and going through the round of Lent year after year. An outsider has no practical way to grasp it. As in so many other ways, Orthodoxy is maddeningly unregimented, with no official, easy-access beginner's guide. Just asking questions about the details of the fast won me many a lecture about not understanding the "spirit" of Orthodox asceticism, which is not works-righteousness but exercises to strengthen the soul. I didn't have a regular confessor to guide me then, and the rest of the parish was looking to my husband for their direction. Eventually we just landed on a regimen that felt practical for us and stopped worrying.

The first Lent was very strange; I was eating desserts so artificially concocted that they had no natural ingredients at all, but I was fasting. The second Lent I learned to expect this strangeness and survived the seven weeks as if it were a grinding race.

This Lent has been relatively easy. I know there is an end in sight. The restrictions on kinds of food have not been particularly irksome, and if anything I have relaxed my fearful vigilance of the previous years.

For example, I've learned that I don't have to be unduly scrupulous while traveling; honest fasting must be balanced against inconveniencing the host, appearing to show off, and plain reason. But the first year I still retained a Western legal-transaction view of such disciplines and feared wrath and obscure defilement if I transgressed. During this time I was in Manhattan to speak at a college and was taken out to dinner at a restaurant beforehand. There I searched the menu for something, anything, I could eat and came up at last with French onion soup. It would be loaded with cheese, but it sounded preferable to any other offering. In fact, it sounded scrumptious.

But when the waiter came to take my order, he asked me a question I've never been asked before. "I'll have the French onion soup," I said, and he asked, "And do you want the cheese with that?" Do I want the cheese with that? What? I'd never heard of French onion soup without cheese. Hot, gloopy cheese is the whole point; the soup is just platform. But since he had asked, conscience gave me no escape. "No," I lied, miserable. "No, I don't want the cheese with that." Soon I was looking into a bowl of watery gray-brown broth in which floated a few shreds of transparent onion tissue. It looked like dirty dishwater, and it looked like I felt.

This Lent has been easy in that the lack of variety isn't bothering me. However, I am eating in fairly unrestrained quantity, probably as a compensation. On Sunday Gary and I went to a luncheon at the Greek Orthodox Cathedral. I ate everything available, down to the parsley. Gary glanced over at my plate; it looked like I had licked it. "Well, you get *your* dessert," he said.

When meat, fish, and dairy are all eliminated, people wonder what is left for us to eat. First, large amounts of bread. We bought a breadmaker just before Lent began, and it grinds away day and night. Lunch is a peanut butter sandwich or a baked potato; dinner is a vegetable soup or pasta with tomato sauce. We've discovered that there are many recipes that are none the worse for leaving out eggs and milk, so we enjoy extra-white, crumbly pancakes and very crisp chocolate chip cookies. (Milk chocolate has milk in it, but semisweet chips are okay.) Last year we used fake cheese, but it's so unpleasant and rubbery that we decided to forego it this time. At last Sunday's coffee hour we had two kinds of fruit salad, bagels, corn chips with salsa, and sautéed potatoes.

Then there's the beans.

I am not a cook. One of the gifts I give to my family is that I don't try to cook. Every afternoon I sit here at the computer tapping away until Gary rings the dinner bell.

He always enjoyed cooking, and I always found it intimidating, a complicated chore that I was sure I would flub disastrously. We worked out an arrangement accordingly when the children were small. I would do most of the child care: bedtime, bath time, baby feedings, doctor visits, most diapers, getting up at night to soothe away a bad dream. Gary would do the cooking, dishwashing, and most of the grocery shopping. This has turned out to be a good deal for me because the children are going to grow up, but we're always going to eat.

Gary knows a lot about food—he still has to instruct me when he sends me out for pork chops—and he definitely knows beans.

During Lent, our house is full of beans—green, red, gray, and white. Beans are soaking in a pot on the stove in preparation for the next soup; garbanzo beans and pesto make a cold salad; navy beans and chopped scallions for another cold salad; more lentils than anyone could want.

My Byzantine Catholic friend, Connie, cooks (a phrase that rings to me like ". . . navigates warships") and early in Lent came over with a twenty-five-pound bag of navy beans. All she wanted to do was share them. I welcomed her at the back door but inwardly began to fret. What do you do with raw beans? How do you store them? Should I get a plastic bucket, or do they need to breathe? A big paper bag? But would bugs get in and eat them? Should I put them in the refrigerator? Should they be kept moist or dry?

I realized that Gary was urgently needed in this situation. I hollered up the stairs to him, trying to conceal my panic. What I wanted to say was, "Help! Help! Someone is trying to bring beans into the house!" Sure enough he appeared, brave and competent as ever, and poured half the bag of beans into a plastic bucket. Everybody needs a hero, and mine is the guy who knows beans.

*Sunday, April 9*
*St. Mary of Egypt Sunday*

FIFTH WEEK OF GREAT LENT

# Crones and Starlets

Carolyn's icon of Mary of Egypt is completed, and it leans up against the brass candlestick on the altar. She is a wild woman, fierce, gray hair flying out around a weathered face, her bony arm raised aloft. An old dull-green mantle passes over her left shoulder and under her right arm; it is her only covering.

She was only a girl of twelve when she left her parents' home and went to the great city of Alexandria, losing herself swiftly in pursuit of debauchery. She became a singer, an actress, and a sexual athlete of inexhaustible appetite. At the age of twenty-eight she saw pilgrims embarking on a trip to Jerusalem and, with flippant curiosity, decided to tag along. As she told some of the young men, Take me along; though I don't have the money for a ticket, I'll pay you back in my own way.

At Jerusalem she accompanied the crowd to the Church of the Holy Sepulchre but found herself mysteriously restrained at the door. While the others crowded in, she was unable to move forward. Shaken by this, she withdrew to a corner of the courtyard, and an understanding of her own sinfulness began to sweep over her. She saw an icon of the Blessed Virgin and, weeping, prayed for help to live a life of penitence.

Fifty years later, about 430 A.D., a monk named Father Zosimus was spending a solitary Lent in the desert beyond the Jordan, when he was startled to see a white-haired human figure. As he moved toward it, it ran away and then cried out, "Father Zosimus, I am a woman; throw your mantle to cover me that you may come near me."

Mary told him her story; she had lived alone in the desert, without seeing another human being, since the day she wept outside the church. The first seventeen years, she said, had been the hardest. She had been tormented continuously with thoughts of the luxuries she'd formerly enjoyed, but prayer had sustained her.

Mary made Father Zosimus promise not to tell her story until after her death. They parted but agreed to meet the following year so that she could receive communion. When Father Zosimus returned the third year, he found her dead body stretched on the ground, and he buried her there in the desert. The often-skeptical editor of *Butler's Lives of the Saints* pronounces the core of this story "not incredible."

In Carolyn's icon, Mary is severe and withered, an ideal of the type feminists call "the crone." The wise old woman who has risen above socially assigned roles is taken to be a particularly forceful symbol of women's power. Read correctly, the thinking goes, stories about witches and wicked stepmothers are actually attempts by a repressive society to denigrate older women and relegate them to helpless dependence.

This thinking is fairly new. When I was a young feminist, in the first days of the movement some twenty-five years ago, we never heard about crones. Crones seem to have risen to popular awareness, coincidentally, just about the time that lots of us once-young feminists are looking across our own Jordans at menopause.

Mary is wise and strong and could be a feminist icon. But her character was formed in self-abandonment rather than narcissistic self-fulfillment (though one could argue that it is only in self-abandonment that we can ever be truly fulfilled—this has been phrased, "he who loses his life will find it"). Some strands of current feminism have been aggressive about acquiring and wielding worldly power; Mary's strength is based on vastly different principles. If this venerable crone were to speak today, her message might not be welcome in those camps.

But in a visual age, crones are never as welcome anywhere as younger, fleshier spokespersons. Actresses are as popular now as they were 1500 years ago, when young Mary trod the boards. I live near enough to Washington to hear the regular gasp of exhilaration when a pretty package from Hollywood arrives on Capitol Hill. Power doesn't impress that crowd anymore, but glitter does. Movie stars who've portrayed farmers have actually been invited to give expert testimony on agricultural matters. Starlets attract the popping flashbulbs at political fund-raisers, while the senators stand by gaping. I saved a typical clipping: a young actress's rambling press conference concerning loyalty to the president, the appeal of her own breasts, and a contorted tale of beating cancer with "positive thinking." The press prefers a spokesperson like this to a wise old crone for obvious reasons: she's earnest and silly, she has no credentials for the field she's addressing beyond the general studies degree of mere fame, and she's talking about her breasts.

I'm trying to picture this actress weeping outside a church. Or after fifty years of prayer in the desert. It could happen; it's happened before, after all. I wish I could reassure her, if she's ever felt such a call, to follow it. There's plenty of desert east of Hollywood, only a few days' walk away. They say that the first seventeen years are the hardest. Go for it.

# 3

## HOLY WEEK

*Wednesday, April 19*
*Holy and Great Wednesday*

HOLY WEEK

---

## Anointing for Healing

Holy Week is 501 pages long. My husband's Greek-English prayer book begins with Palm Sunday evening, but the week actually starts the day before, Lazarus Saturday, when we commemorate the raising of Jesus' friend as a foreshadowing of Pascha. Some parishes will anticipate Lazarus Saturday with a service Friday evening. That's the Orthodox way: can we add a few more icing roses to the top of this cake?

On our Palm Sunday it was Western Easter. We stepped outside the building and made a circuit around it, bearing our palms; Michael also had some pussy willows, which the Russians carry in place of palms (no palm trees in Russia). This street shows a shabby side of Catonsville: old, narrow frame houses leaning together, some wearing a decades-old facelift of brick-pattern tarpaper. There are several churches, mostly small nondenominationals, and one massive Roman Catholic church. There's a bar and a liquor store.

We walked around the building singing "Holy God." No one looked out their windows, but a few cars passed by. When we got back inside, Gary said, "I'm sure people were thinking, 'I've heard of people being an hour late for church when they change the clocks, but a whole week?'"

Monday through Wednesday in Holy Week the Matins services are called "Bridegroom Matins," because of the troparion:

> Behold, the Bridegroom comes at midnight, and blessed is the servant whom He shall find watching; and unworthy is he whom He shall find heedless. Beware, therefore, O my soul, lest thou be borne down with sleep, lest thou be given up to death, and lest thou be shut out from the Kingdom. Wherefore rouse thyself and cry: Holy, Holy, Holy art thou, our God, through the Theotokos have mercy on us.

Most Orthodox churches offer Bridegroom Matins on the previous day—Monday Matins on Sunday evening—because Orthodoxy counts days from sunset to sunset. Most Orthodox begin their Paschal service with Matins before midnight on Saturday; we'll have our Matins in the morning instead, in order to accommodate ReVisions's calendar. After the Paschal feast we'll have Vespers, at about 10:00 Sunday morning. In Orthodoxy I'm always singing, "I've got my Vespers in the morning and my Matins at night."

But we actually have Bridegroom Matins in the morning, 7:00 A.M. at Basil's house. Wednesday is commemorated as the day Judas betrayed Jesus and also the day the harlot washed Jesus' feet. The two figures are juxtaposed elegantly throughout the day's Matins service:

> While the sinful woman brought oil of myrrh, the disciple came to an agreement with the transgressors.
>
> She rejoiced to pour out what was very precious, he made haste to sell the One who is above all price.
>
> She acknowledged Christ as Lord, he severed himself from the Master.

She was set free, but Judas became the slave of the enemy.
Grievous was his lack of love!
Great was her repentance!
Grant such repentance also unto me, O Savior who hast
suffered for our sake, and save us.

The day's hymns are suffused with a wondering horror: how
could Judas have betrayed the Lord? He stood in his presence and
felt his love; what evil could undermine that?

O misery of Judas!
He saw the harlot kiss thy feet, and deceitfully he plotted to be-
tray thee with a kiss.
She loosed her hair and he was bound a prisoner by fury, bear-
ing in place of myrrh the stink of evil: for envy knows not even
how to choose its own advantage.
O misery of Judas!
From this deliver our souls, O God.

Wednesday evening is the annual service of Holy Unction, during
which we hear seven Epistles, seven Gospels, and seven prayers over
a vessel of oil mixed with rose water, before being anointed for healing. The fragrance of roses is heavy and comforting. It's been an un-
seasonably hot day, and the windows are open and unscreened; the
window shade to the right of the altar flaps way in, then way out
again with the breeze. Outside on the broken-brick sidewalk two
teenaged girls are having an argument next to the pay phone.

Margo is trying hard to get us aloft; the choir is sinking, singing
ever slower and more and more flat. She passes around a note ad-
vising us to think cool, think of iced lemonade; singing slowly
would make us hotter. She always looks brisk and neat, with the
freshness of a perpetual ingenue. I've often thought that Margo
perfectly personifies the word *pretty*, with its American undertones
of clarity and simplicity. Her soft, wavy hair lies on the shoulders of
a lace-collared blouse that looks freshly ironed, and her eyes are
bright. Somehow she does this all the time, even on a gummy day
like today when I feel like something found under a theater seat.
For her sake, we all do our best to straighten up and sing right.

This is a healing service, and the Scripture readings recount miracles and promises of healing and forgiveness. One of the prayers includes a recurrent Orthodox theme: the priest is not a holy figure with divine powers but an "unworthy servant" trembling before his responsibility.

O Lord our God . . . who has called me, thy humble and sinful and unworthy servant, entangled in manifold sins and wallowing in the lusts of pleasures, to the Holy and exceedingly lofty degree of the priesthood, and to enter within the innermost veil . . . Do Thou, the exceedingly good King, hearken unto my prayer in this hour . . . and vouchsafe healing unto Thy servants, who are weak both in soul and in body.

As we file forward, Gary makes the sign of the cross on our foreheads and palms with a cotton swab dipped in the blessed oil. All of us need anointing, not only those who bear a physical sickness; everyone has some impairment of soul, everyone needs empowering to do the work God has given them. For me, a writer, it's more literally the hands and the head, because that's all I've got. I sit at my computer most of each day, tapping, listening to David working out new songs on the guitar, seeing a basketball fly up past the window from where Stephen is playing a solo game below. Watching, absorbing, percolating, trying to transmit it all back on a little square screen. No tools to do this with but fickle, ephemeral words, stacked on one another like figments in the air. Sometimes I think I'd feel more satisfied at the end of the day if I could display some visible, concrete object my hands and head had made, no matter how humble—even if it was only a well-crafted chili dog. But with my cooking skills I'd never make one worthy of the title, "World's Number One!"

---

# The Reading of the Twelve Gospels

The phone rings at 5:00 P.M. "Khouria? This is Yia Yia." It's Lillian; *Yia Yia* is the affectionate title the Greeks give to grandmothers, while granddads are *Papou.* She goes on, "Let me speak to Father, please. We have got a real mess over here."

I find my husband downstairs talking on the other line, taking notes on a prior piece of bad news: a priest, his wife, and six kids who were coming to spend Pascha weekend with us have just been in a major collision. Though the car flipped over, apparently no one was seriously hurt, but they are undergoing X rays. Someone will have to go pick the family up.

Gary switches lines to talk to Lillian. The "real mess" is this: Re-Visions is having a staff event tonight, and we can't use the assembly room. This is exceptionally bad news, because tonight we're supposed to have a Divine Liturgy followed by a soup supper, then the reading of the twelve Gospels; last year it took over four hours. Calendar flubs like this are rare, but this one is a doozy.

When I arrive at the church, the room we use for worship is set up for a potluck picnic, and scores of people I've never seen before are milling around in shorts and T-shirts, eating fried chicken off paper plates. They look pretty happy.

Crammed in one of the back rooms are the members of Holy Cross, perched on chairs around the perimeter of the room. They look bemused. We can't set up the altar, so we will have to skip the Divine Liturgy and go directly to the Lenten soup supper. Smiling Jeanne was in charge of the meal, but we sent her off to rescue the car-crash family instead, so there is only one pot of soup and a loaf of bread. My son David and I rush off to the grocery store for supplements; on our way back, twenty minutes later, I say to David, "If we get there too late, and they've already finished eating, it will be the last in a long line of stupid things that have happened today." David says, "How do you know?"

We are too late and everyone has finished eating. The ReVisions staffers are gone, and Basil's team is setting up the temple as fast as it can. "Hey, we saved you guys a bowl of soup," Basil says.

But once the service begins, things fall into place. The Service of the Twelve Passion Gospels, held on Holy Thursday evening, is actually "by anticipation" the Matins service of Good Friday (in the Orthodox tradition, Holy and Great Friday). After the Trisagion prayers, psalms, and intercessions, we begin the story of the Passion with John's record of Jesus' words to the disciples after the Last Supper. We continue the story by hopscotching from one Gospel to another. Some people follow Russian tradition and kneel for the Gospel readings; some even planned ahead and brought pillows to lay on the linoleum floor. It's good planning: the first reading spans six chapters and is 126 verses long.

Between the readings we chant antiphons and prayers, grappling with the mysteries. What responsibility does Judas bear for his betrayal, seeing it was what "was written of him" before he did it?

CHANTER: The Hebrew youths, O Lord, for the resurrection of Lazarus, hailed thee, saying, Hosanna, O Lover of mankind.

PEOPLE: But law-breaking Judas refused to understand.

CHANTER: Thou didst foretell it at thy Supper, O Christ God, and saidst to thy disciples, Verily, one of you shall betray me.

PEOPLE: But law-breaking Judas refused to understand.

CHANTER: When John asked thee, O Lord, who shall betray thee, thou didst point him out to him by means of the bread.

PEOPLE: But law-breaking Judas refused to understand.

CHANTER: The Jews sought thy death with thirty pieces of silver and a kiss of deceit.

PEOPLE: But law-breaking Judas refused to understand.

CHANTER: At the washing of thy disciples, O Christ God, thou didst urge them saying, As ye have seen, so do ye.

PEOPLE: But law-breaking Judas refused to understand.

CHANTER: Thou didst tell thy disciples, O God, Watch and pray, lest ye be tempted.

PEOPLE: But law-breaking Judas refused to understand.

CHANTER: When thou didst help thy disciples at the Supper and knewest the intent to betray, thou didst reproach Judas for it, knowing the while that he was incorrigible; but preferring to make all know that thou was betrayed of thine own will, that thou mightest snatch the world from the stranger. Wherefore, O long-suffering one, glory be to thee.

Gradually the light is leaving the sky. The birds' wild evening flight and squabbling subsides. The windows on either side of the altar are open and cool spring air spills in. Above the altar, the high window's many panes turn dark, then shiny black. "And it was night."

READER: What caused thee, O Judas, to betray the Savior? Did he set thee aside from the disciples?

PEOPLE: Did he deny thee the gift of healing?

READER: Did he take supper with the others and send thee away from the table?

PEOPLE: Did he wash the feet of the rest and pass thee by?

READER: Of how much goodness hast thou become forgetful?

Reading follows reading; we alternately kneel and stand, sing and listen. The end of the fifth Gospel brings us past the trial and begins the walk to Golgotha. Our antiphons now contrast the disciple who was lost and the thief who was found. The good thief is a constant figure in Orthodoxy, a symbol of our being saved strictly by God's mercy not our own worthiness.

The thief, still on his cross, uttered a little song. Whereupon he found great faith and was saved by a single glance. First, he opened the doors of paradise, and then he entered in. O thou who didst accept his repentance, O Lord, glory to thee.

At this point the readings come to a pause. The lights are extinguished, and now the sky through the high window takes on the lurid purple-yellow of a city night. A large wooden cross, about six feet high, has been set up near the altar. My husband censes the cross repeatedly, then lifts it onto his right shoulder and begins a slow procession around the interior of the church. All are kneeling, some prostrate. The choir sings in a hushed and melancholy tone:

> Today he who hung the earth upon the waters is hung on the Tree.
> The King of the angels is decked with a crown of thorns.
> He who wraps the heavens in clouds is wrapped in the purple of mockery.
> He who freed Adam in the Jordan is slapped on the face.
> The Bridegroom of the Church is affixed to the Cross with nails.
> The Son of the Virgin is pierced by a spear.
> We worship thy Passion, O Christ. Show us also thy glorious Resurrection.
> When she who conceived thee, O Christ, saw thee hanging on the Cross, she cried out: "What strange mystery do I behold, O my Son? O Giver of life, how dost thou die, nailed on the wood in the flesh?"

When he reaches the altar again, my husband lays the wooden cross on the ground. He takes the icon of Jesus' body, the one Carolyn painted, from atop the altar and lays it in place on the cross. A hammer and nails rest near the base of the cross.

The choir reaches the end of the antiphon, and Gary takes up the hammer and nails. In the silence he drives a nail through the palm of the icon-Christ, with three ringing blows. I am crying, but Hard-working Jeannie is really crying, bent double near me on the floor. Her sobs are wet and noisy and break my heart even more.

Gary moves to nail the other hand, then the feet, each time with three sharp blows. He lifts the cross, with its burden, back into place and once more censes it.

As the choir resumes singing the antiphon above, everyone lines up to kneel and kiss the feet of the Christ-icon. What awful idolatry this must seem from outside—or at the least, awful sentimentality. I don't care. I love him so much and feel so overwhelmed at his death for me. How far, far from him I had wandered, and how undeserving I was of his grace! Getting in line to kiss those feet seems a small way to release the heart-bursting mix of sorrow and joy I feel.

We return to our places, return to the Gospels. Most of us are still creaking to our knees for every reading. After the sixth Gospel we sing the Beatitudes and after the seventh recite the penitential Fifty-first Psalm, attributed to King David's remorse over arranging a faithful soldier's death so he could seize the man's wife. After the eighth Gospel, we hear this:

> Having beheld her Lamb being led to slaughter, Mary, the ewe, followed him in the company of other women, troubled, and crying thus, "Where goest thou, my Son? And why hastenest thou to finish this course? Is there, perchance, another wedding in Cana to which thou hastenest now to change the water for them into wine? Shall I go with thee, or shall I rather tarry? Give me word, O Word, nor pass me in silence, O thou who didst keep me undefiled; for thou art still my Son and my God."

The twelfth Gospel brings us to the end—for now. Joseph of Arimathea has asked for the body of Jesus and has laid it in his tomb. The last verses we hear tonight describe the final, crushing effort of earthly strength against Jesus: "Pilate said to them, 'You have a guard; go, guard it as well as you know how.' So they went and made the sepulchre secure, sealing the stone, and setting the guard." We sing a few more prayers and intercessions, then leave the darkened church in sober silence.

It feels like we have just completed the first act of a play, one that will wring us thoroughly over the course of several days. For a preliterate people, such acting-it-out must have had the effect of engraving these truths on their hearts. For a too-literate people, accustomed to facile words zinging past us in print, television, and advertising, the simple, deliberate stage directions break down our sophistication and reduce us to tears and awe.

I gather the kids and prepare to leave. On the way I meet Smiling Jeanne. She whispers that the car-crash family is fine; she and Frank have taken Dad and the six kids to a hotel. Mom is a little dinged up but appears otherwise fine and is staying in the hospital overnight just to be sure.

As we move out to the car the night air sidles close. Around us the sky is fringed with unnatural city light; Baltimore is grinding away, just a few miles east. But straight above, beyond the limbs of the big tree, a few stars are winking. A suspended feeling of quiet pervades, blankets us all. I give way to the spreading peace.

Then I realize I forgot the unused dinner groceries and run back inside.


*Friday, April 21*
*Holy and Great Friday*

HOLY WEEK

---

# The Lamentations

The first service tonight is Great Vespers. We gather before the altar, where the large wooden cross still stands, bearing the crucified Lord. But there is something else there as well, a two-tier wooden bier about four feet high. The top and much of the lower level are densely covered with flowers, work done by Michael and other parishioners after last night's service. Underneath the bier two poles run through brass hoops, so that four men can carry it on their shoulders in procession.

The stichera verses offer a glimpse of wild grief:

Today the blameless Virgin saw Thee, O Word of God, hung upon the Cross, and she mourned within herself and was sorely pierced in her heart, and she groaned in agony from the depth of her soul, exhausted by smiting upon her breast, with hair disheveled, and cried out wailing, "Alas! My Divine Son. Alas! Light of the World. Why, O Lamb of God, has Thou departed from mine eyes?"

Wherefore, also, the armies of the Heavenly Hosts were seized with trembling, and cried out: O incomprehensible Lord, Glory to Thee.

Yet hints of hope can't be kept out. We hear readings from the chapters of Isaiah that describe the Suffering Servant and his final vindication and the ending of the book of Job where all is restored. Paul tells us that the foolishness of the cross is what "God has chosen to put to shame the wise."

The Gospel reading is a long composite of the Passion story from all four evangelists. When we reach the point that Joseph of Arimathea asks for the body of Jesus, there is a pause. Hardworking Jeannie and her husband, Vince, move forward to the cross; while Jeannie holds an open spread of white fabric, Vince pulls the nails from the icon, lifts the body, and lays it upon the shroud. In the silence we can hear Jeannie starting to cry again.

Gary takes the wrapped figure from them and lays it upright on its side behind the altar, leaning against the wall under the blackboard. It looks so small and useless. A breeze from the open windows flutters the white fabric, which falls away at the bottom. The small brown feet are pierced with perfect, round holes, and marked by narrow streams of red paint.

After a few more prayers, Gary takes the epitaphion and bears it in procession around the interior of the church, while we sing of the entombment of Christ. This epitaphion is a borrowed one, an icon printed on heavy silk with a fringe of gold, and shows Jesus lying in the tomb. Gary lays it on the lower level of the bier, where the fringe laps up against the flowers. We sing:

When Joseph, with Nicodemus, brought Thee down from the Tree and beheld Thee dead, naked, and unburied, he mourned outwardly and grievously, crying to Thee with sighs, and saying: "Woe is me, sweet Jesus, Whom but a while ago, when the sun beheld suspended upon the Cross, it was shrouded in darkness, the earth quaked with fear, and the Veil of the Temple was rent asunder. Albeit, I see that Thou willingly endurest death for my sake. How then shall I array Thee, my God? How shall I wrap Thee with linen? Or what dirges shall I chant for Thy funeral?"

As Vespers comes to a close we line up, as is our habit, to kiss the icon of the feast; this time, it is the epitaphion lying in the bier. I see that the smallest children are being lifted in by their parents, to reach over the flowers. When the choir finishes singing we get to join the end of the line, and at last it is my turn. I kneel and lean into the dark space crowded with flowers, stretching to kiss this image of Christ. It is like entering the tomb. This private, solemn moment seems like the pause I need; Holy Week is a lot of hard work, especially for the priest's family, especially for the choir. In the pause before the next service I sit on a folding chair at the back of the church, gazing at the bier and not really thinking anything.

A half hour or so later, the group reassembles for the anticipated Matins of Holy Saturday and the Lamentations. Deep in the night of Good Friday, it is already getting hard to keep Sunday out. We sing of the youths delivered from the fiery furnace, Jonah delivered from the whale, the Hebrews delivered through the Red Sea. It's not hard to get a clue as to what's in store for Jesus. Just looking at the tomb reminds us that the tomb was empty and death was overthrown. With all this in mind, it's hard to remember to be gloomy, and some of what we sing transmits jubilantly mixed messages:

The women came to embalm him, weeping bitterly and crying:
Behold the Sabbath transcendent in blessings, in which Christ
hath slept and shall rise on the third day.

The mystery of joy in grief continues. "The tomb is happy," we sing, because it received the treasure of life. What's more, all the faithful who have died are now set free, because on Holy Saturday Jesus descended to Hades and rescued them. The Orthodox icon of the Resurrection does not show the events of Sunday: the empty tomb, the Risen Christ appearing to the women. It shows Saturday's work: Jesus standing on the broken gates of hell, lifting Adam and Eve from their tombs, as the Old Testament prophets stand arrayed behind them. In irrepressible anticipation we sing, "The second Adam, who dwelleth in the highest, hath descended unto the first Adam in the uttermost chambers of Hades."

Mourn not for me, Mother, as thou beholdest me in the grave; for I thy Son, whom thou didst conceive in thy womb without seed, shall rise and be glorified.

The earth, O my Mother, hath hidden me by mine own will. And the gate-keepers of Hades trembled at beholding me clothed with a robe spattered with revenge; for I being God, have vanquished my enemies with the Cross.
Let all creation rejoice, and all the earth be glad; for Hades and the enemy have been spoiled. Let the women meet me with spices; for I redeem Adam and all his descendants, and will rise on the third day.

An unusual icon depicts this moment. Jesus is standing in a tomb of carved red stone, eyes closed in death, while his mother stands beside him, cradling him in her arms; it is an upright pietà. But her expression is not one of grief. Though her eyes are shadowed by circles, they are nevertheless wide and bright. Her eyebrows are lifted almost playfully. The hint of a smile touches her lips. Her right hand, resting on Jesus' chest, is open in a rising gesture of pride and motherly delight. The title of the icon is, "Mourn not for me, Mother."

As we come to the end of this, the ninth ode, Basil passes through the standing congregation, handing out taper candles. Margo crosses to the other side of the church and gathers all the children around her, in preparation for a part they will sing alone, while M. David takes her place at the choir director's music stand. As my husband finishes a thorough censing of the church and everyone in it, we all gather around the bier to sing the Lamentations.

The Lamentations are divided into three songs, or stases, set to three different melodies; each is from eleven to fourteen verses long. Of course, this is a shortened version; the complete Lamentations runs to a couple of hundred verses. This is Orthodoxy, after all. We begin in a lovely, yearning tone:

> In a grave they laid Thee, O my life and my Christ,
> And the armies of the angels were so amazed
> As they sang the praise of thy submissive love.

After a prayer, the next stasis is sung to a minor-key melody that seems to zigzag diagonally, with a Middle Eastern feel:

> Dirges at the tomb goodly Joseph sings with Nicodemus,
> Bringing praise to Christ who by men was slain,
> And in song with them are joined the Seraphim.

Another prayer, and then the final stasis, which has a delicately springing, joyful tune.

> Every generation
> To thy grave comes bringing
> Dear Christ, its dirge of praises.

When we reach the fifth stanza, the children are supposed to sing alone. There are about fifteen of them, nearly all girls, and Margo is afraid they will be too shy to do much more than mumble, so she's there to fill in the gap. But they sing out with admirable volume:

> Myrrh the women sprinkled,
> Store of spices bringing,
> To grace thy tomb ere dawning.

They sing this several times, while my husband walks through the congregation, sprinkling the bier and all of us with rose water. The children smile and shake their heads as the cold, fragrant water hits their faces. We are all edging into smiles.

Children and congregation alternate the final verses of the stasis, then M. David sings the Eulogetaria, a hymn that really lets the cat out of the bag.

> The company of angels was amazed, when they beheld thee numbered among the dead, yet thyself, O Savior, destroying the power of death, and with thee raising up Adam and releasing all men from Hell.

We respond: "Blessed art thou, O Lord: teach me thy statutes."
M. David continues, in a ringing voice of authority and fervent joy:

> Wherefore, O women disciples, do ye mingle sweet-smelling spices with your tears of pity? The radiant angel within the sepul-

chre cried unto the Myrrh-bearing women: Behold the grave, and understand; for the Savior is risen from the tomb.

Blessed art thou, O Lord: teach me thy statutes.

Very early in the morning did the Myrrh-bearing women run lamenting unto thy tomb; but an Angel came toward them saying: the time for lamentation is passed; weep not, but announce unto the Apostles the Resurrection.

In this drama we are moving from darkness to light very gradually; in a few moments, we will be mourning again. It is a distinct departure from my experience as a Protestant. Even in our highly liturgical Episcopal church, as soon as we finished Good Friday services we started stripping off the purple hangings and hauling in the lilies, getting the church prettied up for Easter. There was no transition. As a result, the impact of the Passion drama was blunted and somewhat artificial, as if we were swiping off a frowny-face mask and tying on a happy one.

But now from Palm Sunday to Pascha we Orthodox have a total of eleven services; last night's alone lasted three hours, even without the Divine Liturgy. As we stand here together for the third long night in a row, we are weary and hungry from fasting and have been weeping and singing together for a long time. We have had time enough to drink deeply of the Passion mystery. In these hymns tonight we begin to glimpse the coming joy, peeping out like crocuses through the snow. But there's no rushing it. We will linger another day in this Saturday between-times, a very quiet time. We know our Lord is freeing the captives in hell, but we have not yet seen him with our eyes. The stillness is luxurious; the waiting is delicious.

After the Great Doxology, Jay and Basil lift the bier by the front poles, while Michael and Vince take the back. It is very topply, alarmingly so: four feet high, two feet wide, and overstuffed with towering flowers. What I don't learn until later is that the brass hoops that secure one of the poles are coming loose. Yet the men manage, by leaning and ducking, to get the bier out the door of the assembly room, out the narrow doors of the building, and down the concrete stairs that pass between two close walls.

We circle the exterior of the church, my husband and altar-boy sons with incense in front, then the bier, then the choir and congregation following with our lighted tapers. We sing "Holy God, Holy Mighty, Holy Immortal, have mercy on us," as we go. It is the funeral procession of God.

As we come back around to the front, we pass a man talking on the pay phone. The procession moves solemnly by him, priest and altar boys in vestments, incense, a flower-decked bier, fifty people holding lighted candles and singing a dirgelike hymn over and over. The man looks surprised. He keeps talking into the phone, but his eyes are wide and wary.

The men wedge the bier back inside the door of the building, then hold it high as we pass beneath, bowing low, uniting ourselves with Christ's death and symbolically entering the tomb. At last the bier is safely deposited in front of the altar again. My husband removes the epitaphion and places it on the altar.

We hear three more readings. Ezekiel's vision of the valley of the dry bones doesn't do much to keep the secret. Paul admonishes that "Christ our Passover has been sacrificed; therefore, let us keep festival . . . with the unleavened bread of sincerity and truth." In the Gospel reading, the chief priests and Pharisees ask Pilate to secure the tomb so that Jesus' disciples don't steal the body "and the last imposture will be worse than the first." Pilate tells them, "'You have a guard; go, guard it as well as you know how.' So they went and made the sepulchre secure, sealing the stone, and setting the guard." It is the same Gospel we heard at the end of last night's service. I think there may be a little gloating going on here.

At the end of the readings, Gary replaces the epitaphion in the bier, while M. David sings:

When he saw that the sun had hidden its rays, and the veil of the Temple was rent at the death of the Savior, Joseph, approaching Pilate, pleaded with him, crying out and saying,

Give thou me this Stranger, who from his youth has wandered like a stranger.

Give me this Stranger, whom his kinsmen killed in hatred like a stranger.

Give me this Stranger at whom I wonder, beholding him as a Guest of death.

Give me this Stranger who knoweth how to take in the poor and strangers.

Give me this Stranger that I may bury him in a tomb, who being a Stranger hath no place whereon to lay his head.

Give me this Stranger, to whom his Mother, beholding him dead, cried, "My Son and my vitals be wounded, and my heart burns, as I behold thee dead, yet trusting in thy Resurrection, I magnify thee."

In these words the honorable Joseph pleaded with Pilate, took the Savior's body, and with fear wrapped it in linen and balm. In a tomb he placed thee, O thou who grantest to all everlasting life and great mercy.

We all file forward one last time to kiss the epitaphion, and Gary stands nearby, handing each one a flower from the bier. The family who had been in yesterday's car accident is here, none the worse for wear except for Mom Debbie's impressive black eye. As they pass through the line one of the younger boys tries to refuse the flower he's offered: "I don't want that one, I want a *white* one," he says, while his dad hisses at him to behave. "No, you want *this* one," Gary says in daddy solidarity, with a firm smile. The boy goes off pouting and tries to find someone to trade.

As the evening comes to an end, some are cleaning up while Basil, Michael, and others prepare to hold vigil at the bier all night. Jared's little sister, Lydia, and brother, Billy, are sitting on the floor near the altar, waiting for their daddy, Jay. They are having an obscure theological argument: "It *is* God." "No, it isn't." "Daddy says it *is*." Greta, the littlest, sits with them, above the fray, sniffing her flower vigorously and admiring it to fragments.

# The Liturgy of St. Basil

This morning we have the evening vesperal service, in the continuing topsy-turvy I've come to expect. This vespers is joined to a Divine Liturgy, but instead of the liturgy of St. John Chrysostom it's the liturgy of St. Basil, which is more ancient and more extended (St. John essentially took the received text and edited it down a bit). The vesperal stichera teach the significance of the day:

> Today Hades cried out groaning: My power has been trampled on; the Shepherd has been crucified, and He raised up Adam; I have been deprived of those over whom I ruled, and all those whom I swallowed in my strength I have disgorged. He Who was crucified has cleared the tombs; and the power of death avails not.

We hear as readings the Genesis creation story and the entire book of Jonah, followed by the story of the three youths in the fiery furnace. We sing the Hymn of the Three Young Men, then hear St. Paul's words: "All who have been baptized into Christ Jesus have been baptized into his death."

Before we hear the Gospel, Gary moves through the congregation scattering fresh bay leaves on the floor. He had worried about finding those leaves; over the course of the week he had visited old-fashioned vegetable markets in the city and health food stores in the malls searching for them. At last they turned up in the produce department of our everyday grocery store.

"These leaves are a symbol of the Resurrection," he explains as he goes. "They'll remain here, on the floor, throughout our Paschal liturgy tomorrow. Don't try to be helpful and sweep them up. You're supposed to tread on them; the fragrance the crushed leaves release is a reminder of the Resurrection." Little Greta is ignoring this advice, on her knees, scooping all the leaves she can reach into a pile.

Then comes the Gospel, the last chapter of Matthew, which brings us from the arrival of the women at the empty tomb through the Great Commission ("Go, therefore, and make disciples of all nations") and the Ascension. It concludes, "Behold, I am with you always, even to the end of the world." The news is definitely out now.

In place of the hymn that usually precedes the eucharistic prayers, we sing one that even many Protestants know:

> Let all mortal flesh keep silence, and with fear and trembling
>     stand,
> Ponder nothing earthly-minded, for with blessing in his hand
> Christ our God to earth descendeth
> Our full homage to demand.

We sing this to the melancholy seventeenth-century French melody we used in the Episcopal church. I always thought it was a lovely communion hymn, with a deeper impact than many; I didn't realize that the words had been sung for fifteen hundred years.

After liturgy, the rest of the choir stays behind to practice for tomorrow, while I race off to a busy day. An e-mail buddy, Rod, is coming in at the train station to spend the night and have Pascha with us. He has been a committed Christian only a couple of years and is a convert to Catholicism. Rod is a reporter at a big Washington newspaper, and his arrival brings with it a gust of breezy twentysomething cosmopolitan life. It's pretty dashing to a woman with kids who'll be twentysomething themselves before long.

I enjoy bringing non-Orthodox friends to liturgy. From the first time I did it I've been keeping a secret tally: "Will they kiss stuff?" When the mission was only a few months old I brought my first out-of-town guest, my friend and editor, Marvin. Since he was staying over a Saturday night, I presumed he'd join us for Vespers, out of curiosity or simple politeness. To my surprise, he was deeply reluctant. Marvin is a dedicated convert to a conservative branch of the Presbyterian church, and it began to dawn on me that he might actively *object* to Orthodoxy.

I recalled the typical Protestant anxiety about highly liturgical churches: once in the slippery world of symbolism, you could find yourself participating in overwrought proceedings of theological questionability. On the level plane of words—Bible memory verses and three-point sermons—you can know pretty clearly where you stand. But once a guy puts on golden robes and starts swinging incense around, things become murkier. Still, I reasoned, Vespers is the least threatening Orthodox service, just thirty-five minutes of standing together, singing prayers and Scripture in harmony.

Since Marvin was my houseguest I was able to prevail and even prodded him to stand near the front with me, though he clearly would have been more comfortable in the back or even in the parking lot. I tried to keep the service nonthreatening, and I refrained from crossing myself any of the dozens of times prescribed. The service was sweet reasonability itself. That is, until we hit the part I had forgotten—the *kissing* part.

At the end of the service my husband held up a brass cross for the people to venerate, and they lined up to do so. I whispered to Marvin that people go up and kiss the cross "if they want to." On this Saturday, everybody in the church apparently wanted to except us, so it was a little awkward.

The line to the cross led right past a stand with the icon of the feast, and most people paused to bow and kiss that as well. Quite a few went on to kiss the cross, then kissed my husband's hand. A brief, nonchalant way of explaining all this to a Presbyterian was not springing to mind.

I was thinking that, as far as I've been able to observe, Presbyterians never kiss, at least not in church. Orthodox eagerness to do so probably looks obsessive—even like idolatry. For, I must admit, we kiss a lot. We kiss icons, crosses, and Gospel books; we kiss the edge of the priest's garment and kiss his hand, kiss the chalice, and kiss one another. (Only practical concerns, I'm sure, deter us from kissing the censer.)

It reminds me of being a little girl of three or four, barefoot in my white nightgown, going around at my parents' party to kiss all the guests good-night. I could hear someone chortling, "She's a regular kissing bug!" There is exuberance and generosity in the way we Orthodox scatter kisses around, cherishing the things and people that bear God to us.

How can we honor material things, cloth and icons, wood and paint this way? We are like the lover in the old hit song who complains that his girl went "leaving just your picture behind, and I've kissed it a thousand times." It's not the paper photo that he's in love with but the person it represents. But because it does represent his love, he cherishes and honors the photo, wearing it out with kisses. The holy, invisible Lord surrounds us and we grasp for his elusive presence, kneeling down awestruck with our foreheads to the floor, tasting heaven on the eucharistic spoon, laying kisses on his image and one another and most anything else we can get hold of.

From the outside, Orthodoxy probably looks stuffy, esoteric, and rigidly ritualistic. But once inside, it turns out to be a box full of Kissing Bugs. We feel such gratitude to God for saving us, such awe at his majesty, such joy in the fellowship of the saints, that we respond from the heart. It's not superstition requiring us to relinquish formal, ritual kisses. We find ourselves in our true home in the church, astonished and overjoyed to be welcomed at this glorious feast. Like a child in a nightgown, secure in her father's house, we go scattering our kisses with simplicity and love.

I meet Rod the Reporter at the train station. He swings his backpack into the back seat and clambers in, dressed in sandals and shorts on this warm spring day. He's brought a dress shirt for liturgy, which he carefully ironed before putting it in the backpack. (Bachelors.) On his cap is a pin of Tintin, the Belgian cartoon reporter.

We set off toward home, plunging instantly into ceaseless conversation; observers would doubt that, in our small on-line circle, we already exchange e-mail several times a day. But we're two Southerners trapped in a world of tight-lipped Yankees, and it's a relief to ramble on freely.

In the kitchen preparations for Pascha are already under way. Gary had been worrying about dyeing the hundred or so red eggs he'll hand out after liturgy tomorrow, but fortunately Lillian and Hardworking Jeannie have taken care of that task; trays of red eggs are stacked by the back door. The egg is an ancient Easter symbol; though it appears dead as a stone, new life unexpectedly chips its way out. (Not in the case of hard-boiled eggs, of course, but it's the thought that counts.) The eggs are dyed red to represent Christ's blood; I've heard that, traditionally, this is done with beets or the skins of red onions. At the conclusion of the Paschal service, worshipers file forward to kiss the icon of the Resurrection and the cross. As the priest hands each person an egg, he says, "The blessings of the feast be upon you." During the feast the eggs are part of a traditional game—two players knock their eggs end to end, and the one with the unbroken egg is champion. The tournament continues around the room until only one player is victorious.

Gary takes Rod with him to make some last-minute preparations at the church and to lay out a linen tablecloth with our wedding dishes, silverware, and candelabra. He also stashes some champagne in the big steel refrigerator. We will be having a very heavy meal, with bubbly, before 9:00 tomorrow morning.

Meanwhile, the kids and I have an important annual event to celebrate: the first postfast grocery shopping trip. It seems daring to wheel a cart in the door of the store, stop before the meat case, and *pick up a package of bacon*. We clear out the dairy case, tossing into the cart cheddar, Swiss, cream cheese, cottage cheese, eggs, three jugs of milk. Down the aisles we sail, plucking forbidden fruit—cream of chicken soup, canned tuna, and a giant tub of ice cream. It takes two carts and more money than I want to think about.

Once home we begin making dairy-rich vegetable and dessert dishes to bring to the Paschal potluck. The meat will be prepared and provided by Hardworking Jeannie, who has taken up a collection in order to spare the rest of us the trouble. (She's also cooking a luscious tenderloin that has been donated by an anonymous member of the parish, a gift for the priest and choir.) As Megan assembles her cheddar-potato dish, David makes deviled eggs, and I mix spinach with sour cream. Stephen tries to persuade us that it's close enough to Pascha—we can have a little now. The rest of us emphatically disagree.

When Gary and Rod return, we have our last meal of the fast before turning in for an early night's sleep and the next day's early rising.

Our seventy-year-old house has a gracious dining room, but we always seem to wind up in the bright yellow breakfast nook, no matter how many are coming to dinner. It's an eclectic space. The table is a battered old piece, with turned chestnut legs that suggest it began as a nice dining table. But along the way it was reduced, bit by bit: the chestnut front and back are now joined by black cherry sides, and the top is just two wide planks of northern pine barn siding. After this reformulation, the table spent some time in a workshop, as the deep saw-grooves along the edge attest. When my dad and I refinished it some twenty years ago, it took pure lye to burn through the thick crust of paint, and we pulled some thirty nails out of the top. Now, resurrected, it's a dining table again.

There are four exuberant art deco chairs I picked up at the Salvation Army and painted bright blue. Two other chairs are faux-grained plank seats I found cheap in a flea market stall; I later saw their sister in a Williamsburg folk art museum. On one wall of the niche hangs a plywood trumpeting angel, multicolored and obsessively inscribed with religious admonitions, by the folk artist Howard Finster; on the other is an imposingly large canvas of a whimsical, surreal café scene, painted by my friend Marilyn. The windows at the far end are crowded with shelves of potted herbs, and icons march down the window frame. The little space is too small, too crowded, too bright, too mismatched. We greatly prefer it to the real dining room.

Tonight Gary prepares spaghetti with oil, garlic, and black olives, and we pass around a loaf of fresh-baked bread. Rod is young, full of curiosity and enthusiasm, and makes an excellent foil for boring old people who want to talk about how much they love being Orthodox. Talking is a restful way to recap the seven weeks just past. I have another helping of pasta and feel tired and happy. Lent is finally over, and Pascha is only hours away.

# 4

# PASCHA

*Sunday, April 23*
*Pascha*

## Pascha

I can't say we got off to a good start. Gary was up at 4:00 A.M. and gone shortly after, but the rest of us began arising at 5:00 for the 6:00 service. The problem started when Stephen was first in the shower about 5:15 and continued until he was last out of the shower roughly a half hour later. (An older home has many charms, but one-and-a-half baths is not one of them.) Fortunately, Rod had showered the night before; the rest of us would just have to wait till after church. While the problem wasn't dire, it was annoying, which Stephen heard about in detail. My curly hair gets comical flat places overnight and requires a thorough sprinkling to fluff out (though results still vary, and people are always telling me, mistakenly, that I have a new hairdo. No, my hair is just like the Lord's mercies: new every morning).

So Megan, David, and I were somewhat frumpy and grumpy on Pascha morning. This was amplified by the regular communion fast, which means not only abstinence from food but also from drink, including that ignition-turning first cup of coffee. Still, it could be worse. A woman who grew up Greek Orthodox and converted to Protestantism told me that in her childhood the Sunday rule was that nothing could touch your lips before communion. No lipstick, of course, but she wasn't even allowed to brush her teeth. There's a choir I wouldn't want to sing in.

We drive through the dim streets of Catonsville and turn down Winter's Lane. The drowsy houses still have their eyes closed. A couple of the churches had put out banners last week for their Easter; in front of one parking lot is a stretch of sagging blue vinyl with the words *He Is Risen!* in white. It is damp with dew.

I wonder again how so many churches can bear witness to Christ in Baltimore, week after week, year after year, and Baltimore can still be so unchanged. Murder, robbery, drug use rise; basic civility steadily drops. Yet here are all these churches, all this prayer; further downtown, it's a bar and a church and a bar and a church, block after block, interspersed with bombed-looking row houses and shabby men sitting on the marble steps all afternoon. The churches have long, long names (Ascended Up on High Deliverance Temple of Prophecy) and the bars have short names (Nite Lite Lounge), and they coexist untroubled by each other's presence.

Maybe without the churches the city would be worse; maybe they at least offer some restraining influence. Still, these thoughts are damp and far from triumphal. The sky has brightened from navy to a vibrant royal blue. It looks more charged and insistent than I feel up to just yet.

We pull up beside ReVisions's door to let the kids out, each one hauling offerings for the potluck meal. "The last time I was up this early, I was going to bed," says Rod. He looks pale and a little dazed. I remember being young and single, back when I had a social life. "What were you doing?" I ask, nostalgically. "Oh, I wasn't thinking of anything in particular," he says. "Just in general. I never get up this early."

Inside the church I stand at the edge of the choir, on the other side of the altos, to hostess Rod through the service book. Most people are holding unlit taper candles, but I feel crabby and refuse one, since I have enough to worry about in this complex service without trying to hang onto something that's on fire at one end. We work through preliminary offices for an hour, taking turns solo-chanting the Odes as M. David points to us, one after another. These recapitulate the Old Testament events foreshadowing the Resurrection: the Exodus, Jonah and the whale, the three young men in the furnace.

You could highlight the Resurrection as a personally salvific event or as evidence of Christ's deity or in many other ways, but this morning we are emphasizing it as proof of the defeat of hell. We cheer it as we would news of a military victory:

Foreseeing thy divine humiliation on the Cross, Habakkuk cried out trembling, "Thou shattered the dominion of the mighty by joining those in hell as the almighty Lord."

When hell encountered Thee, O Word, it was embittered. Seeing Thee as a mortal man deified, marked with wounds yet having almighty power, it cried out at Thy awesome appearance.

Isaiah saw the never-setting light of Thy compassionate manifestation to us as God, O Christ. Rising early from the night he cried out: "The dead shall arise. Those in the tombs shall awake. All those on earth shall greatly rejoice."

Yet for all this rejoicing, the church is still undecorated, and after a few more prayers all the lights are extinguished. My husband lights the Paschal candle from the vigil light on the altar, then brings it out to us, saying, "Come, receive light from the Light that is never overtaken by night; come glorify Christ who is risen from the dead." People light their candles from his, then pass the flame toward the back; it ripples across the gray room and illuminates faces along the way. Some look hopeful; some look serious; some look just tired.

Now I wish I had taken a taper. I send Megan to grab one for me. Then, led by Gary and the altar boys, we leave the church and process around it outside, singing slowly in a rumbling minor key: "Thy Resurrection, O Christ our Savior, the angels in heaven sing. Enable us on earth to glorify thee in purity of heart."

As we round the corner of the building and step into the street, a sharp wind comes whistling by. The dawn is coming up gray and chilly. My throat feels a little raw. We clutch around us our light spring jackets and fumble with the tapers; the wind blows mine out and I relight it several times before giving up.

Outside the doors of the church we pause; my husband turns to face us and begins the Gospel. In Mark's version, the women went to anoint Jesus' body but instead found in the tomb "a young man sitting on the right side, dressed in a long white robe." He told them that Jesus is risen and instructed them to tell the disciples, but they were terrified and fled the tomb "and said nothing to anyone, for they were afraid." The earliest versions of this, the earliest Gospel, end abruptly at this point.

It's an odd gap between that small vignette of fear and retreat and all that came next: the Apostles' relentless courage unto death, unascribable to mere fond memories of a really nice dead guy; the preaching of the Gospel across the Mediterranean bowl, the persecutions and martyrdom, the establishment and rise of the Church, and finally the disintegration of Christendom in these times, perhaps a prelude to full-circle persecution and martyrdom. But at one mesmerizing moment, the news of Christ's resurrection was held by a handful of women who were too scared to tell anyone. But tell they did, and the story went on unreeling, and now we are standing outside in the windy dawn, on a shabby street in a little town, half a world away and two thousand years later.

It's time to start shouting! My husband announces:

Christ is risen from the dead, trampling down death by death, and upon those in the tombs bestowing life!

We sing it back to him, for the first of what will be hundreds of times before Pentecost:

CHOIR: Christ is risen from the dead, trampling down death by death, and upon those in the tombs bestowing life!

PRIEST: Let God arise! Let his enemies be scattered! Let those who hate him flee from before his face!

CHOIR: Christ is risen from the dead, trampling down death by death, and upon those in the tombs bestowing life!

PRIEST: As smoke vanishes, so let them vanish; as wax melts before the fire!

CHOIR: Christ is risen from the dead, trampling down death by death, and upon those in the tombs bestowing life!

PRIEST: So the sinners will perish before the face of God; but let the righteous be glad!

CHOIR: Christ is risen from the dead, trampling down death by death, and upon those in the tombs bestowing life!

PRIEST: This is the day which the Lord has made; let us rejoice and be glad in it!

CHOIR: Christ is risen from the dead, trampling down death by death, and upon those in the tombs bestowing life!

Gary turns and bangs on the door. He says loudly, "Lift up your heads, O ye gates, and be lifted up, O ye everlasting doors, that the King of Glory may enter!"

Jonathan is waiting inside; his wheelchair makes it a little more troublesome to get in and out of the building, so he assumes this role in the drama. We hear his voice through the closed door: "Who is the King of Glory?"

Gary replies, "The Lord who is strong and mighty, the Lord mighty in battle. Lift up your heads, O ye gates, and be lifted up, O ye everlasting doors, that the King of Glory may enter!"

Jonathan asks again, "Who is the King of Glory?"

Gary says, "The Lord of Hosts! He is the King of Glory!"

We all burst into song: "Christ is risen from the dead, trampling down death by death, and upon those in the tombs bestowing life!"

Singing this refrain over and over, we file back into the church. It is transformed. Every light is blazing, and Michael and several helpers have been scurrying to set flowers everywhere. The rising sun brings gold through the window. I am beginning to feel like it's really Pascha.

We begin singing the Odes, many pages of brief hymns praising the Resurrection. In the middle comes a quiet, mournful piece, which I have trouble singing because I get choked up. Margo holds her palms up to hush us, allowing our voices to swell and subside as the riverlike melody flows by.

> Before dawn the myrrh-bearing women sought, as those who
> seek the day, their Sun,
> Who was before the sun, yet had descended to the grave.
> And they cried to each other, "O friends,
> Come let us anoint with spices his life-bearing yet buried body,
> The flesh which raised fallen Adam and now lies in the tomb.
> Let us assemble and, like the Magi, let us hasten and let us
> worship.
> Let us bring myrrh as a gift to him who is wrapped now,
> Not in swaddling clothes, but in a winding sheet."

Now the piece begins to build; I have penciled black dashes of emphasis above each syllable. It ends with a full-flowering, mighty major chord.

> "Let us lament and cry: 'Arise, O Master!
> And bestow resurrection on the fallen!'"

The lovely and effective arrangement of this traditional song nearly qualifies as drama; I'm not surprised to see it is Russian. The melodies we sing are a multicultural buffet: Arabic, Greek, Russian, Alaskan, French. Though the sideways, linear Byzantine music takes some getting used to, the Russian versions are very approachable. They echo Western European elegance, just the way Peter the Great would have wanted it. For variation, we sing the Paschal troparion, "Christ is risen from the dead, trampling down death by death, and upon those in the tombs bestowing life," to several different melodies. The Romanian version lilts like a minuet, while the Ukrainian sounds cheerful and sturdy, like a Handel waltz.

At the end of the Odes we sing everybody's favorite, "The Angel Cried." Our first year, when we were all new Orthodox and had no idea what we were doing, this Paschal hymn stood out among all the confusing pieces as something glorious, exultant, and very, very singable. The melody we use—bright, brisk, and joyous—is also Russian.

The angel cried to the Lady full of grace,
"Rejoice, rejoice, O pure Virgin!
Again I say, rejoice!
Your son is risen from his three days in the tomb.
With himself he has raised all the dead.
Rejoice, rejoice, O ye people!
Shine! Shine! Shine, O new Jerusalem!
The glory of the Lord has shone on you.
Exult now, exult and be glad, O Zion.
Be radiant, O pure Theotokos,
In the Resurrection,
The Resurrection of your Son."

This is getting really good. We've gotten to about the halfway mark of the morning's three-hour service, and Megan runs to the kitchen to put her potatoes in the oven. Rod is keeping up in his service booklet and seems to be tolerating the early hour pretty well. When it comes time to sing again the "Let God arise! Let his enemies be scattered!" I'm ready to belt it out. After all, Margo told us at our first rehearsal to pencil at the top *Bombastic.*

We hear the Gospel reading for Pascha, the prologue to the Gospel of John, and then my husband reads the sermon. This same sermon is read in every Orthodox church on every Pascha, the Sermon of St. John Chrysostom. It is brief and blooming, full of the freedom for which Christ has set us free.

If any man be devout and love God, let him enjoy this fair and radiant triumphal feast.

If any man be a wise servant, let him enter rejoicing into the joy of his Lord.

If any have labored long in fasting, let him now receive his recompense.

If any have wrought from the first hour, let him today receive his just reward.

If any have come at the third hour, let him with thankfulness keep the feast.

If any have arrived at the sixth hour, let him have no misgivings, because he shall in no wise be deprived.

If any have delayed until the ninth hour, let him draw near, fearing nothing.

If any have tarried even until the eleventh hour, let him also be not alarmed at his tardiness; for the Lord, who is jealous of his honor, will accept the last even as the first; he gives rest unto him who comes at the eleventh hour, even as unto him who has worked from the first hour.

And he shows mercy upon the last, and cares for the first; and to the one he gives, and upon the other he bestows gifts.

And he both accepts the deeds, and welcomes the intention, and honors the acts and praises the offering.

Wherefore, enter ye all into the joy of your Lord, and receive your reward, both the first and likewise the second.

You rich and poor together, hold high festival. You sober and you heedless, honor the day.

Rejoice today, both you who have fasted and you who have disregarded the fast.

The table is fully laden; feast sumptuously. The calf is fatted; let no one go hungry away. Enjoy the feast of faith; receive all the riches of loving-kindness.

Let no one bewail his poverty, for the universal kingdom has been revealed.

Let no one weep for his iniquities, for pardon has shone forth from the grave.

Let no one fear death, for the Savior's death has set us free: he that was held prisoner of it has annihilated it.

By descending into hell, he made hell captive. He embittered it when it tasted of his flesh. And Isaiah, foretelling this, cried: "Hell was embittered when it encountered thee in the lower regions."

It was embittered, for it was abolished. It was embittered, for it was mocked.

It was embittered, for it was slain. It was embittered, for it was overthrown.

It was embittered, for it was fettered in chains.

It took a body, and met God face to face. It took earth, and encountered heaven.

It took that which was seen, and fell upon the unseen.

O Death, where is your sting? O Hell, where is your victory?

Christ is risen, and you are overthrown. Christ is risen, and the demons are fallen.

Christ is risen, and the angels rejoice. Christ is risen, and life reigns.

Christ is risen, and not one dead remains in the grave.

For Christ, being risen from the dead, is become the first-fruits of those who have fallen asleep. To him be glory and dominion unto ages of ages. Amen.

I'm beaming now; I look around the church, and we're all smiling. This is what we waited and fasted and prayed for, and it has all come true. We are at the heavenly banquet table, surrounded by all the saints gone before, and it is Pascha morning, for all the world and for all time. We stand in a stream of light; the years will turn and we will age, and our earthly bodies will fail, but we will never leave this eternal stream of praise. Orthodox before us and after us will sing and say and chant the same words we do today; we are only the blessed caretakers of it for this fleeting generation. It is a joyful privilege.

By 9:00 we're sitting in the back room, where folding tables are spread and decorated for the meal. The atmosphere is one of giddy camaraderie, the natural result of arriving at this bright day after so many long weeks of waiting and praying together, though the amplifying effect of champagne cannot be dismissed. The Mathewes-Greens take some good-natured kidding for bringing our fancy dishes and silver, since most everyone else opted for easy-cleanup paper plates. Everywhere pairs of people are knocking the red hard-boiled eggs together, end to end. Last year Basil made a lot of noise about being the undefeated champion at this traditional Paschal game, until Carolyn crunched him and won the title. This year the children are collecting all the adults' eggs and playing a high-pressure tournament, with Hardworking Jeannie's daughter, Mary Catherine, the ultimate winner.

We feast on beef, pork, lamb, and fried chicken, and Hardworking Jeannie brings Gary and me some of the special tenderloin. The buffet table is so overloaded that some dishes have to be placed on the shelf underneath, and all the desserts must wait out in the kitchen. Gary stands to thank everyone he can think of, and when he's through, Basil gets up and urges everyone to be grateful that we have Gary as our priest. Gary is abashed, but Basil commands that we all stand and sing the traditional Orthodox song, "Many Years." This song fills the all-purpose role that "For He's a Jolly Good Fellow" does in other cultures. The crowd rises and sings, with warm smiles:

> God grant you many years,
> God grant you many years,
> God grant you many, many years!

When we can't eat any more, it's back into the church for Agape Vespers. During this service we read the Gospel in many languages: Lillian starts us off in the official Greek, then my husband reads the English translation. Jonathan reads the same words in Latin, his wife Barbara takes German, and Sheila reads in French.

When Vespers concludes—just when a nap seems most urgent—there's all the cleaning up before we can leave. I scurry back and forth from the kitchen to the ramp outside the front door, depositing plates and baskets to be carried to the car, then have to move them because, like a dummy, I forgot that Jonathan would need to use the ramp to get out.

As the kids climb back in the car with the empty casserole dishes and silver trays, I look up at the sky. It's white-blue, and the sun is directly overhead; noon. When we arrived this morning, six hours ago, I was pretty grumpy, but now I'm happy and exhausted. We stood for about four hours of worship, singing almost continuously, then feasted on fabulously rich food that we hadn't tasted for weeks; we laughed and wept and hugged.

Not that it can't all be done more efficiently. At the Presbyterian church near my house the sign last week read: "Sunrise service 7:00 A.M. Fellowship breakfast 7:30 A.M." Easter service over in a half hour? Is this possible? It reminds me of the joke about the microwave fireplace—you can enjoy a whole evening in front of the fire in just eight minutes. I guess there was a time when getting in and out of church briskly was important to me. When it's this sumptuously good, though, I'm glad for it to linger.

By midafternoon we have all napped and showered and eaten seconds and thirds. Parishioners have pressed most of the leftovers on us—this is one of the advantages of being the pastor's family— and there are so many casseroles and aluminum trays that they can't all fit in the refrigerator. I stand barefoot in the kitchen admiring the deep aluminum pan of sliced roast beef resting on the stove and think about getting a plate, knife, fork, then just start picking the slabs out and eating them with my fingers. It is luxurious.

The one thing we had missed today was, ironically, a traditional Pascha dessert, kulich with paska. Kulich is an eggy Russian bread made with candied fruit, and paska is the spread that's dolloped on it, a blend of cream cheese, ground almonds, sugar, and other goodies. Last year we had too many of these (including a kulich made in a bread machine, which seemed like cheating). This year, no kulich at all, but Barbara made a lovely paska, molded and topped with the traditional flowers. Paska is very rich, almost a creamy soft candy; Gary and I each had a spoonful on our dessert plates at the dinner, then brought the rest home on a paper plate.

That afternoon we are sitting in the living room, snoozy and happy, laughing about the day, when I hear Rod come down the stairs and go into the kitchen. A few moments later he joins us; he is carrying the plate of paska and eating it with a big spoon. You can't say our houseguests don't feel at home. The sight of that supersaturated paska—the kind of stuff that used to inspire my dad to say, "I can hear my arteries slamming shut"—disappearing by the mighty spoonful strikes me as very funny. Then it starts to seem like a good idea. When Rod sets down the half-finished treat, I pick it up and dig in. This is how Pascha should be.

# Peter Aslan Is Born

We can all die and go home now, because the most perfect baby ever born has arrived. Jan and Don, the second of the couples we were praying into parenthood, have been blessed by the arrival of their son, whom they've named Peter Aslan. I have known many, many C. S. Lewis fans in my time, but this is the first time I've heard someone do what now seems an obvious idea: use *Aslan* as a middle name.

It is marvelous to have a first child, a first son, arrive in Bright Week. From all descriptions Peter is extraordinary, a genius, talented, handsome, kind, thrifty, reverent, all things to all parents, especially his. Funny, about eighteen years ago, I held my squalling daughter in a hospital delivery room, and I could have sworn she held all those titles.

# Sheila's Painting

"You won't like this one," Sheila says. "This one is kind of a Crucifixion." We are up in the loft of her rambling old house, amid scents of cat litter, incense, and warm summer night. I am going to a conference in a few days; I wanted to look through her paintings and select some slides to take along to show to a friend who collects Christian art.

Not many people collect or value or even know the existence of serious Christian art. This is one reason that Sheila, a widow, takes in boarders and scrambles to a half-dozen part-time jobs in spite of health problems requiring home dialysis. Adversities hone her like flint. She is slim and quick, with sharp brown eyes and graying hair that flies out with abandon. She wears gauzy cottons and tie-dyes, and her home is similarly bohemian, a congregation of mismatched furniture, Indian bedspreads, and creaky wooden floors. Visiting Sheila is for me strongly nostalgic; I feel like I'm back in my college days. My house is of the same era as this, and my furnishings are mostly thrift shop treasures, too, but it doesn't work like Sheila's. Her house is carefree; mine looks too intentional.

Downstairs the faded bamboo print wallpaper is nearly obliterated by her vivid paintings, portraits, and abstracts. Up here she has stacked more canvases across the stairwell. They straddle the waist-high railing, and she turns them down one at a time for me to see. Already a stack of four or five lie like pancakes, and, after the warning, she gently turns down one more large abstract piece.

The canvas revealed behind it is horrible and then, after a beat, horribly sad. Against a vague seascape of pale blue and rose is suspended a withered corpse, not human but animal. It is a cacophony, gray shreds of leather skin and narrow white bones. The harmony of the body is wildly disrupted, and a claw-tipped forearm appears to emerge from the ripped bag of abdomen. Behind the head a blue line levels the horizon, and above it floats a pale golden sky.

The contrast between the distant tenderness of the background and the wracked torment of the corpse clears a space for quiet sorrow. The head bent double on the broken neck is bullet shaped, with jutting teeth. "Is it a rat?" I ask.

"I think it's a squirrel," Sheila says. She goes to her bedroom and retrieves a weathered board, on which is fixed a pathetic little corpse. It is identical to the one in the painting.

"I found it in a bag of peat moss," she goes on. "Perhaps a cat had hidden it there to keep till later. I hung it on the outside of the garage for two or three years, then brushed it well with a toothbrush. It's quite clean."

We gaze at the little figure, then back to the canvas. The torn, frozen squirrel is an emblem of helplessness. Its gray head is bowed; this is no image of outrage and pain, no shock and vigor of blood, only futility. Behind it the blue and rosy sea is in quiet motion.

Sheila calls this piece *The Groaning*. The apostle Paul wrote in the letter to the Romans, "The whole creation has been groaning in travail together until now; and not only the creation, but we ourselves, who have the first fruits of the Spirit, groan inwardly as we wait for adoption as sons, the redemption of our bodies."

"We don't realize how much we've lost," she says with quiet passion. "We don't realize how far we've fallen."

This is a stunning painting, but a viewer might well ask what it means. Sheila's explanation is something of a private reading, moving but not obvious. Christian art is, in general, in a dilemma. The great bulk of painting currently done on Christian themes is produced for popular consumption, Bible story pieces laminated onto plaques and sold in religious book and gift stores. These are usually straightforward depictions of events both real—Bible scenes, for example—and imagined, like the popular image of Jesus embracing a new arrival in heaven.

Is it good art? Apparently it does a good job of what it's trying to do, namely to present scenes to the faithful that will provoke feelings of devotion, assurance, and comfort. Most popular Christian art is, like popular music and popular novels, aimed at a broad sensibility. As such, it's not subtle or complex and usually is ignorant of ambivalence, conflict, and tragedy (though sentimental pathos may apply). Rod the Reporter has a term for a place like a Christian gift store: Irony-Free Zone. Popular Christian art is lambs and children and happy Jesuses. It's not a withered squirrel.

While prospects for serious Christian artists have gradually improved over the last decade, it's still an uphill struggle for most. The constant cozy presence of sentimental, popular art makes it difficult for those who would like to produce more thoughtful paintings on Christian themes. Ones that clearly represent biblical or spiritual scenes have their impact flattened by so many mass-produced versions of the same. One solution is to paint dark, as my friend in Virginia, Edward Knippers, does with his vast, roiling depictions of biblical events. Ed produces scenes that seem to be in constant motion, muddy and violent, and he does not hesitate to show genitalia and breasts. Ed is bringing to literal realization Flannery O'Connor's defense of her harrowing short stories: "For the hard of hearing you shout, and for the almost-blind you draw large and startling figures." The paintings are very large, and they do not fail to startle.

These seem to be the poles currently available in Christian art: comfort or disturb. In a culture where Christianity is tamed and toothless, and popular art seems intent on keeping believers that way, artists like Sheila, Ed, and O'Connor shout an alarm. One might wish for alternative conversations: art that inspires courage, for example, or awe or sorrow for sin. Perhaps such is not yet possible; perhaps the first message, "Wake up!," is still struggling to get through.

Indeed, it's hard for these paintings to find a venue. Of his own work, Ed says, "They're too big for homes, too nude for churches, and too religious for public spaces." Major museums aren't in the market for Bible scenes, unless they're a few hundred years old. Though Ed has had more success than Sheila, the content of his paintings still makes them largely unwelcome in the big leagues.

One artist has broken through into the elite museum world with an explicit Christian message, but he's not a college-educated professional living in the suburbs of Washington, D.C. Howard Finster is a bicycle repairman and preacher from the Georgia hills, a ferocious old man whom secular admirers might mistakenly describe as "simple." Finster has visions. In 1976, a blob of paint spilled on his finger developed a face and spoke to him: "Paint sacred art." His art now sells for thousands of dollars, has been on the covers of magazines and rock music albums, and is enthusiastically received and exhibited widely. According to the American Visionary Art Museum, he's the most widely exhibited living American artist.

Yet his work is emphatically Christian and relentlessly evangelistic. A typical Finster painting is not a canvas but a plywood, cut to shape (angels are particular favorites; Finster sees angels) and painted in a simple, disarming style with bright primary colors. Then Finster writes all over the piece with a black marker, messages that come naturally to an old preacher in the Georgia hills. Sophisticated collectors love it, but one suspects they don't always get it.

For example, in 1990 the Smithsonian Museum of American Art acquired over four hundred works from the collection of folk art connoisseur Herbert Wade Hemphill, Jr. The ensuing exhibit included many works by Finster, including his portrait of Hemphill. Finster depicted Hemphill with a cool-guy 1970s haircut, dressed in T-shirt and jeans, standing with one hand on a cocked hip in a Starsky-and-Hutch pose. The background is filled with giant covers of books, and the books are covered with handwritten messages. Here's one:

> He That Believeth Not Shall Be Damned
> Not A Crown But Hellfire And Brimstone
> If You Only Had One Sweet Son
> And You Gave His Life To Save
> Ten Wicked Men. And They
> Returned And Denied That You
> Gave Your Only Son For Them
> And Said You Child Never Exist
> No One Died For Us Please Go
> Right Now And Call You Child
> To You And Measure You Love For Him
> And Turn And Look At The Most
> Sinful Man You Know And
> Think If You Would Trade Your
> Presus Son For Him. God Is Love

As I type those words tears well up in my eyes again, as they did when I first read them on the portrait hanging on the museum wall. Next to the painting the exhibit's curators had affixed a plaque to help us understand it: "The historical, popular, and biblical subjects of Finster's portraits embody his concept of the inventor as someone whose creative process will provide the world's salvation."

Such obtuseness is nearly beyond belief. Finster has a strong opinion about who provides the world's salvation, and it surely isn't himself. That someone could study, admire, and clearly love these paintings yet miss the point so disastrously makes me wonder about interpretations offered for other paintings in the museum.

There's a strong scent of condescension around a Finster exhibit. I first encountered his work in an urban gallery, where I heard two visitors giggling over a painting. Finster had produced a testimony to the healing of his hernia and in the process had misspelled *truss* as *trust*; spelling is not his strong point. The art buffs clearly thought this was adorable, but they missed the central point the artist was trying to make: God heals! I asked the woman at the cash register if anyone coming to the show had mentioned interest in the religious content; no, she said, eyeing me as if I were someone who should be carefully watched.

For the hard of hearing you shout. Sometimes they still don't hear.

I have a small Finster angel hanging over my desk. Years ago we made a detour on our family vacation to visit Finster's extraordinary two-acre spread of art and sculpture north of Atlanta, called Paradise Gardens. It's a jumbled, junkyard kind of place, and as one of his signs explains, the media are part of the message: "I built this park of broken pieces trying to mend a broken world of people traveling their last road."

When I got home I wrote Finster a note of appreciation and mentioned my pro-life work; I asked if he'd ever painted anything on that theme. He wrote back immediately in wavery Palmer script, "My prayers are for you in your work. Glad to see people take a stand for what is right. I will try to make a special angel for you in your work." The box arrived within a week, bringing a flying angel covered with messages like "All Great People Was Once Babys Can't You See." On the angel's outstretched arm is written, "Reach For Life To Save It."

Finster can get away with this. Ed and Sheila cannot; they're not cute enough, not strange enough, not "other" enough to be kept safely at a distance. Serious faith is suspect among many in the elite class, and straightforward representation of explicit Christian subject matter is impaired by the cloying prevalence of gift shop Christian art. Among three possible responses, Ed chooses the most direct, reclaiming the subject matter with disturbingly brutal depictions of biblical scenes. Sheila is more likely to choose the other two paths, painting abstracts that depict spiritual realities (for example, a series of colorful oils representing the daily offices) or representational paintings with private meanings, such as the crucified squirrel.

One of these I fall in love with and decide to buy on the spot: a small canvas filled up with an old brick warehouse, which stands to face the setting sun. The windows are opaque and blazing red; the abandoned building looks forlorn yet full of warm intensity and hidden hope. Near a corner is a small tree, orange and brown but concealing one smudge of tenacious green. Sheila painted this at the first anniversary of her husband's death.

She's surprised that I like it so much I want to buy it; she says that she doesn't often sell a painting. That's one of the reasons I'm here, to gather slides that I hope will appeal to a wealthier collector of Christian art than I. Such collectors are few and far between, and the Christian who wants to produce quality works of art had better have another source of income.

We take a last look at the painting of the broken squirrel. "Sheila, it's very beautiful, and very sad," I say, "but nobody's going to say, 'That would look perfect over the couch.'"

# 5

## PENTECOST

---

# Angry in Church

Anger is not one of my besetting sins. Not that I feel the loss; other pesky temptations keep me busy enough. When a magazine recently asked me to write an article about gluttony, the editor's letter read, "We thought you would be the perfect person." Uh, thanks, I think.

I have besetting sins and pet sins and occasional sins, but anger is a rare visitor. Until this week. For some reason, I'm feeling more peeved, more consistently, than I can remember being for a long time.

Pentecost brings the season of Pascha to a close, and on the evening of Pentecost we observe Kneeling Vespers. On this early summer evening I'm in Basil's living room, standing with a little choir that this time is composed of only me, Carolyn, and Zenaida the alto. And I'm feeling just plain crabby.

The living room is crowded and stuffy. Gary is standing at the altar jammed in the corner, with icons crowding up to the ceiling above it. There are just too many icons in this room. I stand next to the beige-pink wall, by the door that leads to the dining room. The icons keep getting shifted around to accommodate new ones; there are tiny gouges and chips in the plaster where nails were removed. They irritate me.

Carolyn is leading our little choir; she often does when Margo and David are out of town. I suspect that my musical sense is actually a little more accurate than hers, but Carolyn has this advantage: she pays attention. I tend to daydream. I'm always waking up responding, "Lord, have mercy," when everyone else has moved on to "Grant this, O Lord." I think this dreaminess annoys Zenaida; I'll be standing in front of the music stand, lost in space, and she'll reach around me to snap the page over. Some of my earliest memories are of teachers saying, "Mrs. Green, Frederica would be an excellent student if she would only pay attention."

Carolyn pays attention. Her eyes are wide, and her frame is narrow and sinewy. She has the beauty of a forest animal and is just as skittish. Her hands tremble just a bit as she marks the beat or turns the page. Though we're just a bunch of people in Basil's living room, she feels the heat of public scrutiny keenly.

I feel irritated that she's nervous; it makes me feel jumpy, too.

Here's another thing. I came home from a few days' travel and there was an awful smell in the kitchen. No one else in the family could smell it. This is stupid, because I have the worst sense of smell in the family, but when I opened the door under the sink and asked Gary to take a sniff he did, then shook his head. Nope, smelled fine.

I began hauling stuff out from under the sink. It turned out I was right, the details of which I will omit.

Next, Carolyn reads the scriptural account of the day of Pentecost. However, instead of *divers* ("they spoke in divers tongues"), she keeps hesitating, then coming up with *divvers*. I'm bugged by this, but I wouldn't say anything; I wouldn't want to make her more self-conscious.

Zenaida leans over and whispers, "Die-vers." My irritation with Carolyn transmutes into irritation with Zenaida. Oh, leave her alone.

Why am I so cranky? These are all good people, and they're not doing anything wrong. But I feel deeply aggrieved. Earlier today the kids put on a passion play for the church, directed by the Sunday school super, Dr. Pat. Last week Dr. Pat had told us to costume them in basic bathrobe-and-towel gear, which I did; today she snapped at me that "Jesus (David) doesn't look like a Jesus, and the centurion (Stephen) *certainly* doesn't look like a centurion."

I don't see why we have to have a church with people in it. They could just mail their checks in. Gary and I could sit in our living room, with our own little icon corner, and listen to recordings of beautiful Orthodox chant. Maybe have a little wine or cheese and crackers. We could have delightful conversations about spiritual things and be quite edified. When it was time for church, we could phone it in. We could hold church over the computer, on-line.

Except that I'm already in a small on-line circle of Christians, and sometimes I get frustrated with them, too. While I was out of town a squabble erupted over the old heresy of universalism, and now everyone is offended and misunderstood. Especially me, because I've been particularly misunderstood and have the most right to be offended. I have more right than anybody.

Kneeling Vespers differs from the rest in that we kneel, for three long prayers. Other than specified occasions like this, kneeling is rare in Orthodoxy.

I settle down, grumpy, on the thick Oriental rug that lies on top of Basil's brown and orange shag carpet. The first prayer begins:

O Lord, who art immaculate, undefiled, unoriginate, invisible, in- comprehensible, inscrutable, unchanging, unsurpassable, immea- surable, forbearing, who alone hast immortality, who dwellest in light unapproachable, who hast made heaven and earth and the sea, and all created things therein, who grantest unto all men their petitions before they ask . . .

I love being Orthodox, but sometimes, I swear, I wish they'd just cut to the chase.

. . . we pray thee and beseech thee, O Master, who lovest mankind, the Father of our Lord and God and Savior Jesus Christ, who for us men and for our salvation came down from heaven and was incarnate of the Holy Spirit and of Mary, the ever virgin and most glorious Theotokos, who first did teach in words and afterwards did show by deeds, when he endured his saving passion, who did give us, thy humble and unworthy servants, an example, whereby we should offer unto thee prayers with the bending of the neck and knees, both for our sins and for the ignorance of the people . . .

This far into it, and there still isn't a full stop. The wool rug is itchy under my shins. I'll bet this prayer goes on for pages. Then it'll be up and down and incense and chants and another long, long prayer. And we'll still have a third prayer to go.

The rhythm of the prayer begins to put me in neutral. I'm not mollified, of course, and all my just grievances have not been redressed, and I don't intend to give up a single one of them. But the long prayer is a flowing river, swept this way and that by commas, endlessly flowing. After a while I flow along, still pouting but quieter in heart.

Do thou thyself, who art great in mercy and lovest mankind, hearken to us in that day when we shall call upon thee, and especially on this day of Pentecost, on which, after our Lord Jesus Christ had ascended unto the heavens and had sat down at the right hand of thee, the God and Father, he did send down upon his holy disciples and apostles the Holy Spirit, which did also sit upon each of them, and they were filled with his inexhaustible grace, and they spake with other tongues of thy greatness, and they prophesied . . .

It is a lulling flow. I wonder why anger is so sweet. I go through life feeling vaguely guilty for a number of minor things, except for those times when I feel pointedly and miserably guilty for major things. None of this is comfortable. The past is a lot easier than the present. In the present I am cresting up to the front of the unknown every minute and feeling inadequate and feeling responsible for too many failures. Failures of kindness, failures of humility, failures of attention. It is a nervous, uncomfortable place to be. Most of the time I feel like I'm riding a bike over uneven ground, edgy, scanning for the next rock or rut or railroad track. If I could only get five minutes into the future before everyone else, it would be so much easier.

When is this alleviated? Sometimes when we're laughing hard around the dinner table. Or when I finish a big assignment and hit the "Send" key on the computer. Sometimes when a movie or book catches me up, out of this uneven life.

But, oh, how sweet is anger. When I'm angry, I'm not in the wrong. Somebody else is in the wrong, and for once I have peace. A delicious peace that gnaws over the wrong like a lion with a ragged bone. It is delicious and compelling enough that it urges me to accumulate other wrongs and hold them greedily close. I love to be wronged; only then, for that brief moment, can I be sure I'm right. It is intoxicating in its sweetness, this brief joy in being right. It is good to be a victim, because victims are sinless.

Last week Stephen had his first, long-coveted professional acting job: he performed in a video for elementary school kids about bullies. Stephen got to be the bully; he got to push another kid into a mud puddle.

I sat on a folding chair just out of camera range and watched the rehearsals and the taping. (The crew created a mud puddle on a perfectly barren basketball court by scattering a bucketful of dirt around and sprinkling it with a hose.) I could tell Stephen was irritated. The little boy he was scheduled to shove had been performing professionally a long time, was a child model, smug and show-offy, and as Stephen told me later, "a jerk."

The moment came for the big shove, and Stephen ran at this kid with his arms outstretched. Just before his palms contacted the boy's chest, I saw Stephen's face clipped as in a single frame. It was frozen in fury, his blue eyes clear and cold, his stubborn jaw set like a knife. He ran toward this model with all the passion he possessed, rapt in anger; and in his face I saw my own, intoxicated by delicious anger, transformed with a wild, wild beauty.

SECOND WEEK AFTER PENTECOST

---

# My Conversion

Twenty-one years ago today I did the strangest of the many strange things I've attempted in life. I became an active, committed Christian.

When Gary and I met in 1972, I was a pint-sized package of sarcastic hipness and a perpetually indignant women's libber. I was also a lapsed Roman Catholic. As a child I'd had a sweet, childish piety, and at nine I told my parents that I wanted to be a nun. They were witty, educated people who traveled in intellectual circles, and they explained to me that this was neurotic. By high school I was attending the Unitarian Church and beginning a restless search for something that would ring true. After years of cruising circles through Eastern religions, I settled for Hinduism, which I thought had a higher entertainment value than the other brands. I chose it as I chose my clothes; I can't say that it ever chose me or that I surrendered to it in any profound way.

During my college years I lived on Olympia Hill, a site less heavenly than its name suggests. Our Southern city had once been host to a booming textile industry, and a hundred years ago a ramshackle collection of unheated wooden houses had been thrown together beyond the railroad tracks. By the time I arrived, Olympia Hill had developed a mixed population: what my grandmother contemptuously referred to as "po' buckra" (white trash) and hippies from the college.

Country people and blue-collar laborers lived side by side with more flamboyant types. One neighbor, an avant-garde artist, spent a semester working in sweet potatoes (I remember in particular a belt studded with them). Next door to him, a grim Communist was vocally in favor of returning possession of all things to "The People." He came over so frequently to borrow items from us that my roommate took to announcing up the stairs, "The People is here again, and he wants to borrow your stereo."

Down the dirt road was a tiny clapboard Pentecostal church, where on Sunday evenings they would sing and holler, raising dust in the pink twilight air. Across the road the neighbor's hog would sometimes mark the noise and rest his chin on the peeling wooden fence. I sat on the front porch rocker and listened to the congregation's wholehearted joy, sometimes feeling moved to longing tears. How sweet it would be, I thought, to be that simple. But of course, I was too sophisticated for that. You can't return to that childlike ignorance. I had shot too far past that place of wistful piety and could never return.

Gary didn't seem to feel any such longing; if God existed, it was okay, as long as he didn't bother us. As we wound up our college careers, Gary was more interested in making sure he took every philosophy course taught by his favorite professor. It was in one of those last courses that he was assigned to read a Gospel. He chose Mark, because it was shortest.

Then something happened to him as he read it. "It's this Jesus," he said to me, a little bewildered. "There's something about him. I've never encountered anyone like him. It's like he speaks with authority. If Jesus says there's a God, then I guess there must be one."

This was not welcome news to me. I felt pretty hostile to Christianity, which I thought was an oppressive, patriarchal religion that took people away from the real work of revolution. I was already annoyed that so many students on campus were wearing "One Way" Jesus-freak patches on their jeans. I was one of the few wearing a women's liberation patch: the cross-and-circle women's symbol with a fist in the center.

The importance of this image to me had been the occasion of an unsettling experience not long before. I had gone out at dusk with a can of paint to streak a four-foot-high women's liberation symbol on the temporary wall around a construction site. The campus was oddly deserted for the time of day, and I worked undisturbed. Then a young man came slowly up the hill below me, until he stood looking at my work, glossy green on white. Then he looked at me.

"This is not really important," he said. I looked at him amazed, my paintbrush dripping down onto the street. He gestured at the wall. "This doesn't really matter. It's not eternally important. But someday you will find out what is." Then he walked on.

The encounter raised some lingering, eerie feelings, and my irritation with the Jesus bozos increased. Secretly, I was afraid. Those idiots had warped so many minds; was Gary to be next?

No, I was next. Gary was on a leisurely path, pondering Scripture and theology, continuing to search and read, drawn irresistibly from one tome to the next. I was about to turn about-face and rocket down the highway to faith.

We wound up two years of tie-dyed romance with a wedding in the woods; I wore unbleached muslin, sandals, and flowers in my hair. After the vegetarian reception under the trees, we headed off for a three-month honeymoon, hitchhiking and hopping trains across the face of Europe.

On June 20, 1974, we took the ferry from Wales to Ireland, then hitchhiked to Dublin. After dropping our bags at a hotel, we walked sightseeing through the city in the waning light and stopped at an old gray church squeezed into the facade of a city block.

I strolled in the dim interior, past the massive main altar, past the statues. At last I came to a small altar surmounted with a statue of Jesus. The sculptor had depicted Jesus' heart visible in the center of his chest, twined with thorns and springing with flames. I remembered from girlhood the story: he had appeared like this to St. Margaret Mary Alacoque three hundred years ago. He had told her, "Behold the heart which has so loved mankind."

When I came to myself again I realized I was on my knees. I could hear a voice speaking inside. It was saying, "I am your life.

"I am your life. You think that your life is your name, your personality, your history. But that is not your life. I am your life.

"Beyond that, you think that your life is the fact that you are alive, that your breath goes in and out, that energy courses in your veins. But even that is not your life. I am your life.

"I am the foundation of everything else in your life."

When I got up I felt pretty shaky. Nothing like this had ever happened to me before. In a strange way, it seemed like the most real thing that had ever happened, a brutal confrontation with reality. In comparison, all previous life seemed pale.

But I had no idea what it meant. The only sense I could make of it at the time was that, although all religions were of equal value, I would now be a Christian instead of a Hindu. But at the same time I sensed that I wasn't merely making an alternate choice. Instead, a spiritual power had chosen me—a force that I hadn't known existed.

I didn't tell Gary for a week; it took that long to get over the caught-breath, what-was-that feeling of surprise. However, I did immediately become annoyingly nice. I didn't want to leave the hotel room in the morning before straightening up, as a favor to the maid. When we stood by the side of the road hitchhiking, playing word games to pass the time, I would let him win. I felt unexpectedly, unusually happy.

I also felt a pressing need to read a Bible. If this guy Jesus is going to be my boss, who the heck is he? I bought a small King James Version in London and plunged into the Gospel of Matthew. I wasn't pleased. I found a lot to argue with. But a conviction was slowly seeping into me: I didn't make the world, I didn't know everything, and it was time to sit down and listen. The experience in the Dublin church had blown away my neat ideas of the orderly world; I had been forced to admit I was dealing with things I didn't understand. I needed to be taught by someone who did. I kept plowing away at the Gospels, though not without grumbling.

A flash-forward of six months found Gary and me kneeling on the floor of our one-room log cabin while our friend Greg prayed with us. He had introduced us to a new idea: we should formalize our relationship with Jesus by stating in prayer our intention to follow him. My first reaction had been, "But—we're not Baptists." Gary and I had grown up in South Carolina, where "take Jesus as your personal savior" was associated with country folks and shoutin', sweatin' fundamentalists. You mean people in graduate school should do that, too? But it felt right—as if we had been groping along an unknown path, and this would bring us firmly into the light.

That was twenty-one years ago. I cannot explain why I was seized in an instant and swept into the thorn-pierced heart of God.

I know I don't deserve it. Nothing in my life made me worthy; I was far from good or virtuous, a petty, self-centered person who delighted in ridiculing the Lord and his followers. I actively tried to destroy the faith of the simple Christians I met: the apostle Paul only held the coats of those who stoned Stephen, but I was in there throwing rocks. That Jesus would snatch me out of the sea of my confusion and self-will is completely inexplicable. Nothing I can do can ever repay that gift; all I want to do is call others to accept it. Twenty-one years later, I'm still getting used to the strangeness of that moment, a single moment of exploding grace, when I looked at a statue in a Dublin church.

*Thursday, June 29*
*Feast of Saints Peter and Paul*

THIRD WEEK AFTER PENTECOST

# Inspiration Plate

Today we conclude the fast that falls between the octave of Pentecost and June 29; last year it was only two days, but this year it's been ten. Gary is out of town, and Megan is staying with friends, so tonight I'll take the boys to the all-you-can-eat buffet at the shopping center. It's a branch of the chain called Old Country Buffet, but we call it Wide Country Buffet, because the doors are twice as wide as those on every other store in the shopping center. Makes you think.

Today may have historic repercussions, because the pope is meeting with Patriarch Bartholomew to pursue healing of the ancient schism between East and West. To celebrate Christian unity, I bought an icon. Actually, it's a Protestant icon, and it's ceramic. To tell the truth, it's a plate. I bought it at a thrift shop.

I like thrift shops. Most of our furnishings come from thrift shops, and I always scout the dishware. A little souvenir plate from the 1964 New York World's Fair was such a hit that Gary hung it on the kitchen wall by the phone. Not long ago I picked up a clever piece: a gold-rimmed white plate that had a message printed in the middle, designed to be hidden until hubby has eaten away his meal. It reads, "How about you doing the dishes tonight or how about buying me a Crosley automatic dishwasher?" The question mark is lime green and hovers, gigantic, behind the message.

Today I found a plate that showed a pink-lipped Jesus with tumbling golden brown curls gazing upward into a stream of pale yellow light. He is wearing an unfocused, benign expression, but his halo of short yellow dashes suggests surprise. There are vague pastel colored shapes behind him, reminiscent of stained glass windows, so maybe he was in church when this picture was made.

On Jesus' white blouse is written in gentle script, "Inspiration." I suppose this means that Jesus was feeling inspired just then. When he returned to the next meeting of his men's Bible study, and they asked, "When did you feel closest to God this week?," this is the moment he'd describe.

Is this an icon? If so, it's not a very good one—too sentimental, too soft, and too ahistorical. But it could no doubt fill the role of an icon for some Protestants. They would hang it on the wall, in the dining room, much as we put icons in our icon corner. It would remind them of spiritual realities and make visible the constant presence of the Lord in their midst. Perhaps my disdain is mere snobbery. This image of Jesus is nothing if not sincere.

But what to do with it? The plate is resting here on my desk by the computer, and it poses a challenge. Kiss it or put a sandwich on it?

## Stephen's Opinion

It's a hundred degrees outside, and this old house is not air conditioned. Someone gave us a big bag of collard greens, but as much as we love them we can't withstand the heat it would take to boil them for a couple of hours. We give the bag to our next-door neighbors, an elderly black couple. They can cook, because their house came with an extra stove: a 1927 gas model down in the cool basement.

We have a single window-unit air conditioner, and it cools my office and our adjoining bedroom; some heavy summer nights all three kids sleep on my office couch and floor. This afternoon Stephen comes in and flops on the sofa. The humidity is making his hair go in whimsical waves, which is serious business to a thirteen-year-old. He says, "I figured out why I like being Orthodox better than belonging to a Protestant church."

Last night he had attended, for the first time, a junior high youth group at a large church nearby. As a home-schooler, he needs a chance to make friends in his age group, and this seemed like a good idea; our youth group at Holy Cross numbers only a dozen, mostly girls with (I suspect) varying-intensity crushes on Stephen.

"What happened," he goes on, "is they read a poem about Jesus, like it was a letter from him. He was saying stuff like, 'I made the sunrise for you, and you didn't get up in time to notice, I gave you this beautiful day and you just went on your way.' It was signed, 'Your friend, Jesus.'"

Stephen frowns. "It was actually a pretty good poem, but I don't like how all they ever do is put him on the same level with us. It's always like"—here he holds out his hands, flat, parallel to each other—"we're here, and God is here. But actually, it's more like this.

We're here"—a hand at chest level— "and God is here." A hand high, by his ear.

"It's like it's all about how Jesus can serve us. But it's supposed to be about how we can serve him. Like the old hymns we had before, starting with 'Jesus loves me, this I know'—it's all about me, about us. But the Orthodox hymns are about him, about the great things he's done.

"Think about it! He died on the cross for your sins, two thousand years ago! You should get down on your knees and thank him for his mercy! Not just be treating him like a pal."

What I can't figure out is why a kid would prefer a tough, God-centered gospel. "Why do you like that better, Stephen?" I ask.

"Well, don't you?" he returns.

"Yes, but I'm actually not sure why. Why do you think you do?"

Stephen looks at me. "It just seems a whole lot more *appropriate* to me," he says, seriously. "Think of all he's done for us. They say, 'Jesus loves you so you should be glad.' But I think it's 'Jesus loves you and you should be glad, and you should try to show it in every way you can all the time!' Like the two-hour church services and fasting and confession and all that. He deserves it! And, like Megan says, 'It's like boot camp.' It's what we need, too!"

This rings a bell; Megan has boot camp on her mind, because that's where her recently acquired boyfriend, Michael, is right now. In May we spent a week at the beach with my Byzantine Catholic friend, Connie, and her family but didn't reckon what could happen when her son and my daughter spent some extended time together. Now Megan wants to go next fall to the Virginia college where Connie is director of student affairs and Bill's on the faculty. I'm a little relieved that the tantalizing Michael himself will be on a navy base, several hundred miles away.

Back to Stephen's serious gaze. "Well," I say, "a lot of people's attitude toward life now is like that of a consumer, shopping for the best movie or tire or hamburger. I guess when people think about how to attract nonbelievers to Christianity, they naturally emphasize how much good it will do them, as if it were another product. This is what people are used to, after all, being sold stuff on the basis that they'll like it or enjoy it. What's going to attract some-body to this tough, boot-camp God you describe?"

"Well, I think that God by himself is appealing," Stephen says. "You could just describe all the great works he's done. That ought to attract people."

I've been wondering if this is so. Don't we all get tired of being pampered? Aren't we looking for a God who is bigger than we are? Don't we, in fact, want to be challenged to grow stronger, to grow into men and women worthy of admiration, not remaining chil-dren to be indulged?

"Well, Stephen, you may be right," I say. "I hope so."


*Saturday, July 29*
*Martyrs Callinicos, Theodotia, and Children*

SEVENTH WEEK AFTER PENTECOST

---

# Green Linoleum Floor

One advantage of knowing Big City Reporters is that they know further Big Shots; last Sunday Rod visited and brought to church a brilliant jet-setter, a woman recently returned from Greece. Today, over breakfast, I hear of her reaction to Holy Cross: it was nice in many ways, but "not like worshiping in a thousand-year-old monastery."

No use protesting that. I close my eyes and try to picture monks moving through the interior of an ancient church, try to imagine the ancient prayers sung in a place that better suits their solemnity and beauty. To go from that to our propped-up, pushed-together worship space must be quite a contrast.

Still, I've never thought of our humble setting as a disadvantage. It's pup-tent Orthodoxy, making do with the best we can, with can-dlesticks from someone's attic and a table from someone's garage. I know what a beautiful church looks like, but ours is just a different kind of beauty. It is the beauty of a scrapbook quilt, made of the tatters of best loved clothes. It is the beauty of a bunch of dandelions on the kitchen windowsill.

These thoughts prompt a tangle of reflections on aesthetics. Beauty is not solely in the eye of the beholder; God dictated very specific and very elaborate appointments for the tabernacle in Moses' time. The beauty of a stark New England church was not anticipated, nor was that of a gray-on-gray Gothic cathedral. It was to be exuberant in gold and scarlet, swathed with costly fabric and trimmed with bells.

We can't come near that. At our Sundays-only rental site, improvements might only make things worse. A fresh coat of paint wouldn't make this schoolroom look any more like a thousand-year-old monastery. The building's owners had the linoleum floor stripped and waxed, and now it glows nuclear green.

I know what a lovely Orthodox church looks like, stately, fragrant, and ringed with images of the saints. Here, the saints who surround us are only small, laminated plaques set up on the windowsills. The fragrance of incense is washed out every week by the fragrance of Lysol.

Our only loveliness is Orthodoxy itself. We set out like a jewel the liturgy, the music, the Scriptures—the ancient faith, and our own faith born so recently in our convert hearts, still learning. We make this church every week, bolting together the icon stands and pushing the altar out of from the corner. We pack up and take down every week, like desert wanderers seeking a home. Our very labor is part of the offering, part of the beauty. The best beauty is truth itself. A jewel looks stunning set on black velvet, but here it is displayed on simple muslin. There is nothing to distract from the purity of Orthodoxy alone, the faith of the ages.

It's not quite true that the saints around us are only small icon plaques. I stand and sing every Sunday in the midst of saints, Hardworking Jeannie and Basil and Sheila and Jonathan, with my own sons and husband arrayed in gold beside the altar. It is enough. Someday we will have our own home, and Carolyn will paint us icons all around the inside, making visible the larger heavenly community we cannot now see. But for now, this is enough. And this is beautiful.

# Confession at the Monastery

My e-friend Terry always ends his posts with C. S. Lewis's favorite farewell to friends, "Under the Mercy." Our buddy Chris recently sent me a copy of a post to Terry, which he closed with, "Over the Mercy (and through the woods)."

Today the Mathewes-Greens are sailing through the woods in search of Mercy. We are in the Dormition fast, which begins August 1 and runs to the 15th, the feast of the "falling asleep," or Dormition, of the Virgin. There are four major fasts in the Orthodox year: Lent, Dormition, Nativity (which runs from November 15 to Christmas), and Apostles (from All Saints, a week after Pentecost, to the feast of Sts. Peter and Paul, June 29). The latter fast varies, of course, with the date of Pentecost; last year it was only two days.

We aim to go to confession at least four times a year, during these fasts. Confession is a little trickier for the priest's family than for other parishioners. Anyone at Holy Cross can make an appointment with Gary any time or just stay after Vespers on Saturday night. But we can't confess to our household dad, so we make this hour-long journey through the Maryland hills to see the priests at the Orthodox monastery in the shadow of Sugarloaf Mountain.

This monastery—also named Holy Cross—began with two priests who came out of the Byzantine Catholic church years ago. They started with three old homes in a rough section of Washington (the average on their block was one murder a week), and they turned one into a book and icon store and another into a residence for women monastics. The third was their own residence, with the garage turned into a chapel.

Back when Gary was first considering Orthodoxy I made an appointment to talk to one of these priest-monks, Father David. I wanted to know what Orthodox spirituality was like. I described my prayer discipline to date and explained that for years I had been going for spiritual direction to a somewhat liberal Roman Catholic laywoman.

Father David was alarmed. He warned that spiritual misdirection is fearfully prevalent and possibly demonic. I was skeptical; this sounded pretty paranoid to me. Father David is a handsome, earnest man, lean and intense, and he talked at length. I was miffed by that; how could he know what I needed unless he stopped talking and listened? It hadn't yet dawned on me that I would have to stop talking, myself, and do a lot of listening to understand Orthodoxy. I didn't know how much I didn't know; I didn't realize that most of what I needed to learn wouldn't be found already lodged inside my smug little heart.

Then Father David began to explain about the need for discipline, one example of which was standing for worship. (What, you stand for worship?) He explained that you must stand still, with your weight equally balanced on both feet, and not shift back and forth. Sure, it's uncomfortable at first, but that is what discipline is like, as we strive to master our longing for self-indulgence and become one with God.

This was too much for me. I went home and told Gary that I didn't think I could become Orthodox. It was too weird.

Some months later we visited the same monastery for Vespers. I got to meet the head monk, Father Abbot Joseph. Father Joseph is as different from Father David as possible: large, jolly, with a teasing manner. In the movie version he would be played by Dom DeLuise.

The usual inscrutable Vespers service began, and I tried to remember when to bow and what to kiss and to stand completely straight. But then Father Joseph swirled through, vestments floating behind him, and plopped down on a bench near me. "Siddown!" he hissed at me. "Siddown! Go ahead!"

Full of misgivings, I sank down on the bench. Was Father David going to skewer me? But didn't Abbot Joseph outrank him? What's the deal here, anyway?

Needless to say, nothing happened. Except that I learned something about Orthodoxy: it is tremendously individualized. The disciplines exist in a continuum, and you just keep trying to do a little more, as you're able. Now I stand all the time for worship but shift around as much as my restless feet need to; that's where I am on the curve.

The little monastery continued to grow, and the neighborhood continued to deteriorate. It was decided to move the residences but not the store. They were able to buy a defunct Roman Catholic monastery out in the Maryland countryside, and it is there that we are flying today. Gary steers the old station wagon down the narrow road and around the hills faster than I would, but his reflexes are better than mine.

It's yardwork day at the monastery, and Father Orestes is working with a crew of people who are members of the parish here. He is wearing a black cassock, which doesn't seem the thing for loading wheelbarrows in the blazing heat. "Won't Abbot Joseph allow you to wear jeans for this kind of work?" I ask. Father Orestes is puzzled for a minute. "Oh, sure! I can wear anything I want!" he says. "But I want to wear this. It's important for people to see us in our cassocks." It is an old one, at least, with paint stains and a ragged hem.

Father Orestes is a small man, maybe all of thirty, with a bright and eager demeanor. He sometimes fills in when Gary is out of town and is a delightful preacher. His small face and brilliant eyes are almost overcome by bushy red hair: a fluffy border escaping from his hat and a beard scraggling up his cheeks like climbing roses.

No one wants to go first for confession, so I go first. Instead of waiting in the parlor as usual, the other M-Gs sit outside in the shade and swat gnats. It's like an oven in the un-air-conditioned house. The other night, we hear, Father Orestes left his sweltering upstairs bedroom and came downstairs to sleep on the sofa in the living room, hoping for a few degrees' respite in temperature. Abbot Joseph came down sometime later, for the same reason, and in the dark sat down on poor little Father Orestes. It's a funny story, but given the disparity in size, I guess it could have been what the paper would have reported as a "freak accident."

Father Orestes and I enter the dark chapel and sit on a bench to the side, near the icon of the Virgin. My confessions don't change a lot as the months go by, but I have had some encouragement since my Lenten confession. Does it count when temptations get weaker? Or is that just a sign that I was doing so badly God gave me a "time out"? At any rate, I'm grateful. We talk awhile, discuss helpful spiritual reading, and then stand before the icon of the Virgin. Father Orestes places the end of his stole over my head and prays for the forgiveness of my sins. That's the good part.

When I leave Megan takes my place. I go for a walk down the path toward the woods, between a double row of trees that was previously a Stations of the Cross, when this monastery was Catholic. The fourteen stations had been abstractly rendered and mounted on slim black iron poles some twenty or thirty years ago. Now they are rusted and bent. Some have been pulled up and laid on their sides for disposal; we don't do Stations of the Cross.

At the end of the grove I enter the woods proper and follow the overgrown path for a mile or so until I tire of clearing cobwebs with my face. I don't think the spiders enjoy this, either, and I lift one from my hair and lower it to the path. When I rejoin the family, David's taking his turn with Father Orestes. He's been in there a long time, and we all agree that it's probably not Silent Dave doing all the talking. Stephen goes next, and Gary is last.

Soon we're in the car again, scooping around the country roads, in and out of view of the mountains. The three kids are in the back and playing a silly game: when a curve throws them together they exclaim, "I love you, man! You're the greatest!" and when it pulls them apart they mutter, "Uh, I changed my mind, never mind." It's a stupid routine, but they are loving it, and Megan, in the middle, is laughing continuously and helplessly. It's hard to believe they're teenagers; this is a preschoolers' game. And it's hard to believe they get along so well. But they have always known how to have fun together.

The sky is growing heavier and darker; rain must be on the way. But inside the car it's giddy as a bubble. Whatever weight we brought to the monastery we were able to leave behind. Father Orestes goes back to his yardwork, pruning and hauling and bringing good things out of the sullen ground. I suppose it's all the same work.

# Daughters

The heat wave has broken hundred-year records, and now the wave is broken, with rain pounding the asphalt and whipping the trees around. This morning I tried to pick my way toward the church around the yawning puddles, with an umbrella held down tight enough to function as an awkward hat. At last I sacrificed dignity to common sense and ran barefoot through the parking lot with my sandals in my hand.

It was cold in the air-conditioned building. Today is a special, somewhat melancholy day for me, because it is Megan's last Sunday with us worshiping as a family; when we return from vacation she'll be off to college before the next Sunday comes. I can recall her as a six-month-old, sitting propped up in the pew next to me at Gary's first church. She was a jolly, beaming child who attracted strangers like a magnet. I picture her sitting on the pew with her little legs stuck straight out, with the tiny lacy socks and shiny black shoes at the end.

Today I look at her standing, as usual, by herself: Dad and brothers are at the altar and I'm standing with the choir. No lacy socks and shiny shoes, but sopping wet Birkenstocks (she didn't reason as I did about the advantages of running over barefoot) and a slim rayon skirt topped by a generous knit-silk top of dusky blue. She has silky brown hair and her dad's golden brown eyes, and this particular shade of blue has always looked good on her. I recall a pinafore dress this color in about size four and a Christmas velvet a little larger with a pink ribbon at the neck. Funny how they seem still fresh, part of a continuous clothing story, as if I could have gone to her closet this morning and picked them out. I'll bet she doesn't remember them at all.

Transfiguration Day, and I am thinking about the miniature transfiguration I've been privileged to witness, from a baby to a child to a young woman. It is marvelous and beyond full comprehension. It also feels incomplete, like I missed so much or neglected so much; it runs infuriatingly through my hands like sand. How to call it back and do it more thoroughly? Do it right? How to capture every moment and read it to the end? But that is over now, and she's going away from me, standing there alone, already gone.

We have a couple of visitors; Father Robert is here, an Episcopal priest from another parish. There's also, in a blast from our past, one of our roommates from seminary days. Ted has had some difficult times; he and Mary divorced, and their only child, a daughter, was killed in a car accident.

While at a gigantic convention last fall, I was startled to see Ted's picture in the meeting's journal; he was also attending and would be receiving an award for his new book on African American spirituality. I was in town only for the day, but I prayed that the Lord would somehow have our paths cross—though out of five thousand attendees it seemed unlikely. As I went into the room where my panel would be presenting, Ted was waiting outside. He had come, unaware I would be there, to learn more about Orthodoxy.

When a conference brought him back up to the Washington area this week, we invited him to church. He braved the thunderous weather and unfamiliar roads to be here today, and he stands familiarly through the service. Ted hasn't aged at all, though he's slimmer, a trick that strikes me as very unfair. He always had a quiet presence; to be near him is to be somehow stilled. He's a little amused, and a little sad, in almost equal measures.

I keep looking at Megan. Years ago I dreamed I was singing in the choir at our last Episcopal church, standing in the loft at the back. Then I heard a clear soprano voice sail out in a high silvery solo.

I looked around and it was Megan, singing a hymn of praise. I feel like I'm still waiting for that dream to come true.

When we get to the Cherubic Hymn before the long Eucharistic Prayer begins, I feel an urgent need to go stand by her, for this last time. I whisper my departure to Carolyn and Margo and scoot across the room. Megan is very satisfying to squeeze; we're both short and well padded. It's wonderful to be next to her and sorrowful to say good-bye. A mother's sorrow.

Carolyn's newest icon is complete, and it's leaning against a candlestick on the altar. It was just begun when she displayed it for us during her Lenten presentation on painting icons; then the Virgin's face was a blank brown-green, but now she wears a look of breathtaking sweet sorrow. She holds her child in her right arm, and her head is bent over his protectively. Her eyes are large and dark, full of thunderclouds, at the brink of streaming tears. Jesus has passed an arm around the back of her neck and with the other hand reaches up toward her cheek; his face is pressed against hers in a child's gesture of comfort. But she is sad.

When we go into the coffee hour I get to greet Ted more thoroughly, and we bring each other up to date. Father Robert comes over, and I ask how his children are doing.

Well, his daughter, he says with a sigh. She's better. She's joined Alcoholics Anonymous. She never did finish college, but she's got a job. For the first time she's self-supporting. "I never expected my children to turn out like this," he says. "This is not what I ever expected for them, when I was imagining their future."

I look from Father Robert to Ted, who is nodding in sympathy. I bet Ted would love to have a living daughter, even if she was in A.A. I have sorrow because my daughter is leaving, is taking one more step away from me on the journey that began the day she was born. But my sorrow is not like the sorrow Father Robert has for his daughter, and it's not like the sorrow Ted has for his. It's not like the sorrow of the Mother in the icon on the altar. How can we compare the weights we bear? Megan, across the room, is chatting with the other teens and picking virtuously at the nonfat offerings on the table. It's the last time I'll see her here a member of this community. All of parenthood is letting go; I clutch at a lock of hair, a swatch of blue fabric, but it slips out of my hand. I am grateful that my loss, so far, has not been as brutal as the loss other parents have had to bear. Letting go breaks my heart a little, but it hasn't broken my fingers.


*Sunday, August 13*
*Maximus the Confessor*

NINTH WEEK AFTER PENTECOST

# Orthodox in Florida, Closed Communion

On the road again, vacation time, and we get to visit other Orthodox churches. This was a big gap for me when I first became Orthodox. Much of the point for my husband seemed to be the sense of belonging to a universal and timeless church, of being enmeshed in that communion; however, I had seen only a few churches outside our little mission, and I had no idea what was typical and what was peculiar. I felt strangely dislocated. I could walk into an empty Episcopal church on a Tuesday afternoon and analyze the congregation's style, preferences, and income level, but the context of Orthodoxy was a blank to me.

The more I learn of this context, the more I'm charmed by its variability, even peculiarity. Good taste does not always prevail, which is oddly endearing. One church I visited years ago had completed its iconostasis by wiring along the top stuffed white doves with glassy eyes, the type that might decorate tables at a froufrou wedding reception. I suppose these were to represent the Holy Spirit. When Gary was in the Holy Land last winter he visited an ancient church with beautiful old icons; one newer item of wall decoration was a novelty clock designed to look like a giant wristwatch. I hate to ask what that was supposed to represent.

Today we visit a new congregation, younger even than we are. We leave my mom's home on one side of this giant Florida city and drive nearly all the way across it to a church that has been meeting only a year. We inscribe our names in the creaky new visitors' book, which looks just like ours did nearly three years ago. We pick up photocopied, comb-bound liturgy books, just like the ones we used before graduating to loose-leaf binders. There are about thirty adults present, and they nearly overwhelm us with welcomes. This is like a flashback. Holy Cross, this is your life.

But this part is not our life: they have a building. It's not theirs yet, exactly; the church currently belongs to a Byzantine Catholic congregation whose numbers have dwindled. The Catholics rent it out on Sunday morning and hold their own service in the afternoon; they're in the market to sell.

A building like this is a mixed blessing, I think. It's large enough, open and airy, but just a little tacky—enough to be discouraging to a fussy character like me. The sixties have left their mark. The white ceiling swoops up at a jazzy angle, punctuated by hanging chandeliers that feature a sleek cone of teak and five spindly gold-toned arms. Florida has left its mark, too: the wall behind the altar is frescoed with icons, but the colors are swimming pool shades, lime green and sky blue, like a bag of tropical fruit candy. I'd like to have my own building, already painted with icons, but what would I do with this building and these icons?

The priest is recently ordained; previously he was in some aspect of construction or engineering. He's Florida-blond and tanned but with a New York accent, and he reads us the Gospel story about the time Jesus wocked on worter. He's nervous, obviously worried about getting everything right. I remember how worried Gary was at first; there's a lot to remember and many ways to get it wrong. "He's a cute priest, too," Megan whispers, seeing me take notes. "You can write that down."

The parish is Orthodox Church in America (which has Russian roots), and the priest was born in the faith, but he talks like a convert. Last night he had told Gary on the phone that he likes the South better than the New York town where he went to seminary. "Up there, when you're standing talking in the checkout line and say 'Praise the Lord!' they just stare at you. Down here at least *somebody's* going to say 'Amen!'" The sermon has a homespun evangelical flavor, too; the priest compares building a congregation to building a house. The bricks are the worship, and the mortar is love, and the Holy Spirit is the electricity. "I don't really want to say this, but I guess in a way confession is like the building inspector."

As we reach the time for communion we reach the tough part— letting visitors know that if they're not Orthodox they can't receive. Last night my brother-in-law Brent had sat across from me at a Japanese restaurant and expostulated angrily on how he felt when denied communion at my sister's Catholic church. Louisa explained, "Brent grew up Lutheran, he served as an altar boy, he's always believed it's really Jesus in the bread and wine. He was really insulted that they wouldn't let him take communion. Like his faith wasn't good enough."

I recalled how much anguish, even anger, this caused at a conservative ecumenical conference I attended last May. When I was a Protestant it angered me. My assumption was that communion was for those who understood it (as well as any human can understand it), who approached with awe and repentance. Being turned away felt like my faith and devotion were being found substandard.

Now I think I understand. Communion doesn't just link you vertically with God but horizontally with his Church. As he was incarnated in a specific body, we belong to a specific body and live our Christian lives in a specific community.

Taking communion in a church means accepting the doctrine and disciplines of that church and putting yourself under its headship. The chains of accountability stretch upward from priest to bishop to patriarch. This linking is not mere bureaucratic formality but has a purpose: defending the faith, preserving Orthodoxy, vigilantly hewing to the path of truth. Right handling of Christian truth in turn preserves the Eucharist, ensures that what we receive in the chalice is indeed the Body and Blood of Christ.

The link from the cup to doctrine to the teachers of doctrine is a natural one. Each priest or bishop is bound to handle the "faith once delivered" with care, teaching it and passing it on entire, responsible to others above and below him. Jesus praised the centurion for understanding that having authority derives from being under authority. Only such vigilance ensures that the faith of the Orthodox is uncorrupted through the centuries. Only such vigilance ensures my safety as a daughter of the church.

Communion, therefore, is not merely about the individual communicant's relationship with God, which may be impeccable, or one's understanding of the sacrament, which may be profound. It is also this: have you committed yourself to this community of worshipers? Are you under the authority of this bishop? Do you bind yourself under the discipline of this church?

Every other aspect of a Sunday morning liturgy we may share with visitors; in many churches, they may even partake of pieces of the blessed bread, for only the center of the loaf is consecrated with the wine. But this intimate moment, receiving communion on the golden spoon, is only for those who have made that commitment, are "card-carrying members." At a conference I attended last May, Orthodox and Catholic speakers protested that open communion was like premarital sex—a premature sharing of intimacy before commitment. It seems a good analogy.

The problem, at root, is differing understandings of what the Eucharist is. For many of my Protestant friends, it's a symbol of Christian unity, something transcending denominations. Some would even say it's irrelevant whether partakers believe the elements really become the Body and Blood of Christ. The agreement to follow Jesus as Lord is what unites us, and communion is a celebration of that.

Orthodox and Catholics simply disagree. The Eucharist for us has a different meaning, one that may be unfamiliar to our "separated brethren" but for which we must ask respect. To us, the Eucharist isn't a symbol of unity across denominational lines; it isn't a symbol at all. It is the Body and Blood of Jesus Christ. We take this so seriously that we always precede reception of communion with fasting, the hearing of Scripture, and regular confession to a priest; surely no one would be so presumptuous as to demand to receive our sacrament without submitting to these same disciplines. Likewise, we precede reception of communion with a rite of chrismation committing ourselves to the Orthodox Church. It's another mark of our respect for the sacrament.

The unity we have with him and with one another is not a unity of feelings but a unity of faith—a unity of a specific faith, one ensured by the faithfulness and accountability of our leaders now and through the ages. Our formal commitment to one another and submission to the church keeps this faith intact, and that commitment must come before any communion can be shared. The analogy to marriage fits. Unless you're willing to pledge yourself to the community, it's not communion after all.

All this is still awkward for us to express. For those who see communion differently, being asked to respect our disciplines will inevitably sound like rejection. Megan points out the passage that appears in the church bulletin at this point. It asks non-Orthodox to refrain from taking communion, then says, "This is not a judgment on any non-Orthodox. We love you. We ask that you take some of the blessed bread."

"Isn't that sweet?" she says. "'We love you.'"

<br>

*Sunday, August 20*
*The Prophet Samuel*

TENTH WEEK AFTER PENTECOST

# Orthodox in Charleston, From Western to Eastern Rite

Today we're driving again, this time from our rental beachhouse on the seacoast outside Charleston, South Carolina, up the interstate to North Charleston. Gary and I grew up in Charleston, and North Charleston was the industrial, trailer park region just beyond the pale. It's the place where streets have names like Ashley Phosphate Road.

It's where you can pick up a fifties-era Methodist church for under six figures, so we are going today to worship with a new

Antiochian mission, St. John Maximovich. Like us, these folks are nearly all converts, and the priest had a long career in the Episcopal Church. At a conference a few weeks ago Gary learned that, when he was chrismated in 1993, the percentage of convert priests was about 45 percent. Now it's 78 percent. Converts are changing the face of this church.

The full name of this parish is St. John Maximovich of San Francisco; it's startling to have a saint named after an American city. He died in 1966 and was canonized (the Orthodox call it "glorified") in 1994; these things can happen much more quickly in Orthodoxy than in Catholicism. St. John was an eccentric figure, stern and often cryptic, and a wonder-worker, and the combination has won the affection of many. A photo of him shows a bent man with a wild graying beard and hair, wearing a fierce expression and holding a staff as he makes his way down the street. The caption reads, "Archbishop John as he typically looked as he walked the streets of San Francisco."

I love this photo; it's so countercultural. I guess I'm still a hippie at heart. I'm always urging Gary to grow out his hair and wear his cassock everywhere; don't you want to be as challenging as St. John of San Francisco? The answer is, I'm afraid, no. Gary still wants to spend an afternoon puttering around a record store and not look completely strange. I guess I'd feel the same.

One of the stories about St. John concerns an orphanage he started in Shanghai. Mrs. Shakhmatova, who ran the home, had scolded him one day for continuing to bring home children when she hadn't enough food for the ones already there. After this tongue lashing, he sadly asked her what she needed most and she said, "Everything, but at least some oatmeal!" There was nothing in the house for breakfast.

All night long, she said, she could hear him praying, throwing himself to the floor in loud prostrations. When she dropped off to sleep toward dawn she was awakened by the doorbell. There stood an English importer who had a surplus of oatmeal and who wondered if he could donate it to the orphanage. As she stood gaping, they began to cart in bag after bag of the stuff. St. John came down the stairs at this point and, with a single glance of reproach, went out to say his prayers.

The little church of St. John is brick and sturdy, with a simple beige interior. The parishioners have constructed an iconostasis by setting up black metal folding screens ("only a hundred seventy bucks at Montgomery Ward!" the priest, Father John, cheerfully tells us) and affixing to them color-photocopied enlargements of icons. Necessity is the mother of invention, and this parish's inventive coping is admirable, though I hope original icons will be theirs before long.

Though the parish has been functioning about a year, this is an important service; it is their first as an Eastern Rite congregation. Last year we attended a service with them, in a parishioner's expansive living room, and it was a Western Rite liturgy, one that is essentially similar to the old Episcopal Book of Common Prayer. The Antiochian jurisdiction allows parishes to choose Western or Eastern Rite, but they must choose one or the other and not alternate.

Last year Gary was eagerly looking forward to participating in his first Western Rite liturgy; he'd grown up high church Episcopalian and thought it might be a sweet reunion with his roots. But we both went home that day disappointed. A year in Eastern worship had changed us. Instead of the Eastern seamless flow of music, the Western liturgy (like most Western worship) joins hymn, reading, sermon, and prayer in succession. The result now had a jerky, box-car feeling to us. There seemed to be "dead air," empty spaces when you had stopped doing one thing and were getting ready to do something different. I'd never noticed this before, back when I thought a high Episcopal service was about the loveliest thing on earth. But in comparison with the fluidity of the St. John Chrysostom liturgy, it felt halting and laborious.

Also, the familiar words seemed to continuously remind worshipers of what they had lost. "We didn't leave the Episcopal Church, it left us," I often hear recent converts from that church say bitterly. With the Eastern Rite, the bitterness wears off as the joy of Orthodoxy comes on, and soon the old denomination's troubles just seem a bad dream. But with Western Rite, I'm afraid, those already struggling with bitterness may feel the hooks reset every Sunday.

Last year I was honored to be seated next to Metropolitan Philip at a luncheon. He asked me which rite our mission had chosen, and I said, "Eastern; we thought Western Rite would be too ethnic." Too immersed in crumpet-scented Anglophiliac ethnicism, too hooked into what we were leaving. We wanted something new and something we genuinely believed was more beautiful.

After a year of the Western Rite, St. John Maximovich Church has made the same decision. They have been scrambling this week to give the church Eastern appointments, and Father John is still trying to learn the liturgy. Today Gary will celebrate the liturgy, our boys will acolyte, and Megan and I will be a tiny choir. It's a going to be a virtual Mathewes-Green experience.

Megan and I set up a music stand in front of the left-hand pews. (Yes, this old Protestant church building has pews. Will they take them out?) Being the choir is a big responsibility in the Eastern Rite, very unlike the choir's role in a Western church. There, we'd lead the four or five hymns out of the hymnbook, sing the occasional responses, and perform an anthem at the offertory. Here the choir leads the congregation in singing the entire service, beginning to end. It is a headlong experience, flipping from one page to the next and singing, singing, singing for ninety minutes. The choir, I think, is busier than the priest. When we first became Orthodox, M. David would smile at us at the beginning of service and say, "See you at the end."

It feels like a heavy responsibility to provide the entire liturgy nearly single-handed while a congregation of thirty people tries to follow along in photocopied booklets. I run along just fine, supported by Megan's pure young soprano, until I hit the Resurrection Troparion of the week. There are eight of these, rotating a different one each week, and they constitute nearly the only part of the liturgy that changes. When I spoke at a women's retreat at a parish in Pennsylvania, one cradle Greek in the audience was fretting that her friend had quit Orthodoxy for an evangelical church because the worship was more lively. This friend was telling her that she just had to be able to sing different hymns, not the same old thing every time. Another member of the audience piped up, "What's she complaining about? The Resurrection Troparion changes every week!"

This week it's Tone 1, "While the stone was sealed." It has a zigzaggy tune that to my unsophisticated ear sounds like the Arabian Nights. I've been singing this every eight weeks for almost three years, but when I get into the second half I think I zigged when I should have zagged. Suddenly I'm singing a tune I've never heard before. I try to make it sound exotic, and I pray that no one in the congregation can read music.

As we come to the end of the service I feel an unexpected joy that we've been able to do this single-handed. The five of us M-Gs have provided a Divine Liturgy by ourselves, with the congregation of St. John Maximovich supporting us all the way. It is the last time we'll worship together for a while, us five. I give Megan a good hug at the end.


*Sunday, August 27*
*Venerable Poeman the Great*

ELEVENTH WEEK AFTER PENTECOST

---

# Presbyterian in St. Louis, Stuffiness vs. Awe

A speaking engagement has brought me to St. Louis, and this gives me a chance to stay with my friend and editor, Nick, and his family. They want to bring me to their church this morning, which means I can have the shocking experience of eating a Danish and drinking a cup of coffee on Sunday morning. This will be a first for me; I don't think I've ever been to a Presbyterian church before.

It is huge. It is a palace of brick and white columns, nearly new, spanking clean. Construction machines have gouged out fresh, deep pits in the earth for expansion. The parking lot goes on to the next county. The effect is of rolling expansiveness, confident growth.

Inside we climb the stairs to the balcony and sit behind the sound crew, two people hovering over a bank of black knobs and switches. A television monitor displays what the people in the over-flow room are seeing. We've gotten our seats just in time; the balcony and the floor below fill to capacity. Nick tells me that there are usually nine hundred to a thousand on Sunday morning, with about half returning on Sunday night.

The soaring walls are palest pink with white pilasters. The chandeliers are magnificent. I look at my watch; about now our little group of seventy worshipers is taking communion, in that funny little schoolhouse with the green linoleum floor.

"Wow," I whisper to Nick. "I'm just thinking, this is so different from my church."

"Oh, yours is more high church?" he asks. The question seems so odd that I have to ask him to repeat it.

"No," I reply, "it's not that. I guess, in terms of stuffiness, we're about on the same level. But we just have a dinky, borrowed space. I was just thinking how big this all is and how new and impressive." Though this isn't exactly what I'd want for our church, I'm envious all the same.

We begin with a few lively praise choruses; Nick whispers that our other editor, Marvin, who's the same-brand Presbyterian, would hate this. I guess the bouncy tunes are silly and lack the dignity of the fine old hymns. You could also argue that they're theologically questionable, emphasizing the security of the worshiper more than the majesty of God. I can't argue with that.

But from my perspective, there's nothing sacrosanct about "dignified" hymns a couple of hundred years old. All of those four-lines-and-a-chorus hymns now have a man-made quality to me; they're all us talking about various aspects of God or ourselves. In comparison, the ancient liturgies have been washed through multiple centuries and cultures and have stood mostly unchanged; what endures has the scent of eternity. It's stone-washed worship.

Not that I have any illusion that our prayers were written by angels rather than men; in one sense, ours are just as man-made as this morning's Presbyterian fare. But because of the multiple distances of geography and generations, Orthodox liturgy for us Westerners is more free of contemporary cultural markers. The truth of the faith stands out more boldly when it's not set amid familiar, reassuring tokens of good taste and religiosity. Separating current cultural faith from eternal faith is awfully hard to do from inside the mesmerizing culture; that's why I told Metropolitan Philip that the Western Rite was too temptingly ethnic for us.

I sing the praise songs with gusto, ripping right into the ones I know and applying myself diligently to the ones I don't. I just like to sing. And I have to admit, four-lines-and-a-chorus is more fun to sing, more physically satisfying, than the delicate free-verse compositions of the ancient Church. There we have to blend our voices subtly so that no one's stands out; Margo is always shushing me. Today I enjoy standing in the front row of the balcony and booming out over the vast field of worshipers below.

Way down below there is a flowing expanse of stage, with the empty chairs for the choir lined up in lengthy rows. No choir today; rehearsals for the new year are about to start. The choir director and her husband do a humorous routine soliciting new members. Instead of full choir, two fine male soloists handle the musical duties. What strikes me as odd, though, is that the stage with all its chairs is completely unoccupied except for a man sitting just right of center. Turns out this is the pastor. As the service progresses he gets up and says a prayer or makes an announcement or (at the end) preaches a good long sermon, but when he's in neutral he's just sitting there.

I'm not sure why this seems odd to me; lots of time during our service my husband is just standing there, praying or singing along while the choir and congregation go through a hymn. Then it hits me: there's no altar here. At our church, everything points to the altar, a visual anchor for our attention, reminding us of the presence of God. Here, with no choir filling the rows of chairs and nothing else to focus on, we all look at the pastor. He looks back at us; he's the only person facing this direction. Well, here we are.

He's an attractive, well-spoken man, comfortable in his authority and flashing with good humor. The initial prayer he offers is addressed to God and dwells on our unworthiness and need for repentance and God's grace. The content is impeccable, but there's something about it, perhaps the delivery, that makes me think the pastor believes we need to hear this more than God does. He's probably right.

Why does this seem different from prayers at home, other than the fact that it's spoken while we incessantly sing? I can't quite put my finger on it. There are more songs, more prayers, and readings from Scripture. I'm enjoying the service, but somehow it still feels preparatory, like we haven't gotten down to business yet.

I suddenly realize that I'm waiting for that special seasoning of humility and—intimacy. The prayers of the Eastern Rite are so tender, so personal, so forgetful of self and riveted on God that they have an intimate touch. It's a context in which falling on your face in prostration seems appropriate; indeed, it seems the only reasonable response to God's mercy and majesty. I can't imagine that happening here. What they do they do well—great teaching and fellowship, and the music is a gas. But it feels to me like preparation for a payoff that isn't going to come.

After service I meet a lot of nice people; it sure is a friendly church. And an active one: people are breaking up into different small groups and Sunday school classes. Nick and I slip away to get me to my airplane. On the way out I pass in the hallway a carved wooden table inscribed "In Remembrance of Me." Yes, Nick tells me, this is the altar. They carry it into the church when they're going to have communion. For an Orthodox, it's a shocker to see the altar stashed away like this; it looks to me forlorn. Yes, some people see the Eucharist differently than we do.

We arrive at the airport with time to spare and settle down for lunch in a cafe with a thunderingly loud jukebox. We ask to have it turned down, but the waitress informs us that it's their policy, it has to be this loud. I SAID, IT'S OUR POLICY . . . I wonder how having music too loud for conversation increases the sale of food, but I'm sure it must.

Nevertheless, we are able to have a conversation by means of shouting and occasional use of semaphore flags. I explain that I had a new insight at church today. It's that there's such a thing as a stuffiness scale, and different churches (as well as whole denominations) fall at different points on the scale. The high church Episcopal practice I used to know would lodge at the top: acolytes drilled to turn in perfect unison, the altar party symmetrically spaced, kneeling and rising as one, the congregation reciting psalms antiphonally with a four-beat pause between the lines.

I expected Orthodoxy to push this fanciness through the roof and was surprised to find it more relaxed, less stuffy. The first time we attended an Orthodox Sunday liturgy they were expecting Gary and brought him behind the iconostasis to observe. I slipped into the pew with Megan and the boys, but about ten minutes later an usher came up and asked if I'd like the boys to acolyte.

The idea astonished me. In the Episcopal Church, one of the things the rector regularly hears complaints about is a poorly trained acolyte falling a step behind or failing to bow as low as the others. David and Stephen had never even seen an Orthodox service before, much less had the appropriate training. Besides, the service was already under way.

But the usher kept beaming and assuring me it was all right; he seemed to view this as an offer of hospitality, a way of making us feel at home (it was an Antiochian Orthodox church, and those folks with Middle Eastern roots are unstoppable when it comes to hospitality). But would the priest approve of suddenly having two new, raw acolytes? The usher said he'd go ask. And to my amazement he did exactly that: went behind the iconostasis, behind the altar, and conferred with the priest, while the choir sang away.

Minutes later my bewildered boys were wearing acolyte robes and holding candles. It was a pretty strange experience for them, they said later, one that consisted mostly of strangers in vestments hissing or clucking at them, grabbing them by the shoulder and pushing left or right.

Whatever Orthodoxy may be, it's not stuffy. My confessor, Father Orestes, told me about the time he attended evening services at the beautiful Episcopal convent near me. He was admiring the lovely way the sister puts out the candles on the high altar: she stands in the middle with a long, long snuffer and sweeps to the far right, extinguishes a candle, then sweeps back to center, and pauses with the snuffer upright. Then a motion to the far left, tap the candle, back to the center, pause.

Father Orestes said, "This is how an Orthodox monk would do it" and "Pfff! Pffff! Pffff!," made loud blowing noises. "All the while he'd be doing what I call the 'soup-server' cross," and he rapidly and repeatedly crossed himself, as if flinging out ladles of soup. "The Orthodox would say, 'Ah, what a holy man!' and the Episcopalians would say, 'Gasp! The barbarian!'"

On the stuffiness scale, as I'd said before, our church is probably the same as Nick's. But there's another scale of measurement, which is awe. How does the service gather worshipers into the presence of God? In a high Episcopal service there is a great sense of God's dignity and majesty; matters are charged with gravitas.

In Orthodoxy it's more intimate, less dignified; more tender, less formal. The intimacy is with God; we speak prayers of repentance, charging ourselves as the chief of sinners, bowing to the ground in humility. Each of us cries out for mercy, reminding ourselves of our unworthiness before God and his overwhelming, unmerited love. It's intimacy, not just formality. He's not just an impressive CEO who really, and I mean this, is a great guy who deserves our deepest respect. He is The One Who Sees, who sees us naked and helpless, and the one who saves, through the extraordinary gift of the blood of his Son. No wonder we're on our knees with our foreheads on the floor.

I tell Nick that from my humble perspective, we just barely peeped onto the awe scale today. We talked a lot about God, and much of the talking was well said and useful for spiritual growth. But we didn't actually bow before him and repent and cry out for mercy—not in the way I mean. Do you guys have another service where you do that?

"Well, did you hear the first prayer?" Nick asks. "That was more like what you're talking about."

"That was more like it than anything else," I say. "That was a pretty good prayer." I think I'd better shut up about this. I don't want to sound ungrateful for hospitality, and it was a really fine church with friendly people and lively music and a meaty sermon. I just wonder if they get hungry for that prostrate-in-worship part.

FOURTEENTH WEEK AFTER PENTECOST

# Mental Darkness

When does the year begin? New Year's Day is on the calendar, but maybe it was really at the solstice a week before, when the depths of darkness was broken and the days began getting longer, a distant foreshadowing of spring. Spring itself marks a new year, as cruel April stirs the bones again and forces out new life. The Western Church year begins with the first Sunday of Advent, around the beginning of December. Long after our last schoolday, most of us retain a lifelong sense of the first day of school as a bittersweet marker of new beginnings. We celebrate the start of new years over and over throughout the calendar, with a special gold star on our birthdays.

The Eastern Church adds another date: September 1, our New Year's Day. Our parish feast comes just two weeks later, on the fourteenth, the feast of the Elevation of the Holy Cross. Two events are commemorated this day: the discovery of the cross, which had been buried under three centuries of Jerusalem debris, by St. Helena; and the recovery of the cross by Emperor Heraclius after it had been stolen by the king of Persia. On this second occasion, in 629 A.D., the cross was "elevated" for the adoration of believers, at the Church of the Resurrection in Jerusalem.

As the cross was the symbol of the Eastern empire, the Fourteenth of September constituted a national holiday something like our Fourth of July. The Troparion of the Cross originally celebrated political and military victory but now is taken to refer to spiritual warfare:

> O Lord, save thy people and bless thine inheritance.
> Grant victories to all Orthodox Christians over their
>   adversaries,
> And by virtue of thy Cross, preserve thy habitation.

At Holy Cross we sing this every week, after the Resurrection Troparion, in the space appointed for the parish's patronal hymn. I think of it as our fight song. When I visit another parish and we sing a different hymn—to St. John Chrysostom or St. Matthew or whoever is the parish's patron—it always takes me by surprise. Who says there's no variety in Orthodox worship?

As with the events of Holy Week, we celebrate this feast on the evening before. On this Wednesday night we're gathered in our familiar room at the ReVisions building, with a men's civic association meeting down the hall. We look stranger to them than they do to us; they look quite normal. We have a Divine Liturgy, then follow it with the adoration of the cross. My husband carries through the church a silver tray piled with stems of fresh, leafy basil, on top of which reclines a brass cross. When he places it on a table in front of the iconostasis, we line up to prostrate and kiss the cross.

Jay is here with his kids, and autistic Jared is having a hard time. He's been more restless lately; on Sunday he was lunging a bit, and I could see a newcomer, a woman who came in and sat alone in the back, leaning out to stare at him. Jared comes nearly up to his dad's shoulder and is getting bulky; with a sudden surge he can pull his mother, Heidi, off her feet.

Usually he's silent, but tonight he's vocalizing a little, with a "bub-bub-bub" sound. He's wearing a lavender Mickey Mouse T-shirt and smiling in that disorienting way he has—a smile sometimes broken with trills of laughter, his eyes gleaming and excited. As Jay walks him up to reverence the cross he's unusually resistant and thrashing. I come up and take Jared's right hand and help Jay bring him to the front.

What is God doing in Jared? I can understand how physical illness, and even the process of dying, can yield hard blessings. But mental illness I can't comprehend. It seems to change the very self in a way bodily suffering does not. The "there" that is there is altered at the root. I know God loves Jared and is mysteriously saving him; God set him in a loving family and meets him every Sunday in worship. But why this suffering, this way? Where's the silver lining? What good does it do?

These are silly questions; why should I imagine things the way they aren't and judge reality by them? Reality is always better than fantasy, because in reality you can actually change things. In fantasy, the screwdrivers don't work.

The evidence for mental illness is around me. All week long this room is used by people with psychiatric disabilities, and their work is on the walls. They have just had an art contest, and the paintings pinned up have names like *Crazy Box, Eye of the Storm,* and *In the Middle of Nowhere.* On a list of the contest's awards I find that the one judged "Most Original" was titled *St. Maria of Squirrel.*

Here's a strikingly good *Self-Portrait,* sketched with a pencil, a tilted oval face that looks like a smooth-carved Brancusi. But the expression on the face is sad, almost bitter; the eyes are pinched shut, and shadows lie deep along the edge. The bottom of the paper is ripped and crumpled; I imagine it had to be rescued from the artist.

On the blackboard next to the art display this is written in chalk: "Spookie monster I love you. Reck this place down, call a recking crew." The first *reck* is crossed out, and above it is written in the same hand, *build.*

What a lost place this is, in the middle of nowhere, in a crazy box, in the eye of the storm. Can God reach them there? Though we go to the uttermost parts of the sea, he can find us there. But when we go to the uttermost parts of our minds it is much further. And we take our very selves along for the ride.

Some of the mentally disabled send postcards back. In his Sunday sermon Gary had recounted this story: he was in the local music store and heard music so beautiful over the system that he thought, "Could this be a Mozart I've never heard?"

When he asked at the desk, the cashier handed him a newspaper clipping. The music was by Hikari Oe, a severely brain damaged young Japanese man. Hikari is partly autistic, with impaired vision, is subject to seizures, is incontinent, and rarely speaks. He writes music like an angel.

When Hikari was born in 1963 he had a growth that made his head look double in size. Doctors advised his parents that lifesaving surgery would leave him a vegetable, and it would be better to let him die.

During the weeks he pondered this terrible decision, Hikari's father, Kenzaburo Oe, went as a journalist to Hiroshima. He was struck by the lives of bomb survivors, people who had every reason to commit suicide yet chose to live. He and his wife decided they had to give Hikari the same chance; Kenzaburo later said that he might have chosen suicide himself if Hikari's needs had not given him a reason to go on.

Kenzaburo Oe turned from journalism to fiction, he said, in order to give his son a voice; many of his novels involve characters with similar disabilities. But as Hikari grew, he progressed from a fascination with birdsong to learning to play Chopin and Mozart on the piano, and by the age of thirteen he had begun to compose his own works. So far two recordings of his compositions have been released, and his *Hiroshima Requiem* was the theme for a television special produced by his father. As the younger Oe began to express himself in music, the elder announced that he would cease writing fiction, because his son had at last found his voice. Kenzaburo Oe was subsequently awarded the Nobel Prize for Literature.

Gary told this story to illustrate the biblical injunction to love one another. As I thought about treasure hidden in Hikari Oe, I looked at Jared, twitching and grinning in his father's grip. I could see the newcomer sitting in the back, peering around at Jared. But when we went back into worship I forgot about her, and it wasn't until the end of the service that I looked around again. She was gone.

The story of Hikari and Kenzaburo Oe might be too perfect, too sweet, if it were not for this: Hikari's music is laced with sadness. Kenzaburo Oe titled his liner notes for Hikari's second album "A Soul Wailing in Darkness"; he uses the phrase three times in the brief essay. He and his wife are shocked and troubled, he says, by the pain evident in Hikari's music. As a writer, the father is especially frustrated, for his native medium, words, are of no use in comforting his son. "We have to face up to the fact that this voice is present within him," Kenzaburo says. The longing to find a way to comfort Hikari does not cease: "As long as I live together with Hikari, I shall continue to be taxed by this question."

Kenzaburo Oe closes his essay with an interesting idea. He quotes Simone Weil that prayer "is the orientation of all the attention of which the soul is capable towards God. The quality of the attention counts for much in the quality of the prayer." Music commands Hikari's complete attention, in fact, seems to be his only medium of communication; listening while his work is performed soothes him, makes him "the very image of contentment." Might it somehow "lead him towards his own unique mode of prayer"?

The soul wailing in darkness cannot be comforted with words; the father's overbrimming heart can in no way reach his son. But God hears, and God knows. How feeble our connections to one another in this life, impaired by sin or sickness or the dazzling darkness of mental pain. But in his light there is no darkness at all; our connections, tenuous and hazy now, will one day be full and free, on that day when the shadows flee away.

*Saturday, September 23*
*Conception of the Prophet, Baptist, and Forerunner, John*

FIFTEENTH WEEK AFTER PENTECOST

# The Jesus Prayer

I don't have an icon for today's feast, the Conception of John the Baptist, but I do have one of the Conception of the Theotokos. The thing is, she was conceived the regular way. So the icon shows her parents, Joachim and Anna, standing and embracing; behind them is a narrow bed with a blue striped cover and an embroidered pillow. The couple looks serious yet tender. Anna has stretched up on tiptoe to press her face against her husband's, with her arm around his neck. At the Orthodox Cathedral in Wichita, Kansas, the pair appears on the iconostasis, so that among the images worshipers see as they look toward the altar is a married couple in a tender embrace. When a depiction of natural human love is given such a place of honor, it calls into question the caricature that Christians are opposed to sex.

A couple of weeks ago Holy Cross sponsored a two-day retreat on the Jesus Prayer, also known as the Prayer of the Heart. We found more interest than we anticipated; every space was booked within days of the announcement, and a waiting list began to form. People want to pray, I guess, but tend to be plagued by fears they're doing it wrong. The appeal of the Jesus Prayer is that it is so simple.

Many people encounter this prayer for the first time in Salinger's *Franny and Zooey,* where the distressed young woman describes it to her bored boyfriend over a restaurant lunch. Franny had been reading *The Way of a Pilgrim,* an anonymous Russian work of the mid-nineteenth century. In that book the pilgrim narrator recounts his desperate longing to learn to "pray without ceasing" and his wanderings across the country in search of someone who could teach him. A wise monk, whom the pilgrim takes as his *staretz* or spiritual father, instructs him in the prayer and gives him *The Philokalia,* a collection of writings on mysticism and the spiritual life composed between the fourth and the fourteenth centuries.

The pilgrim recalls the conversation:

> "Read this book," [the staretz] said. "It is called The *Philokalia,* and it contains the full and detailed science of constant interior prayer, set forth by twenty-five holy Fathers. The book is marked by a lofty wisdom and is so profitable to use that it is considered the foremost and best manual of the contemplative spiritual life. . . ."
>
> "Is it then more sublime and holy than the Bible?" I asked.
>
> "No, it is not that. But it contains clear explanations of what the Bible holds in secret and which cannot be easily grasped by our short-sighted understanding."

The staretz compares the Bible to the sun and *The Philokalia* to a small piece of dark glass that enables a person to view its rays.

With this sort of buildup one expects something esoteric and complex, but the prayer is simple. The staretz reads to the pilgrim St. Simeon the New Theologian's instructions in *The Philokalia:*

"Sit down alone and in silence. Lower your head, shut your eyes, breathe out gently and imagine yourself looking into your own heart. Carry your mind, i.e., your thoughts, from your head to your heart. As you breathe out say, 'Lord Jesus Christ, have mercy on me.' Say it moving your lips gently, or simply say it in your mind. Try to put all other thoughts aside. Be calm, be patient, and repeat the process very frequently."

The pilgrim is delighted with this advice but at first finds himself bored, sleepy, and plagued with other thoughts. The kindly staretz encourages him to persevere and gives him a circle of black knotted yarn called a prayer rope, or chotki. The staretz tells him to use it as a marker for repeating the Jesus Prayer at heroic length, beginning with three thousand a day. "'Say it quietly and without hurry, but without fail exactly three thousand times a day without deliberately increasing or diminishing the number. God will help you and by this means you will reach also the unceasing activity of the heart.'" The first two days are hard, but then the pilgrim finds, "I grew so used to my prayer that when I stopped for a single moment, I felt, so to speak, as though something were missing, as though I had lost something. The very moment I started the prayer again, it went on easily and joyously."

The staretz increases the repetition to six thousand, then twelve thousand. At that point, "Early one morning the prayer woke me up as it were. . . . My whole desire was fixed upon one thing only—to say the prayer of Jesus, and as soon as I went on with it I was filled with joy." The staretz is pleased and says,

"Such happiness is reserved for those who seek after God in the simplicity of a loving heart. Now I give you permission to say your prayer as often as you wish and as often as you can. Try to devote every moment you are awake to the prayer, call on the name of Jesus Christ without counting the number of times, and submit yourself humbly to the will of God."

As the prayer moves into the heart it becomes automatic. Later in the book, the pilgrim describes this to a blind man traveling with him:

"Can you not picture your hand or your foot as clearly as if you were looking at it? . . . Then picture to yourself your heart in just the same way, turn your eyes to it just as though you were looking at it through your breast, and picture it as clearly as you can. And with your ears listen closely to its beating, beat by beat. When you have got into the way of doing this, begin to fit the words of the prayer to the beats of the heart one after the other, looking at it all the time. Thus, with the first beat, say or think, 'Lord,' with the second, 'Jesus,' with the third, 'Christ,' with the fourth, 'have mercy,' and with the fifth, 'on me.' And do it over and over again."

This slightly different approach to beginning the Jesus Prayer was appealing to me; I can't imagine counting three thousand repetitions of anything, much less twelve thousand. So about a month ago I began spending a half hour every night listening to my heart beat out the words of this prayer. At first I didn't think it was possible to hear your own heartbeat, but before much practice I could sense the pulsing, that faint whispering rhythm.

I wake up almost every night to pray, usually about 3:30 in the morning. I've been doing this since I was pregnant with Megan, almost nineteen years. In the early years I'd spend the time reading the Bible and talking with the Lord. Then, for a few years, I read the morning prayer service from the Episcopal Book of Common Prayer, pleased to imagine I was the first person in the country to do so each day.

About ten years ago my Catholic spiritual director told me I was long past time to begin centering prayer, so I should select a word and repeat it endlessly in my mind; later, when I went to the monk Father David for spiritual counsel, he emphasized that if we pray anything except the name of Jesus we open ourselves to unknown spirits. So I began repeating Jesus' name with every exhalation, for a half hour each night. In the last month I've started expanding that to the Jesus Prayer itself. The goal is to focus on those recurring words, not on any other prayers or intercessions, not on Bible study or theological truths; you have all day long for that. For this half hour, just fall into the presence of God like warming your hands before a fire, without a conscious thought in your head.

Tonight I rise as usual, about 3:15. Gary, lying next to me, is snoring in a low blubbery way, one of the sweetest tender sounds of my life.

I sit up and stretch my toes to the floor from our high old four-poster bed. Fall is coming on and it's getting cold, and throughout the house haphazard window management has left some open and some closed. The radiator at my bedside ticks furiously as the thermostat, downstairs in the dining room, duels with an open window nearby. I pad across the worn, flattened Oriental rug; where it's trodden away to bare strands, smaller rugs are laid randomly on top. The floorboards in this seventy-year-old house creak underfoot.

My office is in the next room, through a connecting door; it must have been intended as a nursery. Through the window over my desk I can see the slender moon wasting away. The old slate roof of the garage looks blue in the light. It's never dark in the city. Down below, Molly the cat is patrolling the driveway.

I sink onto the sofa, one my parents bought when I was a baby; I have a photo of myself and my mother on it when I was about four. About twenty years ago Gary and I reupholstered it with the cheapest remnant fabric we could find, a faded and mismatched paisley brown. It's part of the general scrapbook effect here: to the left of the window over my desk is a bulletin board studded with photos of friends and *Zippy* comic strips that Rod the Reporter keeps sending me and that I don't really get; to the right, the painting by Sheila of an abandoned warehouse in brilliant autumn light, and several icons including the perennial King of Glory. Along the windowsill lie an old heart-shaped cookie cutter I found when we were cleaning out my grandmother's house, old glass bottles that double as vases when my roses are in bloom, and more icons. On the desk, in addition to the beige complement of electronic devices fed by three phone lines, are pens in a red mug made by a friend who died of cancer. Between two fluted white marble bookends are my old red Bible, calendars, phone directories, a U.S. road atlas to plot travel, a regional-restaurants guide to accompany the road atlas, and a fine, fat thesaurus.

On the radiator, next to four years' worth of author's-copy magazines, is an old pink teapot I found at a thrift shop; I placed it here just so I could look at it when bogged down in writing and be encouraged by its cheery bulbous shape. My dad's thirties-era toy train runs along the green bookcase. Megan's old wooden high chair, which Gary painted with a rainbow before she was born, holds a six-inch stack of scrap paper. Next to it, a thunderstorm painted by a young David and two of his more recent still lifes. A framed Mother's Day message from a younger, but always emphatic, Stephen: "You are vary nice mom! p.s. I relle mean it!" On the bright blue filing cabinets, boxes of envelopes, business cards, an iron, a watering pot, tools of various trades. Above the sofa, a large religious folk art embroidery that I found crumpled in a bin of curtains at the Salvation Army thrift shop and that they gave me free. And on the sofa, a dozen memory-pillows made from old or sentimental fabric: a square from a favorite shirt, a "cathedral-cloth" print from a Ugandan bishop's wife, heart-shaped puffies made by the kids, a faded lavender pillow slip embroidered by my grandmother. There are several hand-crocheted blankets, baby shower gifts of long ago. And, now, me.

I sit at the edge of the sofa and drape around my shoulders the biggest baby blanket; someone gave this to me before Meg was born, and I remember she'd carefully found wrapping paper and ribbon to match, but I don't remember her name. I hold up the little clock so that the light can strike it through the window: 3:21. Okay, then, go to 3:51. After years of this, a lot of times I find myself automatically surfacing at the end of the period, rising up out of prayer as if from the bottom of a pool. If I pick up the clock and squint at it then, I can see the thirtieth minute appear.

Lord. Jesus. Christ. Have mercy. On me. Lord. Jesus. Christ. Have mercy. On me. Oh, I forgot to cross myself. Okay. Is there anything I need to recollect before the Lord and clear out of the way? Lord.

Jesus. Christ. Have mercy. On me. Lord. Jesus. Christ. Have mercy. Last week, before I got up to speak at a banquet, the pastor asked everyone to pray for an anointing on me. At that moment I realized with a sudden shock that I am very headstrong and rebellious. Maybe this is obvious to everyone who knows me, but it's something I hadn't imagined before. And in fact, I'm not sure what I'm rebellious about. I feel pretty agreeable. I love the Lord and always want to be near him; my whole prayer is to be conformed to him. So I don't know how I'm rebellious. But it hit me like a slap in the face. I could see myself, smug and proud. I feel at a loss, thinking of that.

Don't think about that now. Imagelessness. Lord. Jesus. Christ. Have mercy. On me. Lord. Jesus. Christ. Have mercy. On me. Lord. Jesus. I need to write a column tomorrow, and I think I want to write about how, for years now, I've been getting wrong-number calls for somebody named Daisy. Who is this person? I have a title: "Sweet Mystery of Daisy." I begin toying with ideas of where to go from there, then remember I'm supposed to be praying.

Lord. Jesus. Christ. Have mercy. On me. Lord. Jesus. Christ. Have mercy. On me. Lord. Jesus. Christ. Have mercy. On me. Lord. Jesus. Christ. Have mercy. On me. David has to get his wisdom teeth out. Where is that money coming from? Lord. Jesus. Christ. Have mercy. On me. Lord. Jesus. Christ. Have mercy. On me. Lord. Jesus. Christ. Have mercy. On me. Lord. Jesus. Christ. Where the water came through the hall ceiling, when the tub was leaking, I painted over it, but it shows through. Lord. Jesus. Christ. Have mercy. On me. Lord. Jesus. Christ. Have mercy. On me. Lord. Jesus. Christ. Have mercy. On me. Lord. Jesus. Christ. Have mercy. On me.

Lord. Jesus. Christ. Have mercy. On me. Please show me how I'm rebellious. I want to stop. Make me a better mother. Make me kinder. Help me get out of being in your way so much. Lord. Jesus. Christ. Have mercy. On me. Lord. Jesus. Christ. Have mercy. On me. Lord. Jesus. Christ. Have mercy. On me. Lord. Jesus. Christ. Have mercy. On me.

SEVENTEENTH WEEK AFTER PENTECOST

---

# Another Kind of Fasting

Magda is a priest's wife like me, but a few years older, and she converted a few years earlier. From time to time, when I need advice about just how you do this Orthodox stuff, I call her. Sometimes I'm embarrassed to ask anyone else because it seems like I should know these things by now. Sometimes there are other reasons to feel embarrassed.

"Magda?" I say, "I need to ask you about something. What do you know about sexual fasting?"

"Not much," she says. "I know it's one of our Orthodox things, but I don't know if there's any typical way it's observed. It's not something people talk about much."

"I'd never heard of it before," I go on, "and here I've been Orthodox almost three years. But recently I heard someone say that, when he was in seminary, they were taught to abstain from sex the evening before Divine Liturgy and the evening after—which is why, with married clergy, we don't have a tradition of daily Mass! This guy said you're supposed to abstain every fast day, too—every Wednesday and Friday, and all of Dormition and Nativity and Apostles' fasts, and all of Lent."

"That's a lot," Magda says. "Well, in the *Lenten Triodion* it says the Church's teaching is that during seasons of fasting married couples should 'try to live as brother and sister.' I don't know if most people take that to mean just Lent or every fast day or how hard they feel obligated to try. It's like every other kind of fasting; you do what you can. Paul says in 1 Corinthians 7, you couples might abstain for a season of prayer, but don't strain yourself."

"Fasting the evening before Divine Liturgy, that seems appropriate," I say. "I guess this is not one of those things, like with food fasts, that we can say, 'Oh, those extra-hard rules are for monks.'"

"Well, if I find out anything more I'll let you know," Magda says.

I hesitate. "I'm not sure I want you to."

She says, "Well, I know what you mean. I guess sometimes ignorance is bliss."

It takes us a moment before this strikes us as really, really funny.

*Wednesday, October 11*
*Deacon and Apostle Philip*

EIGHTEENTH WEEK AFTER PENTECOST

# Walking the Land

In the morning mist we're walking around in knee-high grass, between beer cans and cardboard boxes, and feeling delight and amazement. This is our land, or it might be; it could be, any day now.

After the early morning Divine Liturgy at Basil's house we drove over here to look at it. The "For Sale by Owner" sign went up last week, and Hardworking Jeannie phoned for the price; not too bad. Four acres, just a few miles from the Baltimore beltway, sloping up evenly, clear centered and ringed with trees. It lies in a narrow stretch between Catonsville and Ellicott City, a passage that seems nearly rural.

This is a sudden, new idea, but it comes at a good time. ReVisions has started asking us to clear out by 12:15 on Sunday afternoons, which means cutting Sunday school short to take down the altar and clean up. The other land and buildings we've looked into in our shopping around have been too small and required more money. This seems ideal, and a brilliant surprise.

Everyone is surprised but Lillian, who's been watching this corner lot for months, long before the "For Sale" sign went up. "Every time we'd go to the monastery, we'd drive by that lot. And I'd always think, 'Oh, dear Lord, that's a beautiful lot,'" she said. "Something in my heart kept saying, 'You better look into it.'"

But Basil kept telling her, "It's too small, don't bother." Now everything's different. When the true size of the place came out, says Lillian, "Even Basil was stunned."

About ten of us came over after the liturgy. We parked in the small gravel clearing and walked under the trees. Down a little hill at the right side of the lot there is a strip of mud about a foot wide, which the plat proclaims a "stream." Cattails stand above it. An old brick springhouse, roofless, is disintegrating just on the other side. We wonder if this damp spot constitutes a wetland subject to regulation; we joke that Basil and Frank will have to stand here in uniform, guarding the snail darters.

"Father Gregory, look where the sun is coming up," says Smiling Jeanne. "We want to place our church properly."

I look down the road, where the sun is rising in wraiths of mist. Across the street a hill rises smooth and green behind a fence; beyond the hill the land must slope away at length, because the next thing visible is a distant ridge, tree rimmed, blue-gray in the morning light. On the near hill there is a lone broken tree trunk, and below it nubs of gray rock emerge from the face of the hill. Two brown horses are grazing on the side of the hill and one white one at the top, near the shard of blackened tree; it makes me think of the lines from T. S. Eliot's "Journey of the Magi," which describe the green valley where the wise men will find the Birth they sought. There three trees stand against the sky, and "an old white horse galloped away in the meadow." I don't know why, but that "old white horse" always brings tears to my eyes.

Carolyn and Gary and I turn and begin trudging up the slope of our lot, toward the small green house at the back. The wet grass springs droplets against our legs. Jeanne and Joan, less adventurous, get back in Jeanne's car and drive up to the little house's driveway. At the top of the hill we meet them and Basil, Michael, and Frank.

"How about that smell of manure, Father?" Michael asks with a grin.

"I'm Orthodox, I'm not concerned about that," Gary says. "We'll take care of the smell." He swings an imaginary censer.

Joan and I wander past the house toward the stream; here the drop-off is some twelve feet high. "I'm just so excited," Joan is saying softly, nearly to herself. "I just can't get over this. Oh, this is beautiful." She looks around at the sweep of grass, how it plunges to rise in the green hill across the street. The morning sun catches a big round tree and makes it look like a huge yellow puff.

Joan whispers, "This is an answer to my prayers. I can just imagine what this will look like." She pauses, then adds, "Of course, I may not be here." Joan is a young seventy and is in excellent health, but I suddenly think, why not a cemetery? Maybe we can all be here and all be together. Not many people are buried by their churches anymore; it would be a good custom to restore.

Gary is talking to the man who rents the house, and I walk up to join them. Three half-grown black kittens tumble past. Bob has the durable, flatfooted accent of native Baltimore.

"It was all pretty well growed up at one time of the day," he says. "The owner, Mr. Bush, had a fruit and vegetable stand down by the corner. He wanted to put in a roller skating rink, but the county wouldn't let him." In quest of that dream, the land had been cleared all through the center, with trees left to form a stately border.

Bob's doubtful about the trouble we might have laying a foundation. "It's a lotta rock in there. You'd probably have to dynamite."

Gary and I say good-bye to Bob and rejoin the circle of dreamers. I'm worried about the dynamite remark. "That's what dynamite is for," Michael says. Joan, still looking at the grass, says, "Look at all the violets in here."

"Isn't this great?" Frank says, looking around expansively.

"Oh, man, you aren't kidding!" Basil exclaims. "If we don't jump on this—"

We plunge into calculations—if the monthly note is so much, but we continue to rent the house to Bob for that much, and in the meantime we lease a hall to worship in for this much—

"I think we ought to meet here," I say. "I don't know how. Maybe we could meet in the house; that's how we started, in a front parlor."

"We could rent trailers," Frank says.

"Let's go ahead and be on this land," I add.

"That's right, Khouria," says Basil. "You said it."

The light is strengthening, and for the first time our shadows lie cut out on the grass.

"I think we oughta jump on this with all dis*patch*," says Basil. "We oughta do whatever needs to be done, and do it now." We nod. The idea glows within us like a warm cup of coffee.

I make my way back down to my car and drive off dreaming. Half the day my full cotton skirt is wet up to my knees.

*Saturday, October 14*
*Martyrs Nazarius, Gervase, Protasius, and Celsus*

EIGHTEENTH WEEK AFTER PENTECOST

# Orthodox in Chicago, Eugene and the Weeping Icon

A speaking engagement brings me to Chicago, and I spend the afternoon driving circles around the grimy suburb of Cicero. I was here over a year ago to see a phenomenon: a weeping icon. I'd like to see it again, but I take many false turns before I light on the church. In the process I see closed shops, factory walls, gray-smudged city buses. It seems a funny sort of place for God to do a miracle but probably no funnier than a manger.

In April of 1994, as the Friday evening services that precede Holy Week were about to begin, a recently ordained priest saw glistening drops on the iconostasis image of the Theotokos. Father Doug, who had come to Orthodoxy from an evangelical Protestant background not long before, figured that some previous ceremony had accidentally spattered the image with holy water; with those Orthodox, he figured, it could be anything. Then, as he watched, a tear welled up in the image's lower eyelid and spilled down her face.

For the next several weeks St. George Church was open night and day as tens of thousands of pilgrims streamed through. "For seventeen months now, we have been open every day from eleven to five," St. George's pastor, Father Nicholas Dahdal, tells me. The church has purchased sixty thousand dollars' worth of candles for the pilgrims. All that smoke means that the walls and ceilings had to be repainted, but I can see graying at the tops of the windows already. The carpet had to be replaced. Access for the disabled underwent an emergency upgrade.

And still the tears trickled down. The wooden icon, which depicts the Virgin Mary holding the Christ child in her left arm, is part of the iconostasis, so it stands upright and free between the congregation and the altar. When Gary was with me here before he walked behind it and saw just the back of a plain sheet of wood. The tears are oily in substance and leave a double shiny trail down the Virgin's red robe and over the hand of her son, which is raised in blessing. Even when, as now, the episodes of weeping are less frequent, the visible trail of tears remains.

Of course, conversions and healings have followed in its wake, as people were anointed with the tears. Father Dahdal shows me an enamel cross given in honor of the healing of Dellamarie, a woman facing renal failure. Doctors testified that they had no explanation for the reversal of her condition. "The producers flew her and me to California to be on that TV show *The Other Side*," says Father Dahdal.

Over in Ohio, a man heard about the icon and the healings. Eugene drove over for several daylong visits to pray because his wife, Alina, was dying. But Alina was not healed.

Eugene now lives at the church; he is here day and night. Father Dahdal wants me to meet him, a man with a graying beard and a residual Romanian accent. We sit in a back pew to talk, and I begin to scribble notes. "I have no other life now," Eugene confirms. "This is my life."

But first he wants to tell me about Alina. "She was the strongest believer I ever met," he says. "We were twenty-five years in a Communist country where faith is tested daily, to danger of life, even. She would never compromise and never give up."

He goes on, "The last four years she suffered greatly, and the last two years she was paralyzed totally. But she didn't complain one time. 'All is God's will,' she would say. Our marriage was forty years and never one single argument. Our love was based on faith.

"Now her end was coming. I expected that I would mourn her the rest of my life. But when she died I was with her, and I didn't feel any pain in my heart; my heart was calm. I asked myself, Didn't I love her? Yes, I loved her more than myself. I prayed many times that I might take her place. But that was not God's plan.

"Later in the day she died, a joy began to form in my heart. A priest told me, 'What a great joy, now she is with the righteous.' I could feel that already. Since she fell asleep till now I didn't mourn; my heart is full of joy. You couldn't find a card in a store that applies to my situation; they are all about sadness. But I continue to live in that love which didn't die, until my time comes to go be with her forever.

"For unbelievers, death is a tragedy," Eugene goes on, "because their treasure is here on earth. In death, they lose everything, including their own souls. For a believer, as my wife was, death is a victory because her treasure is in heaven. St. Paul wrote, 'Love never dies.' It didn't die. She didn't leave me. Her heart beats in my heart."

After Alina's death, Eugene came to St. George's, worshiping all day and sleeping on a makeshift platform in the basement at night. Father Dahdal quickly discovered that he had no children, no other family, and didn't own his home in Ohio. The priest urged him to come live at the church.

"I am very grateful but afraid of my own decision more than of a fire," Eugene tells me. "I have to pray, and after I pray I believe it is God's will." St. George's now furnishes him with a bedroom and nearly drowns him with the warm hospitality typical of Middle Eastern Christians. Eugene in turn provides prayer and counsel to others grieving and serves, Father Dahdal says, as "an inspiration to us." "I don't see how," Eugene says. "If somebody is an inspiration, it's my wife, not me."

As we talk, a member of the church stands nearby, beaming. "He is so beautiful. He is a holy man," she says repeatedly. "We love him." It's good to see what a loving family Eugene has found at St. George's. But he waves dismissively when someone admires his "wisdom." "I will tell you my wisdom," he says. "First of all, recognize you are stupid. Then turn and rely on him who is true wisdom."

Because Eugene is present every day, the church can remain open, a situation in which everyone wins. "Look what a gift of God means," he says. "A gift for more than one person. A blessing for me, for the church, for every person. I pray for every person who comes here." He adds, in what must be an understatement, "My prayer life is improving."

It doesn't take long for him to return to the story of his beloved wife. "How could I doubt that Alina is praying for me?" he asks. "Look what it means to have such a marriage! Look what true love is!"

As I pack up my notes to leave, he has one more request. "If you write this, don't let the merit be on me. Let it be on Alina."

*Saturday, October 21*
*Soul Saturday*

NINETEENTH WEEK AFTER PENTECOST

# Tricky D's Prayer

A few days ago David had his wisdom teeth out, and he's been feeling poor and achy. His long face balloons out at the jaw with Nixonian jowls, prompting Gary to address him over the dinner table as "Tricky D." David responded, "Well, *you* look like Jerry Garcia." Those dark, twinkling eyes over an expanse of graying beard—yes, we had to admit it's so. So the two of them have been doing "Jerry and Tricky D" routines all night.

Now, with Gary in his study making last-minute sermon adjustments and Stephen up in Boyland (the bedroom that stretches the length of the attic, jumbled with sports equipment, computer, and a son's bed at each end), David retired to Megan's empty room to sleep; he wanted to be nearer us, not up the attic stairs. I settle on the living room sofa with a rental movie, Joan Crawford in a murder mystery.

I have just gotten into the opening courtroom scene when David appears in the doorway asking, "Mom? Can I talk to you for a minute?" There are tears all over his cheeks and a catch in his voice.

"Of course," I say, surprised, and pat the sofa. David is the most tranquil, even-tempered person I know; I've seen him cry only a few times, and that not for many years. He comes over and sits by me on the sofa and manages to choke out the words, "I was lying in bed saying the Jesus Prayer, going to sleep, and suddenly I had a terrible thought. I thought, Maybe I just know God in my mind and don't really love him in my heart. Maybe I'm not really saved." He gulps and bows his head, leaning against me like a falling tree.

What tenderness in this Tricky D heart. I put my arm around him, then ask, "David, do you *want* to love God?" He nods yes, emphatically. "Well then," I say, "don't you see that you must already love him, or you wouldn't want to? Somebody that didn't love God wouldn't be crying because they were afraid they didn't." He nods again, getting quieter.

"Okay, so this is a good sign already," I go on. "You wouldn't have this love for him if he hadn't put the love in your heart, moving you toward him. It's like Jesus says in the Good Shepherd passage, he calls his sheep by name, and they come to him, and no one can snatch them out of his hand. Nobody else can take away your salvation in Jesus, since he's called you his own. Do you believe that?"

"Yes," David says.

"But it never hurts to commit yourself to him again," I continue. "Do you want to pray now and give your life to Jesus and take him as your Lord?" This sounds like pretty Protestant lingo to me, but I don't know how to say it in Orthodoxy yet. When David nods again, we bow our heads, hold hands, and pray. His usual tranquillity is beginning to return.

David has a characteristic peacefulness that spreads out from him like slow motion ripples on a laketop. When he was a baby, holding him would calm *me*. He has a great stillness. I imagine that if scientists measured his brain waves they'd find he just spins at a different rate from the rest of us. His peacefulness is catching.

It worried me when he was a toddler, though. Megan had been a little sunbeam, the kind of rosy child over whom strangers fuss in the supermarket. Stephen was a lightning bolt of intensity, blasting with energy from birth (and probably before). But David—was he autistic? He didn't talk much, didn't smile, didn't engage. He did drool. Most photos from his first few years show a beautiful child with mouth agape, pale blue eyes wide, and a damp ring spreading over his shirt front. Strangers always said, "Aww, he needs a nap." No, he'd just had a nap. This is just David.

One day I took him to the pediatrician and stood over the tow-haired child, pointing down at the top of his head. "Do you see this?" I asked, determined to know the worst. "He's like this *all the time.*" Dr. K leaned back, clicked his pen, and studied little David, who stared back at him openmouthed.

"Yes, we in the medical profession see this condition from time to time," he said. "I've encountered it before. It's called 'laid back.'" He went on, looking me in the eye, "Leave him alone. Stop worrying about it. Let him be himself."

It was good advice. David grew and found his own pace, but he never grew verbal. He paints and draws and writes music but mistrusts the realm of words. Not long ago I described something I'd read that impressed me and said, "Wasn't that great? It was exactly the right word to use."

"How can there be an exact right word?" David protested. "You can have the right number in an equation or the right shade of color in a painting or the right note in a song, but words aren't measurable like that. They're just . . . you can't . . . words are . . ." he fumbled, then looked at me and exclaimed triumphantly, "See?"

Right now there don't seem to be any words to add; silence is comfortable. David heaves a sigh. On the screen Joan Crawford is frozen in a twist of gray, her bitter mouth set. Protest, accusation, defense are ready to spring from the screen. It can wait.

---

# Information Night

Orthodox count days from sunset to sunset, so although the calendar for tomorrow shows a little tiny picture of St. John Chrysostom (hat, halo, staff, and stole, upraised blessing hand, patch of speckled sky, all in one-half inch square), it's already his feast tonight. *Chrysostom* means "Golden Mouth," and he was a gifted orator; he compiled our Divine Liturgy somewhere around 400 A.D. But it's his Bible teaching that I enjoy the most, due to its simple, straightforward tone. Nothing fancy, just a running commentary, verse after verse, unafraid to confront tough questions or seeming contradictions. I could recognize a patch of Chrysostom at twenty paces, I think, because of his running stream of questions: "And what does he mean by this? Why does he say that? Didn't he say the other, somewhere else?" He does his best to answer the questions, but I'm always impressed, in the first place, that he asks them.

Tonight we're back at ReVisions, and the chairs are set out in rows in the middle of the floor, because tonight we're hoping for visitors. We had advertised an evening with a well-known Orthodox author and speaker, but he's lying in a hotel north of town with a wrenched back and all appointments canceled. There wasn't time to put the word out, so the room is filling up: about half Holy Crossers, about half friends, sometime-visitors, and folks we've never seen before. We hold evenings like this a couple of times a year, and from past experience I know that some of these strangers will be joining us as regulars at Holy Cross.

We sing through Vespers a little short on voices; Margo is resting her strained voice, M. David is out of town, Carolyn and Zenaida are at other obligations. Dr. Pat, the other alto, and I sing "Bless the Lord, O My Soul" alone, since there's no one else who knows it; it sounds strange to hear a duet in our church. Michael shares the chanting with Greg, an Episcopal chaplain soon to be chrismated, and Carl, an ex-Catholic and Orthodox seminary grad who'll be joining us if a local job comes through. Greg has a delicious bass voice and Carl a crystal tenor, and we'd sound great if we'd only rehearsed this stuff together a few more times.

A duet sounds strange here; it sounds too show-offy, like a performance. But something else doesn't sound strange to me anymore, though it did at first. When someone is chanting a solo, you just hum along if you feel like it. You could hum the melody or a single low note, called the *ison,* which sounds like the drone of a bagpipe. You can stop or start, do it loud or soft, break into singing along on the words if you suddenly remember what they are. In an Episcopal church people would be whipping around to glare at you, but here it's just participation in worship.

For a few weeks there the Halloween decorations were giving us fits. We get along all right with snowflakes and Easter bunnies, but the big pale green witch behind the altar was too much. Every week we had to take down ghosts and skeletons to make our worship place holy. Now they're gone, except for an orange plastic jack-o'-lantern forgotten behind a pot of Swedish ivy on top of the black filing cabinet.

Tonight it's autumn leaves and turkeys everywhere. Across from me I see a circle of red, yellow, and brown construction paper leaves on the bulletin board, around a sheet of loose-leaf paper inviting ReVisions's clients to sign up for a meal. "You don't have to be alone for Thanksgiving anymore!" says the handwritten message, which has four varicolored turkeys marching underneath. It rebukes me to think how lonely the lives of ReVisions's clients might be, I who am so lucky in love and friendship and family. On the back bulletin board the clients' artworks are still displayed. The crumpled, tragic self-portrait has a homemade prize ribbon, with jagged red ink on torn lilac paper; it reads "Grand Prize 1 +" and includes a sketch of a smaller first-prize ribbon illuminated by the streaming light of two stars. Second prize went to *In the Middle of Nowhere.*

In the absence of a celebrity speaker, Carl and I each take a turn. After I describe my conversion to Christ and journey to Orthodoxy, Carl speaks a little more knowledgeably about the Orthodox Church; after all, he has a recent doctorate in Byzantine history. He is an intense, compact man of Italian background, who strides back and forth as he speaks, gesturing vigorously. He jokes about his Catholic church featuring "polka masses" and how startlingly different Orthodox worship was, "with a beauty that bores at our heart." The first time he attended Orthodox service was the Saturday night vigil before Pascha, all in Church Slavonic, and he found it interminable and incomprehensible; yet he thought, "These people seem to be very patient and very steadfast. Why don't I get it?"

Carl was chrismated on Holy Wednesday twenty-eight years ago. The following Epiphany season the priest came to bless his apartment, as is the Orthodox custom. It was a Friday, and Carl had prepared lunch for the two of them: hamburgers. A few members of the audience gasp; we fast from meat on Wednesdays and Fridays.

"It didn't occur to me," he said. "Having been brought up Catholic, post–Vatican II, we really weren't fasting on Fridays anymore. Well, you know what it was like in the Catholic Church—if you break a law, you go straight to hell, past purgatory, don't stop.

"But in Orthodoxy it's different. You see a real compassion, a genuine love, a sense that as brothers and sisters in Christ we are redeemed not by anything we do. Father Gabe sat down at the table, blessed the hamburgers, and ate with me. Then he said, 'Now Carl, in the future . . . '"

We laugh with recognition. What a freedom there is in choosing to fast, choosing to undertake these disciplines, in the company of others. Nativity fast will be starting in a few days, and we will be meatless for the forty days till Christmas (allowing a break for Thanksgiving turkey).

As the meeting breaks up we move to the fellowship room for platters of snacks that include plenty of cold cuts and sausages, since everyone's clearing out refrigerators. The crowd is jovial, and the conversations go on for hours. As I help clear away the dishes, I carry to the kitchen a casserole dish with just two Swedish meatballs rolling in the bottom. There will be plenty of time in the weeks ahead to wish I'd eaten them.

---

# Plans for the Land, Choir Rehearsal

The wheels of realty grind slowly, and though we've been dancing with the landowner for weeks now, it's unsure when things will conclude. A watershed was passed today; we signed a contract and sent it to the owner's lawyer and transferred funds to cover that first check.

This is enough to have Gary blooming with hope and big plans. He settles on my office sofa and, taking a sheet of scrap paper, sketches the lot. It's roughly rectangular, with a narrower end in front on Frederick Road. Another road marks the left border, and the stream marks off the right, cutting that side in at an angle near the street.

"From Frederick Road going back, the ground rises, then levels off, then rises again," Gary says. "I'd like to put the church in the middle, on that plateau. I think it should be a tall church, but simple—a whitewashed Greek-style church with a single dome over the middle, either blue or red."

He draws it centered on the lot. It seems odd to see it facing away from both streets, facing right toward the woods and stream. "That's east; if the church is going to be oriented, it has to face that way," Gary goes on. "But we can have parking lots above and below it and doors into the narthex on both sides. A Sunday school building behind it, here."

I ask about the old green cinderblock house, currently home of Bob. "Oh, I think we can definitely find some use for it. Maybe that's where we'll put our icon and book store."

The next seventy-five days are the crunch, Gary explains. We have a fourteen-thousand-dollar land use survey to undergo, assessing whether this spot will actually do what we need. We have to figure out what that muddy stream is going to demand of us. I recall Basil saying confidently, "You know, the new czar of the wet-lands for the county, what's-his-name, he's a Greek." Well, then, it's in our pocket.

It's choir night, so I roll on over to Margo's house. "It smells won-derful in here," I say as soon as I come in the door. Margo always puts out a spread on her green faux-marble dining table: tonight it's cider, popcorn, chocolate kisses, and cinnamon doughnuts.

"Oh, you always say that," Margo says. I didn't know I did; I have a poor sense of smell, so it's some kind of testimonial. She's perched on the piano bench, and she and Michael and Carolyn are looking at Michael's photos from his recent trip to the Holy Land. Soon we are joined by Greg as well. He's keeping busy; though still an Epis-copal priest, he spends one night a week rehearsing with our choir and another attending chrismation classes. Greg would like to be-come an Orthodox priest, and his job as a hospital chaplain gives him some leniency to accommodate an in-between period while he's not fully ordained. Making this switch is not impossible; my husband did it.

But my husband had something Greg does not: a wife. Though the Orthodox Church allows married priests, men must marry be-fore ordination or choose lifelong celibacy. The latter option holds little appeal for Greg. In our Antiochian archdiocese a man can marry after he's ordained a subdeacon, but not after being ordained a deacon or priest, and bishops are chosen from the ranks of un-married priests and monks. Greg can be chrismated and become a subdeacon, but after that his plans will go on hold until he finds a bride or determines that God has something else in mind. I've often thought that if I were a young woman looking for a husband, I'd get an apartment near an Orthodox seminary and all those bride-hunting men. I'd hang out in the local coffee shop reading the *Lenten Triodion.*

The current chrismation class, preparing a half-dozen people to join Holy Cross, is being held in the home of Rose and Tom. This is somewhat fitting, since they met each other and began their ro-mance in a Bible class at our Episcopal church. One member of the class is a co-worker of Rose's, Tracey, who grew up without any church affiliation. She and Greg met in class and have begun tenta-tively dating. Maybe history will repeat itself.

Michael has brought some panoramic shots of Jerusalem and postcards of historic churches. The Church of the Resurrection in Jerusalem, a particular site of pilgrimage, was built by St. Helena over the site of the Crucifixion and the Resurrection. It literally covers the geographic site; you go upstairs to get to Calvary, and the Resurrection tomb is downstairs at the bottom of the hill. Up on Calvary, in front of the altar, you can reach through a hole in the marble floor and touch the bare rock.

"I made my confession up there, in front of the Crucifix," Michael says. "When you're standing there, and the priest asks you 'Anything else?,' it sure makes you think!"

"Like Father Gregory always says," Margo laughs. I never confess to my husband, so I didn't know he does this. "'Anything else?' Gulp!"

"You start thinking, 'Well, when I was in second grade . . .'" Carolyn says.

"Maybe you should save something out," I suggest, "so you'll be ready."

"That wouldn't work," Margo says. "After you said it, he'd just go, 'And anything else?'"

Michael tells, too, of the silence. "When you confess to those heiromonks at a monastery over there, they're so used to silence, they'll just wait you out. I stopped once, just to check. The monk did this—" Michael stops, closes his mouth, widens his dark eyes "—for three or four minutes."

What would be going through your mind at a time like that? You'd be frantically searching for more sins to fill the gap. Greg suggests, "Uh, I'm kinda hating *you* right now. . . ."

We turn from the photo album to tonight's music; Advent is coming, and next week we'll be using a different, more melancholy setting of the Trisagion and new hymns for communion and for the kontakion, the hymn of the day. Well, not new hymns exactly; just different ones.

We practice a lyrical hymn I look forward to every Advent:

> The virgin cometh today to the cave to give birth;
> Ineffably to bring forth the Word eternal.
> Therefore, rejoice, O earth, at the message!

With the angels and shepherds give glory to Him
Who shall appear, by His own will, as a young child:
He who is from eternity God.

There are some beautiful Christmas hymns in Orthodoxy, but there are not many to choose from. David likes to say, "As far as music goes, the East has it all over the West at Pascha. But the West has it all over the East at Christmas." We're definitely a Pascha-heavy bunch. Liturgically, Christmas is celebrated on a scale more like Pentecost or Epiphany; it's nowhere near the Queen of Feasts.

Margo takes us through a tough hymn that's a real workout, "We have no hope, no other hope than you; we have no help, no other help than you." It's tough because she insists on every *H* and every *P* being clearly pushed out. I'm thinking that popcorn is not the best thing to go with singing. Other than that, Margo is the perfect, vigilant choir director. I try to remember all the instructions, how to shape my lips on *ah lay LOO ya,* to raise my palate as if holding a hot potato in my mouth, to breathe where the checks are and not in between. I really love this. So the hardest rule to remember is the last one: don't smile; it makes you go sharp.

<br>

*Wednesday, November 22*
*Apostle Philemon*

TWENTY-FOURTH WEEK AFTER PENTECOST

---

# Thanksgiving:
# Litia and Artoklasia Services

Last Saturday, when I went out with a friend for lunch, I mentioned that we were in the Nativity fast (this allowed me to ignore the burgers and order blackened salmon from the menu instead). When she asked what that meant, I replied that we go without meat from November 15 to Christmas, forty days; our parish doesn't observe a stringent fast now like we do before Pascha, though some Orthodox do. I said, "Of course, we make an exception on Thanksgiving. We eat turkey."

"Then what?" she asked. "Do you have to feel guilty about it and go to confession?"

"No," I said, "American Orthodox generally make an exception and feast on Thanksgiving. Because it's a local custom." A minute later I realize how funny this sounds. In Orthodoxy, the vast United States of America from-sea-to-shining-sea is "local."

We'll gather tonight to celebrate, with Vespers followed by a Litia and Artoklasia. This pair of short services gets tagged to the end of a regular service on the eve of a feast or when you want to observe a joyful occasion. We've never done a Litia and Artoklasia before; it's one of the last of the special Orthodox services for us to try. The Litia is a long litany—not much new there. But the Artoklasia, as the name suggests, is a ceremonial breaking of bread.

This version is a special, sweet bread, full of honey and cinnamon, and this afternoon Gary was doing his best to make it. He stood beating the ingredients in the big blue bowl with a wooden spoon. "The recipe refers to this as 'batter,' not 'dough,'" he said, looking a little worried. "They say I have to beat this until it's 'smooth and satiny.'" Looked like it was going to be a long trip.

Next, the recipe called for the batter to be poured into five five-inch-round cake pans. I have never seen a five-inch-round cake pan. Maybe they had them in ancient Constantinople, but they don't have them at Wal-Mart. "Why don't you just pour it out in five big glops onto the two cookie sheets?" I suggested. He did, and the loaves stood up pretty well, though of course we might open the oven later and see five pancakes. Or two pancakes. "After they're baked, I have to cover them with honey and confectioner's sugar," Gary said. "Just to make sure that they're completely impossible to deal with."

I leave to pick up Megan, who has gotten a ride halfway home from college. Fall has set in; it's cool but not cold yet, and the narrow black highway winds under flaming trees. By skipping down back roads and past farms, I am able to beat the holiday traffic. All the way out I sing along with the radio, delighted to be alone in the beautiful Maryland woods. All the way back Megan talks, talks, talks: who's dating whom, how cool poli sci is, how she thinks she wants to cut her hair. Meg has always been a chatterbox, but being away from home seems to have concentrated and distilled the impulse to Olympic-competition quality. We get home in time for a quick dinner, and then Megan decides to take a nap, from which I have to wake her for church. She rises under protest, as grumpy when wakened as she was when she was three.

We arrive at ReVisions under a clear black sky. Inside, a small congregation has gathered, and I slip into the small choir—just David, Michael, Carolyn, and Zenaida. The altar is dressed as usual, and for tonight's flowers we have a clear plastic water pitcher stuffed with small pink carnations and baby's breath. We move through vespers, then into the Litia service. Usually a litany consists of intercessions a line or two long, interspersed with "Lord have mercy," but these are hefty paragraphs. Gary prays:

> Again we pray for every Christian soul, afflicted and weary, in need of God's mercies and help; for the protection of this city and those who dwell therein; for the peace and stability of the whole world; for the good estate of the holy Churches of God; for the salvation and help of our fathers and brethren who with diligence and fear of God labor and serve; for those who are gone away and those who are abroad; for the healing of those who lie in infirmity; for the repose, refreshment and blessed memory and forgiveness of sins of all our fathers and brethren, the Orthodox gone to their rest before us who lie here and everywhere; for the deliverance of captives; for our brethren who are serving and for all who serve and have served in this holy temple, let us say:

And we respond, "Lord have mercy, Lord have mercy, Lord have mercy." There are several long prayers like this, covering everything you could think of, a virtual yellow pages of intercession. After one of them the rubrics call for a fortyfold "Lord have mercy," which Michael intones seamlessly.

The table for the bread is set in front of the iconostasis. The five loaves, with cruets of oil and wine and a small bowl of wheat berries, rest on a silver tray, and they look like giant Danishes. I decide that this is acceptable. The tops are indeed drooled with honey and confectioner's sugar, and I can't imagine what it will be like to pick them up and break them by hand.

After processing around the table and censing the bread, Gary takes the loaf on top and with it makes the sign of the cross over the other loaves. He prays:

> O Lord Jesus Christ our God, who didst bless the five loaves in the wilderness and didst satisfy the five thousand therewith, thyself bless these loaves, this wheat, wine and oil, and multiply them in this city, in the houses of those who celebrate this feast and in all thy world, and sanctify the faithful who partake of them.

Uh oh. The next instruction says, "The priest kisses the top loaf of bread and breaks it crosswise." I look at the gummy, festive surface of the loaf and at Gary's full beard and mustache. Why do the Orthodox have to kiss everything? Maybe this rubric was written for when priests didn't have beards. Wait a minute, this is Orthodoxy, they *always* had beards. I watch, but Gary merely picks up the loaf and breaks it—no kiss. When I ask him later he says, "I forgot."

He chants, "Rich men have turned poor and gone hungry; but they that seek the Lord shall not be deprived of any good thing." The choir chants this twice more, while Gary processes through the Royal Doors with the tray. A footnote in the service book here reads, "If a bishop is present, the omophorion and epitrachelion are removed from him as the clergy enter the sanctuary. After the aposticha, the bishop says the hymn of Simeon the God-Receiver."

I have no idea what this means. It reminds me of a persistent dream I used to have—that I was exploring an old house with winding stairs and funny rooms leading to more hallways and other rooms. I never got to the end, but I had a wonderful time. I know I'll never get to the end of Orthodoxy. It will always be Grandma's attic to me.

Gary breaks up the bread and pours some of the wine over it. Yesterday was the feast of the Entry of the Theotokos into the temple; it is said that, at the age of three, Joachim and Anna took her to the temple in Jerusalem, where (like the child Samuel in the Old Testament) she lived till adulthood. She went preceded by all the virgins of the town, bearing lamps—which would be quite an experience for a tiny girl. While Gary prepares the bread, Michael and David take turns chanting the aposticha of the feast:

> The virgins in your train, holding their lamps enkindled, shall be brought into the Temple of the Lord, O pure Virgin, as foretold by the prophet David. . . .
>
> She is led to the King with her maiden companions.
>
> Having gathered from spiritual meadows a bouquet of various flowers which are words inspired by the Spirit, let us joyfully weave a crown of praises for the Virgin.

The hymn imagines Zechariah, the high priest and father of John the Baptist, prophesying as he greets the little Mary: "Behold, the hope of the afflicted is coming near! She is holy, she is vowed to be the dwelling-place of the King of all! Let Joachim rejoice and Anne dance with glee. . . . The Queen of all, the one whom God prepared from all eternity, has opened to us the kingdom of heaven."

The service ends with the hymn from another presentation in the temple, when Mary brought in her infant son, and Simeon (the God-Receiver) sang, "Lord, now lettest thou thy servant depart in peace." We file up to the front, where Gary anoints our foreheads with the oil, and then we each take a piece of the bread. It tastes pretty good; in fact, it tastes great.

All the way home Megan chatters and chatters. If she pauses for a second, the boys jump in and tease her. Thinking of a recent test score, she begins, "While I was at college I made, uh . . . "

"A turkey. Out of brown paper. We *know*," Stephen says with exaggerated patience.

"You drew around your fingers and colored it in. We *know*," David joins in. "You told us."

She laughs helplessly and brushes her hand across her anointed brow, pauses, then laughs some more. "I was thinking, how come my forehead is oily?" she says. "I was going to play it off, but I was thinking, how come nobody told me there was butter on my head?" I love to hear her laugh.

# Divine Liturgy in Basil's Living Room

We awake to snow on the lawns and the housetops, the first real snowfall of the year. The roads are slushy but clear enough. Gary and I get into the old blue car to drive over to Basil's for the Divine Liturgy. Fat flakes are drifting down; the snow is the heavy, damp kind that's best for making snowmen. Inside the car it is cozy, because those Swedes sure know about conquering winter. The radio is crackling quietly as a soprano's voice climbs up an aria. It is nice being up early in the weather with my sweetheart. The only thing needed to make it perfect is a cup of coffee, but that has to wait till after liturgy.

When we come in I can smell the coffee, already perking in the kitchen. I go first to kiss the icon propped up in front of the fireplace, then turn to kiss Lillian who's seated nearby. She's all in blue today, with a fuzzy sweater, and her red leather Bible is open on her lap. Michael greets us as he passes through, on his way to work; Victor, also a member of Holy Cross, is already waiting outside in the big green service truck. "I'll bet Michael is the only plumber who goes off to work in the morning smelling like incense," Gary says.

The Divine Liturgy can be pretty elaborate, of course, but what we do here on Wednesday mornings is the simple minimum. There's usually a group of five or ten, and we stand informally around Basil's living room. It begins with a half-hour preparatory service that Gary does by himself, as he puts on his vestments and prepares the altar bread and wine. Basil has baked the traditional round loaf, made with only flour, salt, yeast, and water. It's about ten inches in diameter, and in the center is the mark of the carved wooden seal, a five-inch disk. The seal displays the letters *IC XC NI KA*, which stand for "Jesus Christ, Victor," and various small marks representing the church, saints, and angels. After Basil stamps the rising loaf with the seal, he cuts around the border, so the center pops up nicely.

At Basil's dining room table, Gary takes a sharp knife and cuts out the center of the bread, called the "Lamb," and dissects the various portions bearing the seal. This is set aside to be consecrated, and the remainder of the bread is chopped large and placed in a basket.

At 7:30 he comes into the living room, where Carolyn and I are waiting by the music stand. Basil, Joan, Frank, and Smiling Jeanne are standing nearby, while tiny Lillian remains seated. I recall Carolyn taking her turn teaching adult Sunday school on Sunday. She was describing the legends surrounding the death of the Theotokos: a hostile crowd was trying to disrupt the funeral procession, and a man reached out to overturn the bier. At that moment an angel appeared and cut off his arms. Carolyn said, widening her eyes, "And the guy goes, like, 'Whoa!'"

Gary begins: "Blessed is the kingdom of the Father and of the Son and of the Holy Spirit, now and ever and unto ages of ages." We sing back, "Amen," the kickoff for a continuous liturgy of song.

After a litany sprinkled with "Lord have mercys," we sing the first antiphon. The refrain is "Through the prayers of the Theotokos, O Savior, save us." We don't pray to the Virgin as a Savior in her own right, but we continually ask her to pray for us, much as we ask one another's prayers.

A brief prayer, then the second antiphon, with the refrain, "O Son of God who arose from the dead, save us who sing to you, alleluia!" This goes without a break into the ancient hymn, "Only Begotten." It's a minicreed, added to the liturgy by the emperor Justinian in the sixth century:

> Only begotten Son and immortal word of God,
> Who for our salvation willed to be incarnate
> Of the Holy Theotokos and ever virgin Mary,
> Who without change became man and was crucified,
> O Christ our God,
> Trampling down death by death,
> Who are one of the Holy Trinity,
> Glorified with the Father and the Holy Spirit,
> Save us.

Next we sing the Beatitudes as our third antiphon, then the Entrance Hymn, "Come, let us worship and fall down before Christ." Gary comes out from the altar, bows low, then blesses us with the silver Gospel book.

At this point, on a Sunday, we would sing the Troparion of the Resurrection, the one appointed for the week from the cycle of eight rotating hymns. But on a weekday we sing the troparion of the day's saints. Today it's Paramon, who was martyred before 251 (my calendar notes, "and 370 companions"), and Philumenes, who was killed a quarter-century later. That's all I know about them. To think that there were people who actually died for this faith I hold so comfortably, and I barely know their names.

Sometimes there's a second hymn for the same saints, but that one is called a kontakion instead of a troparion; I don't know what the difference is. In both cases, they appear as paragraphs in the worship book, and Carolyn and I just chant them freely. Today there's no kontakion, so we sing our fight song, "O Lord, save thy people and bless thine inheritance," instead.

At this point we sing the Trisagion hymn: "Holy God, Holy Mighty, Holy Immortal, have mercy on us." This echoes the heavenly worship in Revelation 4:8, and like the twenty-four elders we bow each time we repeat it, crossing ourselves. We sing this three times, then a "Glory be to the Father," then sing it once more. Stage directions call for the deacon, if you have one, to shout "Dunamis!" ("with strength") before the final round: "Louder!"

It's time for the Epistle; Basil points out the passage for Frank to read. After three "Alleluias," Gary reads the day's Gospel. Three times in this Scripture-reading portion of the liturgy we are exhorted, "Wisdom!" and "Let us attend!" I suppose even in the earliest days there was a tendency for people to wool-gather in church.

On Sundays we have a homily at this point, but on Wednesdays we plunge ahead and enter the eucharistic portion of the liturgy. It begins with the Cherubic Hymn:

> Let us who mystically represent the Cherubim,
> And who sing the thrice-holy hymn to the life-creating Trinity,
> Let us now lay aside all earthly cares.

During this time, Gary is making preparations at the altar and reciting prayers quietly. At one point he turns and bows to us, saying, "Forgive me, my brothers and sisters." We bow in return, still singing. He goes to the dining table, gathers the elements of Eucharist, and turns for the Great Entrance. On Sundays, he processes with altar boys, incense, candles, and the processional cross, all around the interior of the church and back to the altar through the Royal Doors. Here he goes briefly through the living room before returning to the altar corner, just left of the fireplace. He chants the commemorations as he goes, remembering particularly members of the parish who need our prayers. There is a something to give thanks about: on Sunday afternoon Rose delivered a baby girl, Nicole. It's been eight months since she announced her pregnancy after church, one of our answered prayers. She and Tom are ecstatic and plan to be back in church with their prize on Sunday.

When Gary reaches the altar, we sing the conclusion of the Cherubic Hymn:

> That we may receive the King of All
> Who comes invisibly upborne by angelic hosts.
> Alleluia, alleluia, alleluia.

Another litany, then we exchange the kiss of peace. We greet one another with "Christ is in our midst," and the response, "He is and shall be." We kiss twice, once on each cheek, and some people swing back for a third, trying not to bump glasses. On Sunday you can reach only the few people nearest you, but here we all exchange the peace with everybody. Gary turns from the altar and heads for me first.

After the peace, Gary exclaims, "The doors! The doors! In wisdom, let us attend!" In the ancient church, those who had not been baptized would be dismissed from the church at this point and the doors closed. We are about to recite the Nicene Creed, which no noninitiate could say.

I like hearing Basil recite the creed, because he does it as if someone is challenging him on every line. "I *believe* in one God, the Father Almighty . . . *And* in one Lord Jesus Christ . . . I *believe* in the Holy Spirit . . . I *acknowledge* one baptism for the remission of sins . . ." If they were arresting Christians, there would be enough evidence to convict Basil.

Now, with fear and trembling, it is time for the Anaphora, the prayers of consecration.

"Let us stand well! Let us stand with fear! Let us attend, that we may offer the holy oblation in peace!" Gary chants.

"A mercy of peace, a sacrifice of praise," we respond. We go through the "Lift up your hearts" and the "Holy, holy, holy," then the words of institution. As Gary begins the epiklesis, the prayer that invokes the descent of the Holy Spirit upon the gifts, we kneel or prostrate as we sing:

> We praise thee, we bless thee, we give thanks to thee, O Lord,
> And we pray unto thee, O our God.

After final words of consecration we rise again to sing a hymn to the Theotokos. There are intercessions, then the Lord's Prayer. The "Prayer with heads bowed" comes next. We follow the direction to bow our heads, and Gary prays: "Look down from heaven, O Master, upon those who have bowed their heads to You; for they have not bowed to flesh and blood, but to You, the awesome God. Therefore, O Master, distribute these gifts offered to all of us for our own good according to the individual need of each person." He elevates and breaks the bread, and Basil goes to the kitchen to bring a little hot water to add to the chalice. Then we pray:

> I believe, O Lord, and I confess that thou art truly the Christ, the Son of the Living God, Who didst come into the world to save sinners, of whom I am chief.

A prayer like this now comes easily, but back when I was a just-barely Christian, I couldn't even bring myself to say all of the Nicene Creed. Something like this would have had me contemptuous of the abjection, eager to assert a "divine spark within" that makes us all minigods. Letting go of that self-righteousness and self-delusion was healing. There's relief, even joy, in telling the truth about yourself to someone who already knows and loves and forgives. Not a powder-puff love based on sentiment, but love that knows exactly what I'm worth and sent his Son to die for me anyway. Saying this prayer, and receiving that love, is always a moment of tender joy.

The prayer goes on:

> Of thy Mystic Supper, O Son of God, accept me today as a communicant: for I will not speak of thy Mystery to thine enemies, neither will I give thee a kiss as did Judas, but like the thief will I confess thee: remember me, O Lord, in thy kingdom.

This reflects again, I suppose, the ancient origins of the liturgy, dating to a time when the details of the Eucharist had to be concealed from Christ's "enemies" and shielded as a secret.

Gary takes communion in both kinds, then combines the Precious Body and Blood in the chalice while we sing, "Praise the Lord from the heavens! Praise Him in the highest!" When he turns around he lifts the chalice and spoon, saying, "With the fear of God, with faith and love, draw near." We respond, "Blessed is He that cometh in the name of the Lord. God is the Lord, and hath revealed Himself to us."

The seven of us line up for communion, singing the basic communion hymn, "Receive the body of Christ, taste the fountain of immortality." Carolyn and I go last, handing off the song to each other like relay runners. No one else here has much of a voice, and if one of the two of us isn't singing there's an uncertain mumbling that just passes for song. As we leave the altar we take a chunk of blessed bread, the antidoron, from the basket offered by Basil. But we can't eat it yet; too much singing to do.

When all have received, Gary says, "O God, save thy people and bless thine inheritance." That's our cue to sing a hymn that I noticed the first time I went to an Orthodox service:

> We have seen the true light! We have received the Heavenly
> Spirit!
> We have found the true faith!
> Worshipping the undivided Trinity, for He hath saved us.

Can we say that? That this is the true faith and all? Guess so. It seems pretty daring in a culture where it's deemed rude for anyone to claim possession of objective truth. Our hymn doesn't say that nobody else has any truth at all, just that we're sure we do. While we believe that Jesus is the only way to the Father and that the Orthodox Church today is the same Church he established, we don't presume God is unable to save people who follow Jesus in other churches. But whatever truth there may be elsewhere, we assert confidently that we have found it fully here.

We're getting close to the end now, but there are no shortcuts in Orthodox worship. "Let our mouths be filled with your praise, O Lord," we sing, "that we may sing of your glory, for you have permitted us to partake of your holy, divine, immortal, and life-giving mysteries. Establish us in your sanctification, that all the day long we may meditate on your righteousness."

Here Gary has a couple of longer prayers, so I can take a couple of bites of bread without worrying about spraying crumbs. We sing "Blessed be the name of the Lord, henceforth and forevermore" three times, and with a final "Glory to the Father" we are through. From the first "Blessed is the Kingdom" till now, the minimum Divine Liturgy for a priest and congregation of seven took fifty-five minutes.

Gary consumes the remaining elements while Basil chants postcommunion prayers. As this ends, Lillian asks, "Coffee?"

This is one of the nicer spots of the week. We crowd into Lillian's kitchen and sit around her round table, which is covered with a rose-sprigged vinyl cloth. On the table is a loaf of homemade bread, and we break it and smear the pieces with grape jelly, drawn from the jar with a long iced-tea spoon. We drink coffee and talk. "How come we didn't do that new Cherubic Hymn?" Frank asks, teasingly. "I was rarin' to go." The choir has been trying to introduce a more complex and melancholy version of the "Let us who mystically," and it's been an occasional catastrophe. Carolyn and I decided to do the old familiar today.

"Why, Frank, I thought that's what you were singing," says Gary.

"If I had, you all would have been running out the door," Frank responds.

This old kitchen has a porcelain sink and metal cabinets painted white. It is a working kitchen. All along the windowsill above the sink are nailed up measuring cups, paring knives, basting brushes, and potholders. These last include fancy purple crocheted ones that look like bunches of grapes; Lillian made them years ago. A note on the refrigerator reads, "Find candy thermometer to make Christmas candy."

On the wall is a plate with "My Kitchen Prayer" and another fancy one with a pierced border showing the Last Supper. There's the familiar icon I see in nearly every Orthodox kitchen, of St. Euphrosynus the Cook. He is holding his attribute, a branch full of yellow apples, supposedly a supernatural gift plucked from heaven's garden. A Romanian Christmas carol we're learning begins "At the gates of heaven above, apple trees are blooming sweetly."

There's an icon of Christ holding an open book, and this in fact is the first icon I remember Gary buying, some dozen years ago. On the book it reads, "You have not chosen me but I have chosen you that you should go and bring." Yes, it ends abruptly there, in the middle of an idiom; the conclusion of the sentence, from the Gospel of John, is "forth much fruit and that your fruit may abide." It strikes me as characteristically Orthodox to be unconcerned with getting the full text onto the icon or even getting to a natural break in a phrase. It reminds me of the old novelty office sign: "Plan Ahea."

Meanwhile, Basil is reminiscing. "When I was in school, they didn't like Greeks. I got in a fight every day. The kids would say, 'Go on back home, you foreigner.' I had to bust some chops." He didn't speak English when he started school; Lillian's Greek-speaking mother was caring for the kids while she worked at Pete's Grill.

"I walked back and forth every day to the restaurant," Lillian puts in. I'm surprised; it must be two miles from here. "Till one day, this big collie dog came and ran and put his paws on my shoulders and knocked me down. After that I asked that cop, George, to teach me to drive. He said, 'Oh, Harry's not going to like that.'" Harry was Lillian's husband, and by all accounts the source of Basil's temper. "I said, 'Never mind Harry.' And he did teach me to drive."

It's easy to linger here, but we have to get on with the day. Outside the air is brisk, but it's stopped snowing, though loose flakes are still blowing down from the trees. Gary says, "Do you think the boys are outside playing in it?" I hope so, but I'm afraid they're getting too old to be excited about a snowfall. I never get used to it, though; it always seems a treat to me. We bundle into the car to find out what the boys are doing.

# Tracey's Baptism, Chrismations

This morning Tracey awoke for the last time in her thirty-seven years unbaptized. At the church Gary was preparing for the day, setting out at the back of the room our old metal washtub (draped with a white sheet, covering the word *Falstaff* stenciled in black on the side), and a table with incense, oil, and my great-great-grandfather's silver water pitcher. Matins would begin, as usual, at 8:30, but when it ended an hour later we would have Tracey's baptism before going forward with the Divine Liturgy.

Gary had entertained hopes of an immersion baptism, which is what the Orthodox Church prescribes, though it's not easily provided by a mission congregation meeting in rental space. He had fun going to a couple of feed and grain stores and admiring the horse troughs, asking what they cost. "Of course, I didn't say what I wanted one for," he'd told me. "I waited for them to ask." Though it would have been memorable to push Tracey down in a horse trough, due to logistical factors (How do we fill it? How heavy would it be on those old floorboards? And then, good golly, how do we *empty* it?) the notion gradually dimmed in the light of common sense. We would have to settle for standing Tracey in the tub and pouring lots of water over her head.

Matins, baptism, and then the chrismations. Chrismation, a service involving prayers and anointing with blessed oil (hence the name), is the second of two rites uniting a Christian with the Orthodox Church. The first, of course, is baptism, but people who have been previously baptized usually do not undergo the rite again. Only Tracey will be baptized, but the others who have been going through class will be chrismated with her: Greg (yes, they're still dating), Sheila's daughter, Liza, with her little toddler, Meagan, and Martha, a single woman a little older than me. Steve has also completed classes but is traveling this week and will be chrismated next Sunday. Welcoming new members into Holy Cross like this happens a couple of times a year and is always a joyous occasion.

But I will not be there. At 4:30 A.M. I slapped off the alarm in the home of my friends Julie and Owen, down in South Carolina. I have been attending a conference on the campus of the fledgling Orthodox "great books" college, Rose Hill, but now am going to catch the earliest possible flight home.

The last thing Julie told me last night was, "The coffee is ready to go, just plug it in. And there are Styrofoam cups you can take with you." But when I woke up I felt an inner impulse: don't have any coffee so you can take communion with the new members of Holy Cross.

I didn't want to appear to reject Julie's thoughtful hospitality, though. It sounded holier-than-thou: "How dare you offer me coffee, I'm going to liturgy!" What to do? I perked the coffee, poured half a cup, then dumped it down the drain. I unplugged the pot and took the used cup with me, evidence to discard later. If I were a murderer, I bet I could get away with it.

I get lost in the dark leaving Aiken, get lost on the interstate finding the airport, ditch the car, rush to the plane, and buckle in. I am irritated and start to argue with God. Who can go from 4:30 in the morning, through an hour's drive and two plane flights and a taxi ride, and never take a sip of coffee? Besides, I may get there in time for communion, but I'll never get there in time for the Gospel. I can't take communion if I come in after the Gospel, anyway. This is just stupid.

In the Atlanta airport I have a cup of gourmet coffee, one that tastes like it has big, loud quotation marks around the "gourmet" part and maybe around the "coffee" part as well. It is 7:30; if all goes as scheduled, I'll be getting to church a little after 10:00.

The part I will miss I can see on videotape, since Frank plans to stand on a chair with his son's camcorder and immortalize the day. Later I sit and watch it with Gary. The focus shifts from Carolyn's crucifix to the altar to the silver Gospel book, zooming slowly in and out. "Frank's being arty," Gary says.

We see Tracey standing in the back of the room, wearing a white robe; "That's Greg's alb," Gary says. The alb is the basic Episcopal clergy vestment, which goes under stoles and chasubles. After his chrismation today, Greg won't need it anymore; he won't be an Episcopal priest but an Orthodox layman. He and the other chrismands are standing near Tracey, front-row witnesses to her baptism.

Tracey is tall, with an alert manner, large eyes that reflect amusement and surprise, and short dark hair that looks like it has a mind of its own. So far today, on a scale of one to ten, her nervousness level seems to have reached about six. Gary begins the baptism by breathing in her face three times, then making the sign of the cross over her three times as well. Laying his hand on her head, he prays that God will "remove from her her former delusion and fill her with the faith, hope and love which are in thee. . . . Enable her to walk in all thy commandments. . . . Inscribe her in thy Book of Life. . . ."

Then begins the exorcism. Gary goes on: "O Lord of Sabaoth . . . Look upon thy servant; prove her and search her, and root out of her every operation of the Devil. Rebuke the unclean spirits and expel them . . . speedily crush down Satan under her feet, and give her victory over the same. . . ."

Gary then breathes on her three times again and chants:

"Expel from her every evil and impure spirit which hideth and maketh its lair in her heart.

"Expel from her every evil and impure spirit which hideth and maketh its lair in her heart.

"Expel from her every evil and impure spirit which hideth and maketh its lair in her heart.

"The spirit of error, the spirit of guile, the spirit of idolatry and of every concupiscence; the spirit of deceit and of every uncleanness which operateth through the prompting of the Devil. And make her a reason-endowed sheep in the holy flock of thy Christ, an honorable member of thy Church, a child of the light, and an heir of thy Kingdom. . . ."

"They have a lot of confidence in your breath," I say to Gary. Of course, there's nothing like an exorcism to bring home powerfully how little of this is our doing, how completely it is the power of God. It had better be.

Together Gary and Tracey face the back wall of the church. He asks, "Dost thou renounce Satan, and all his angels, and all his service, and all his pride?"

Tracey answers, "I do."

"Dost thou renounce Satan, and all his angels, and all his service, and all his pride?"

"I do."

"Dost thou renounce Satan, and all his angels, and all his service, and all his pride?"

"I do."

"Hast thou renounced Satan?"

"I have."

"Hast thou renounced Satan?"

"I have."

"Hast thou renounced Satan?"

"I have."

"Breathe and spit upon him."

Tracey gathers up her breath in a dry mouth and manages to spit into the air. Then Gary turns her to face the altar.

"Dost thou unite thyself unto Christ?"

"I do."

"Dost thou unite thyself unto Christ?"

"I do."

"Dost thou unite thyself unto Christ?"

"I do."

"Hast thou united thyself unto Christ?"

"I have."

"Hast thou united thyself unto Christ?"

"I have."

"Hast thou united thyself unto Christ?"

"I have."

"Dost thou believe in him?"

"I believe in him as King and God."

"Dost thou believe in him?"

"I believe in him as King and God."

"Dost thou believe in him?"

"I believe in him as King and God."

Casting out evil spirits is immediately linked to union with Christ. Exorcism is not a parlor game to be played by people tickled with the occult. In one frightening Gospel passage, Jesus describes a person who is delivered from a demon, but because he is left empty the demon returns with "seven other spirits more evil than himself, . . . and the last state of that man becomes worse than the first." When evil spirits go, they must be replaced quickly with the Holy Spirit, Jesus warns, or the consequences can be dire.

A more amusing incident occurs in the book of Acts: a team of brothers tries to cast out a demon with the words "I adjure you by the Jesus whom Paul preaches." The evil spirit responds, "Jesus I know, and Paul I know, but who are you?" and thrashes them till they flee "naked and wounded."

Together, Tracey and the congregation repeat the Nicene Creed. Then Gary asks her again, "Hast thou united thyself unto Christ?"

"I have," Tracey replies.

"Bow down also before him."

Tracey makes a prostration, then rises and says, "I bow down before the Father, and the Son, and the Holy Spirit, the Trinity, one in essence and undivided."

After a prayer, Gary turns his attention to the group waiting to be chrismated. "Do you desire to enter into and abide in the communion of the Orthodox-Catholic Faith?" he asks.

They respond, "I do."

Gary prays over them, then asks, "Do you renounce all ancient and modern heresies and false doctrines, which are contrary to the teachings of the Orthodox-Catholic Eastern Church?"

"I do," they say. Greg and Liza are reading from the same prayer book. Little Meagan, in Liza's arms, has her red hair in a topknot and wears a fancy pink dress with a hem swooped up like drapery. Liza has a comfortable, kindly demeanor and wears a cotton flowered dress that goes well with an easy-chair temperament. But Meagan has the intense, superfocused look of an child with unusually high intelligence. Meagan doesn't miss a trick, and I'll bet she'll drive her teachers crazy. That red hair is a warning flag.

"Do you desire to be united unto the Holy Orthodox-Catholic Eastern Church?"

"I desire it with all my heart."

"Do you believe in one God, who is adored in the holy Trinity, the Father, the Son, and the Holy Spirit; and do you worship him as your King and your God?"

"I do."

You can tell, listening to these prayers, how vital right doctrine is to Orthodoxy. The church spent the first few centuries wrestling out all these beliefs, holding church councils to settle questions, writing creeds. I didn't always value this; at first it just seemed obsessive. That was before I saw theologians in other churches rejecting the Resurrection, the Virgin Birth, and other elements of the faith once delivered. Without a fence around the faith, the orchard is overrun and trampled.

I used to think that the Nicene Creed wasn't much of a prayer—it was just what you said to qualify, like showing your driver's license to cash a check. Then I realized the cost at which our ancestors in the faith worked it out. The Nicene Creed is a gift of the Holy Spirit, won through toil and tears. It is an honor to receive it, to be one of the stream of believers who stand fast by this acclamation as the centuries roll by.

The chrismands are sent to stand up near the altar, while Gary turns to the baptism itself. Tracey's nervousness has risen to about an eight; she rubs her chin, and a wing of dark hair has fallen over her right eye. Gary goes through a long litany, then through prayers exorcising the baptismal water and blessing it. He dips his fingers in the pitcher, making the sign of the cross three times and breathing on the water three times, as he repeats, "Let all adverse powers be crushed beneath the sign of the image of thy cross."

After further prayer over the water, Gary breathes three times on the vial of oil and blesses it. He pours a little of the oil into the water, in the sign of the cross. Then, with the oil, he makes the sign of the cross on Tracey's forehead, chanting: "The servant of God, Tracey Anna, is anointed with the oil of gladness; in the Name of the Father and of the Son and of the Holy Spirit."

He anoints the front and back of her neck, chanting: "Unto the healing of soul and body."

Anointing her ears: "Unto the hearing of faith."

Her hands: "Thy hands have made me and fashioned me."

Her feet: "That she may walk in the way of thy commandments, O Lord."

The instructions in the baptismal service next say for the priest to hold the baptismal candidate "securely upright." This rubric presumes an infant baptism, I suppose; in our case it would be difficult, since Tracey is taller than Gary. She steps into the metal tub, and Gary pours water from the pitcher over her head three times, chanting, "The servant of God, Tracey, is baptized, in the Name of the Father and of the Son and of the Holy Spirit." She sputters and blows the water from her face. Now she doesn't seem as nervous; her face is full of quiet light.

As Tracey steps from the washtub, Smiling Jeanne is right behind her to wrap a white towel around her shoulders, and Jeanne is living up to her name, smiling to beat the band. Gary chants, "The servant of God, Tracey, is clothed with the garment of righteousness, in the name of the Father and of the Son and of the Holy Spirit." Jeanne hustles Tracey off to the women's room to dress; when she returns she'll join the other chrismands in front of the altar for the office of Chrismation. The choir begins chanting through psalms, while we wait for Tracey's return.

I see on the screen a short woman in a red sweater slip into the choir and take out a small notebook and pen. She looks around and breaks into a beaming, excited smile. It's me; I just glimpsed Rose standing with baby Nicole in her arms. Nicole is a few hours shy of one week old, and she made it to church her first Sunday. I've missed another service on this long, packed day—the "churching" of Rose as a new mother, on the first day she returns to church. Nicole's baptism will occur a few weeks later.

There's a Post-it note on the music stand that reads, "Psalms 23, 46, 66, 63, 111, 121, 122. Sing until signaled by Father Gregory."

"What's going on?" I whisper to Carolyn.

"We're waiting for Tracey to finish dressing," she whispers back. "We did the baptism but not the chrismations yet."

Uh oh. I realize, that means, they haven't read the Gospel yet. I shouldn't have had that cup of coffee in Atlanta. Well, maybe I could have communion anyway? No, that wouldn't be right. I had a clear warning about this. Why do I argue with that little voice inside? It's always right. I feel really crummy about this, and stupid.

We sing psalm after psalm. It is taking Tracey quite awhile to dress. Later, she tells me that they couldn't decide how to arrange her scarf; Tracey ultimately wanted to just leave it off, but Jeanne was game to keep trying. As we get to the end of the last psalm, Tracey strides in wearing a white knit dress and a very nice scarf.

The chrismands kneel in a row before the iconostasis, with their sponsors behind them: Margo and David stand behind Greg, Rose behind her old friend Tracey, Hardworking Jeannie behind Liza and Meagan, and Zenaida behind Martha. Meagan is stretched out flat on the floor with her head on her crossed arms and the soles of her little bare feet upturned behind her.

"Rise, stand aright, stand with fear," Gary chants. As Martha stands she flashes a smile of delight that peels off the years. A few weeks ago she came up to me at coffee hour and said, "You know how you say that men come to Orthodoxy for truth, and women don't get it as easily?" She smiled. "That wasn't so in my case. I came because I was searching for truth." Martha is independent, with an incisive intellect. Fifty years ago, she probably looked just like Meagan.

The chrismands look down at their photocopied booklets and recite in uneven unison:

This true faith of the Holy Orthodox-Catholic Church, which I now voluntarily confess and unfeignedly hold, I will firmly maintain and confess whole and in its fullness and integrity, until my last breath, God being my helper; and will teach it and proclaim it, so far as in me lieth; and will strive to fulfill its obligations cheerfully and with joy, preserving my heart in purity and virtue.

And in confirmation of this, my true and sincere profession of faith, I now kiss the Word and Cross of my Savior. Amen.

Gary presents the silver Gospel book to be kissed by each candidate, then makes the round again with a brass cross. Meagan leans out of her mother's arms to land her kisses.

Then Gary tells the chrismands to kneel again and places his stole over the head of each one, pronouncing absolution of sins. Each person has come to our house for confession this week, standing with Gary in the corner of the living room, before icons of Christ and the Theotokos. One icon shows Jesus placing his arm around the shoulder of the weeping Prodigal Son. A scroll tumbles from Jesus' other hand: "For this my son was dead and is alive again, he was lost and is found."

For Tracey it was the first confession of her life, a prospect that she told me beforehand had her pretty nervous. A "whole-life confession"! I advised her not to worry about remembering everything—just hit the high spots, or low spots, as they may be. The important thing is to confess and thoroughly air out anything that is continuing to burden you. Minor items and things forgotten can be covered in the sea of God's forgetfulness.

Gary prays over each kneeling candidate:

> May the God who forgave David through Nathan the prophet, the Prodigal Son, and the weeping woman at his feet, may that same God forgive you all things, through me a sinner, both in this present world, and in that which is to come, and set you uncondemned before his dread Judgment Seat.

As the chrismands stand again, there is a litany and a prayer, and then the anointing begins. Gary starts with Martha and anoints her on the forehead, eyes, nose, mouth, ears, throat, hands, and feet. With each anointing he calls out, "The seal of the gift of the Holy Spirit!" The congregation responds in a shout, "Seal!" That's twelve times for each person, sixty times in all. It's invigorating, shouting in church, welcoming these people into our fellowship. The room is crowded on this cold morning, and full of smiles.

Gary anoints Martha and Liza, then Liza holds up Meagan. "Quick," she whispers, "because I don't know when she's going to revolt." Gary smiles at Meagan and makes firm eye contact; he is familiar with kids and liturgical handling of the same. Meagan returns a focused, scrutinizing gaze. Gary anoints her as he does the rest but a little more quickly, and we all shout "Seal!" every time. Hardworking Jeannie is wiping the tears from beneath her glasses.

When all the chrismands have been anointed, we bow our heads. Gary prays, "They who have put on thee, O Christ our God, boweth also their heads with us unto thee. Keep them ever warriors invincible in every attack of those who assail them and us; and make us all victors, even unto the end, through thy crown incorruptible."

Gary then sprinkles the chrismands with holy water, using a sprig of fir cut this morning from our neighbor Horace's tree. As he spatters each one in the sign of the cross, he chants, "Thou art justified. Thou art illumined. Thou art sanctified. Thou art washed, in the name of the Father, and of the Son, and of the Holy Spirit."

Next, Gary takes a cotton ball and wipes the forehead of each chrismand. After chrismation, the oil is wiped off, though I'm not sure why; I was told that it was so the new believer wouldn't put his trust in the magic of the externals but rather in the Spirit. Of all the anointings, sprinklings, and other such we go through in the course of a year, this is the only one I know that we take time to undo. As Gary wipes each forehead, he chants, "Thou art baptized. Thou art illumined. Thou hast received anointment with Holy Chrism. Thou art sanctified. Thou art washed, in the name of the Father, and of the Son, and of the Holy Spirit."

Gary hands a cross on a golden chain to each sponsor, to be placed around the neck of the newly chrismated. Rose has her arms full of baby Nicole, who's sleeping peacefully throughout; Tracey holds Nicole while Rose fits the cross around Tracey's neck.

Finally, Gary says to the crowd, "Now we will have the tonsuring. In the ancient world, the sign of servanthood was tonsuring, having your hair cut. Since these newly illumined are now Christodouloi, servants or slaves of Christ, we will take a clipping of the tips of a few hairs from the front, back, and sides of their heads—the 'four corners' of their heads. These clippings will be put in the censer as a first offering." Stephen, holding the censer, has been warned to pile on incense to overlay a more pleasing fragrance.

Tonsuring brings to mind a letter from my friend Julianne. When her husband Don (previously known as Don the Baptist) was tonsured, she said it was like the parable of the widow's mite: "The others gave of their abundance, but he gave of the little he had. . . ."

As Gary clips Martha's hair she grins with delight. Liza is characteristically peaceful. Little Meagan gives all her intense attention to the process. Tracey looks like she's straining to hear distant music. And Greg looks very serious. After the tonsuring, and a final prayer, the chrismation is complete. We greet our new church members with a rousing chorus of "God grant you many years."

Before continuing with the liturgy, Gary addresses the crowd. "In the interest of time, we won't have a sermon today. As you know, ReVisions has started asking us to clear the building, plus have everything put away, by 12:15. It's always tight, but the special services today make it even tighter. We'll pick up the Divine Liturgy now with the Troparion of the Resurrection, and when we get to the Gospel we'll just go straight to the Cherubic Hymn." I think about that cup of coffee in Atlanta. I wish I weren't so foolish—and it's not for the first time.

An hour later, the new members have received their first Eucharist, the final hymns have been sung, and Gary makes announcements. Good news: we've signed a contract for the land at last, and next week we'll go over there after church for a short service of thanksgiving.

Also, next week we will chrismate Steve, who was out of town today and missed going through with the rest of his chrismation class. Steve had told me during a recent coffee hour that becoming Orthodox was a momentous decision: "My grandfather converted from Buddhism to Protestantism while he was still in Japan, before coming to America," he said. "That was a real 180-degree turn. I still have, over my sofa, the calligraphy he made of the Twenty-third Psalm. Now, for me to go from Protestant to Orthodox feels like another 180 degrees. I had to read the chrismation service over very carefully. It's really a heavy decision."

Gary then calls forward Rose and Tom, with baby Nicole, and the crowd showers them with applause. Hardworking Jeannie steps forward to say, "And now that you've seen these beautiful new parents, I'm still taking names of people who'll bring them dinner, for one more week." With a final round of "God grant you many years," we adjourn for coffee hour. My second cup of coffee is waiting in there, the one that should have been my first.

Sunday, December 10
St. Joasaph, Bishop of Belgorod

TWENTY-SIXTH WEEK AFTER PENTECOST

## Litia and Artoklasia at the Land

"Do you all know why we're here?" Gary asks.

About thirty of us are standing in a semicircle before him, standing fair and square on our patch of land, under a blazing blue sky, in about three inches of snow. The wind gusts and blows his vestments around, flinging the layers out like petals: on top, a copious black wool cape, then under it the blue and gold brocade phelonion, then the black jibby. (The jibby is a simple robe for nonsacramental occasions, analogous to a cassock. When it arrived from the seamstress it bore a pinned-on note, "Here is your beautiful jibby," so that's what we call it, as in, "I need to wash my beautiful jibby.")

Basil proclaims, "We're here to give thanks to God for this land."

"Yes, and it's also an act of intercession," Gary says. "We have a long way to go. First there's the land use survey, then we need the approval of Metropolitan Philip, and if all goes well we'll go to closing on June 30. A lot of things have to fall into place before then, including raising as much money as we can, to keep the loan small."

It's about twenty degrees out, and the wind is biting. "I think we ought to go ahead and start," I call out. Gary looks toward the road. "Jay and his kids aren't here yet," he says. Most of us came over from ReVisions directly after Sunday liturgy, but people leave there and arrive here at different times. We shuffle in the snow, smiling despite the cold, with noses glowing red. "Think of Russia," says newly chrismated Martha.

Hardworking Jeannie has gone to her car to haul out blankets to pass around. "I got these at the church yard sale," she tells me as she wraps a hot pink queen-sized blanket around Lillian. Jeannie, strapping and vigorous, is easily a foot taller than Lillian and stands behind her arranging the blanket folds until just the tufts of Yia Yia's white hair protrude above the shocking pink. Satisfied, she wraps her arms around the older woman. Lillian pats her arm, saying, "That's my Jeannie!"

"Load it up, David!" Basil is shouting to my son, who's preparing the censer. "Put plenty of incense in there! We're outta doors, and you can't use too much. Fire that baby up!"

Gary begins the service as Jay and his kids pull up. We are going to have a Litia and Artoklasia, as we did just a couple of weeks ago for Thanksgiving. I circle the crowd, taking photos and trying to scribble notes with my increasingly frozen fingers. Gary is facing the small mahogany table, which is draped with an embroidered cloth, and holds two votive candles and a margarine tub full of incense. In front is another, smaller table, with the silver tray and five much more successful looking loaves of artoklasia bread. These are big and hearty, with crosses on top. "Who made the bread?" I whisper to Basil. "Yia Yia," he says proudly.

Behind the table stand Vince and Andy, holding up a large icon depicting the Crucifixion; this was, I think, one of Carolyn's first icons. Unlike the simple corpus, which is nailed to a bare-wood cross, this one is detailed with figures of Jesus, the Theotokos, saints, and angels, and a skull under the foot of the cross. I don't know how long I can keep writing; my fingers are freezing, the ink in the pen is freezing. Just then one of Jeannie's daughters comes up and hands me something small and red; it is her mother's right-hand glove.

Frank has gone to his car for plaid mufflers, which he's draping over the heads of Lillian, Martha, and Jeannie's daughters. Someone puts a crocheted baby blanket around my shoulders. I notice that Andy is wearing Gary's gloves, and my son David is wearing gray knit gloves I've never seen before. We look like a walking yard sale. With a final fight-song rendition of "O Lord, save thy people, and bless thine inheritance," we're through. Doris, next to me, is wrapped in a large blanket with pink roses; as she goes forward to receive some of the artoklasia bread, her blanket comes unwound and trails behind her in the snow. I pick up the end and carry it like a queen's train.

It's beautiful being out here, and everyone is elated, but it sure is cold. I've never seen my sons' noses so red. As we scurry to the car, Greg says to me in his deadpan bass voice, "You know, this is how the Crystal Cathedral got started." I look around at four acres of snow. "Well, we've got the crystal," I say.

# 6

## NATIVITY & THEOPHANY

*Saturday, December 23*
*The Ten Holy Martyrs of Crete*

SATURDAY BEFORE NATIVITY

---

## Walking Around the Convent

If I button the collar of my blue winter jacket, the opening fits just right around my glasses, and I can peer out through the circle meant for my neck. I'm walking around this way in the dark, and I'm glad that it's dark because I'd rather not have anyone see me.

When I finished at the gym, I had an hour to pass before Vespers—not enough time to fight the holiday traffic home. I drove, instead, to the Episcopal convent a few blocks from Basil's house, thinking I'd walk around the grounds here for a while. But my hair was still wet from swimming laps, and I had no hat, which in this twenty-degree chill amounts to a prescription for hypothermia. It seemed like a stroke of genius when I figured that I could slip my arms out of the sleeves and wear my jacket as a sort of misshapen tent. Still, it wasn't the kind of genius you necessarily want people to observe.

I walk down the narrow black road that winds like a ribbon over this hill. The convent is nestled in a pocket of the state park, so it's quiet under the black sky. The grounds are deserted, and all the sisters must be inside. The first big stone building, the guest house, is dark; I'm surprised that there don't seem to be guests for Christmas. Around a curve, then past the smaller wooden house where the chaplain lives. His lights are on, and the home looks cozy and bright. Here I come upon an empty swath of meadow, and I can see my shadow on the road cast by a tall streetlight. Empty sleeves swing, and the top of the figure ends with a blunted shoulder line. It looks like, "Legend has it that every year, on the night before Christmas eve, a short, headless woman walks these hills."

I'm thinking about what I want to ask the Lord to give me for Christmas. If I could have anything I want, what would I want? I recall Eugene in Chicago saying, "I am more afraid of my own decision than of a fire." I am afraid of the things I want, in my foolishness. All I want is God. That seems the only safe thing to ask for.

I hear a cracking on the thin sheet of icy snow, and three deer step across the road in front of me, nervous on their stilty legs. Barrel bodies, but the legs are absurdly fragile. Safe on the other side, they sprint down the slope. In the dark they look smaller than fullgrown, but I can't be sure; they're little more than black shapes in the night.

Up ahead I see the end of a long stone building: the dark flank of the chapel, and beyond it the convent proper. I walk on, ruminating. There are a lot of specific things I could ask for, and a host of petitions are nudging for attention. Sometimes, when I go through this exercise, I ask for the boldest things I could imagine and am frequently surprised to find my wishes coming true. I think this works only when you ask for the right things, however. That happens only when you're in tune with God: listening, receptive, ready to ask for what he wants to give. It amounts to filing an order for goods already on the way, indicating intention to receive.

I make my way around the curve in front of the convent. Windows are lighted in checkerboard fashion. We had our retreat on the Jesus Prayer here, and when I was Episcopalian I visited on retreat several times, staying in the convent and wearing a doily on my head. Silence in the hallways, silence all night and much of the day, silence at breakfast; the crunching of toast sounds unnervingly loud when there's no other sound in the room.

What do I want for Christmas? Lord, I only want to be near you. I just want to draw closer to you, and I want that desperately. I need to be rescued from myself, from my pig-headedness and vanity. I'm so afraid of wanting the wrong things—how many times I've taken willful side paths that delayed me from getting nearer you! Please continue burning away the sin in me. Help me to see you more clearly. Bring me swiftly to your side.

It strikes me that this is an odd thing to want. It would make more sense to want a new car or a windfall of cash or, for goodness' sake, to be thin. Of all the things I could want, though, I most want something I've never seen or touched or even can prove exists. From the outside, I guess, this is like wanting to be George Washington or to live in the second dimension. (Which would, in fact, make you pretty thin.)

Why would I want to be near God? I've never even seen him. Yet I want this far more than any earthly thing I can think of—my children's happiness, my husband's health, the success of Holy Cross Mission. I wouldn't want any of that outside the shelter of God's will. More afraid than of a fire, to ask for any earthly thing. So I ask only for God, and for me to be hemmed and altered to fit his will, his presence.

I always add, "Lord, give me a chance to learn it without the suffering." I know God is going to fit me to his image one way or another, and I have every intention of going along quietly. Years ago I was baby-sitting a four-year-old girl, and we had the following conversation. Naomi told me, "When I was at Julie Schwartz's house I met God."

I thought for a minute. Oh, she must mean a rabbi.

Naomi went on: "But I wouldn't shake his hand."

Me: "Why?"

"Because God shakes too hard."

Your arm's too short to box with God; you need to be careful, even just shaking hands. As C. S. Lewis says of the Christ-figure Aslan in the Narnia tales, "It's not like he's a tame lion." All over the world, millions of times a day, people are praying, "Thy will be done." And I think I can dispute that? Like, "Oh, I'm an exception." If I'm stubborn enough, I can get my will done instead?

Tragically, yes. I recall my theology professor at seminary saying, "I am not free to be black. I am not free to be a woman. I am not free to be three feet tall. But I am free enough to be lost." I may be able to defy the will of God and accomplish my own, in some cramped and narrow way. The edge of that precipice is ever at my side, leering with a greedy grin. No wonder I'm begging: save me from myself, bind me to you.

At the end of the convent building the road loops back. I stop and listen for a train down below in the black forest; nothing. At the wood's edge I hear more deer trample by, but it's too dark to see them.

I tip back and gaze through fixed glasses at the sky. I wonder, still, why I should be so drawn to God. It's not just self-protection; that doesn't work anyway. If it was God's will that I suffer, for my own good or someone else's or just his mysterious plan, I'd accept it. Well, I mean, I'd make a decision to accept it and work hard at staying in the circle of his peace, fighting my natural gift for complaint. It made me almost giddy to realize, long ago, that there was no loss in this life worth fearing; wherever I had to go, I would have the Lord with me.

Many years ago I memorized this Scripture during a nightly prayer session: "For I am sure that neither death, nor life, nor angels, nor principalities, nor things present, nor things to come, nor powers, nor height, nor depth, nor anything else in all creation, will be able to separate us from the love of God in Christ Jesus our Lord." I went back to bed and woke up a few hours later in labor; by noon, David was born. Maybe that's why he's so peaceful.

It's awkward with my glasses being gripped this way; I unbutton the collar and instead drape the jacket over the top of my head. Now I look even more like the headless walking woman. Stopped at the bend of the road, I squint again to make out deer, but unsuccessfully. To the left the ground is white, sliding away in a curve under the black sky. The silence is complete.

Suddenly I remember something I hadn't thought about for years. I was a little girl playing on the swing set in the backyard when I heard a deep voice call my name. It happened a second time. I went inside and asked my mother; she hadn't called me. I went back out and waited.

Nothing. Well, I didn't say this was going to be an *interesting* story. It isn't as good a story as what happened to the young prophet Samuel; after the third call, God gave him a clear and specific message. Of course, it wasn't a very cheerful message: the next morning the little boy had to tell the priest Eli that God was going to destroy his family and expunge his line forever. Not a tame lion. Probably just as well I wasn't given such news to deliver.

But maybe this early event has something to do with my sense that God is shockingly real and infinitely desirable. It's not merely a desire to love God in order to get goodies and avoid pain; he doesn't make any such promises. I want to be near him just in order to be near him.

That, I guess, is the bottom line. It doesn't make any sense I can put into words. It's like, off the pie menu, I want pecan. I want cotton, not wool; crab, not shrimp. I want to be near God, not anywhere else. This doesn't make me any kind of a woo-woo special holy person; quite the reverse. I'm endlessly needy. I can't help what I want. I can't even explain it. Even my wanting him, I know, comes from him.

How strange this is. I've never seen God, so how can it be that he feels more real than anything I've ever known? There's an immediate, breathtaking touch, the presence of one closer to me than I am to myself. As close as I can be to my husband or my kids, there's still a veil. On this earth, you can't really touch any other human, even someone you love very much. There's always that scrap of muffling felt, blunting your touch.

Only God is at the deep heart of it all. Fleeing to him, we wind up closer to everything and everyone he's made. The nearest I can get to the ones I love is by going through God. I meet them there. And so I pray to be brought to him. For good measure, I ask for lots of specific stuff, too, requests for my husband and children, for family and friends, and for my own dreams of the coming year. But for none of this to come true if it would move me a step from him.

Time to head back to the car, or I'll be late to Vespers. I hasten around the rear of the convent. All the lights are on in the big, gleaming kitchen; Holly is near the window, washing dishes, and Mother Catherine Grace is putting something away. I worry that the light cast on the road will illuminate the headless walker and cause them a fright. No need to worry. Instead, I see Holly talking as I pass, then hear her whoop out a laugh. I guess she didn't see me. Or maybe she did.

*Sunday, December 24*
*Feast of the Nativity*

# Nativity

The West calls it Christmas and prepares to the point of exhaustion; today, the checkout woman in the grocery store told me she'd wrapped over three hundred presents. The East calls it Nativity, and it kind of sneaks up on us. The special services during the week preceding it generally go unobserved, and there's no elaborate acting out of events, as with Pascha. A forty-day fast, a service of Royal Hours, a Vespers, a Matins, and there you are. Christ is born.

As far as the choir is concerned, this is a mercy. The plague has run through and left us limp. Last Sunday I got a phone message from Margo: "I hope you're in good voice today, because Carolyn and I both have lost ours." I arrived at church to find two basses (Greg and Michael) and two altos (Zenaida and Dr. Pat). Only one tenor, but Carl has the most effortlessly huge singing voice I've ever heard.

I was the lone soprano. I quickly realized that this was going to be like the old P. D. Q. Bach routine, where two sportscasters describe the action as the New York Mills Philharmonic goes up against the Danish conductor Heilige Dankeschoen in a battle of Beethoven's

Fifth. Today, it was a bunch of parts-people up against the sole melody-toter, and no choir director. It was a struggle to the end.

The room was decked to be jolly. Our choir corner was crowded by a ten-foot tree, garlanded and tinseled. Behind Carolyn's solemn, crucified Jesus, a silver garland streamed across the blackboard, flanked by twisted crepe paper of red, green, and a little blue (maybe they ran out of green). Just beyond each elbow of the icon a single silver ornament dangled from the garland. Looking toward the altar I could see the large icon of Jesus on its stand and beyond it, taped to the black metal cabinet, a cutout of an elf struggling with a candy cane twice his size. Our smaller icons are placed, as usual, on the windowsills and window tops; in between are taped snowflakes cut from white and yellow paper. The yellow is a surprise. I don't have positive associations with yellow snow.

This morning, the eve of Nativity, we returned in slightly better shape. Margo has a bit of a voice, not much. Carolyn has none and tells me she has also lost her hearing in her left ear. Dr. Pat has dropped to a tenor. Greg is too diseased to pass the peace but still sings beautifully and with mellow cheer. I thank God for my durable good health and am aware of what a foolish risk I took last night wandering around in the dark with wet hair.

This morning we had a regular Divine Liturgy, and tonight we gather again for Nativity Matins and Divine Liturgy. It happens that way when Christmas falls on a Monday, generating four or five hours of church today combined. When we drove by the Presbyterian church on the corner I noticed that there were no cars parked out front; maybe they'd canceled their morning service to focus on a midnight celebration. "Wimps," Stephen snorted.

Part of the nonwimp part of being Orthodox, of course, is fasting before liturgy. We fast from food and drink after midnight for a morning Eucharist, and after noon for an evening one. This causes a small problem today, when we have liturgies both morning and evening. The solution: a big, heavy refreshment hour before going home to fast the rest of the day. Megan contributed her famous potato dish, the one we call "Winnie Potatoes" because she got it from her friend Winnie. (Winnie got it from the back of a bag of frozen potatoes.)

I picked Megan up just yesterday; she had lingered at college after exams to stay with my friend Connie because she's still dating Connie's son. Michael was just getting some leave from the navy, and the lovebirds hadn't seen each other for months. They hugged good-bye, then Megan plopped in the car and was completely silent—a sure sign, with her, that something is really out of kilter. I glanced over and saw big tears spilling out over her lower lids. I squeezed her hand, and she held mine in both of hers like a little girl; her hands are soft and plump, with short nails that are pointy like kitten's teeth. Still the round tears came down, until I pulled out a handkerchief from the cubbyhole under the radio. "As long as I've known you," I said, "I could never understand how you can just cry and not wipe your eyes."

She smiled at me then. "Oh, Mom," she said. Then she started talking.

So this morning we had Divine Liturgy followed by a feast of Winnie Potatoes, egg-and-toast casserole, white-frosted doughnuts, shrimp dip and crackers, chocolate cake, and hollowed-out zucchini cylinders stuffed with minced vegetables. Well, it is an odd combination, especially considering that for fifty people it was the only meal of the day. But it was delicious and filling. This is why they call it potluck, I suppose, and most of it struck me as pretty lucky, except the zucchini.

After an afternoon of napping, reading the paper, and gradually getting hungrier, we return for the Christmas liturgy at 10:30. Masses of poinsettias are already banked under the two big standing icons, and they create a brilliant glow. Margo and David are wearing green with red sweaters; Vince does the same, while Hardworking Jeannie is in a red sweater-dress with a green scarf. It always surprises me when men agree to dress to match their wives. It seems a very tender concession, something an anthropologist from Mars would recognize as evidence of profound bonding. There are limits: though Jeannie and Margo are wearing red shoes, their husbands are not. Gary and I are not dressed alike. I'm wearing a simple navy blue outfit, he's in floor-length gold brocade.

We sing the Troparion of the Nativity, which is scattered three times through the evening liturgy. It has a sprightly tune:

Thy Nativity, O Christ our God,
Hath given rise to the light of knowledge in the world;
For they that worshipped the stars
Did learn therefrom to worship thee, O Sun of justice,
And to know that from the east of the Highest
Thou didst come, O Lord,
Glory to thee.

This morning we heard the birth narrative from the Gospel of Matthew. Luke's familiar version focuses on Mary's experience from the Annunciation to the verse that reads, "She kept all these things and pondered them in her heart." According to legend, Luke went to visit Mary in her old age and interviewed her for his Gospel, then painted her likeness—the first icon.

Matthew's version, on the other hand, depicts the events from Joseph's point of view. His bride-to-be is mysteriously pregnant, and he considers breaking the engagement quietly. But an angel tells him in a dream, "Do not fear to take Mary your wife, for that which is conceived in her is of the Holy Spirit." In his morning sermon, Gary pointed out that "Quiet Joseph," so overshadowed in the Gospel story, shielded Mary from shame by taking it on himself, making himself the object of gossip.

Tonight, surprisingly, the Gospel reading is not about the birth of Jesus but about the next event in Matthew's story: the visit of the Magi and Herod's rising suspicion. The three wise men ask Herod for directions to the birthplace of the new king, news that troubles the old king greatly; as a result, "in a furious rage" he orders that all baby boys in Bethlehem under two years old be killed. I cannot read these words, now, without seeing Caravaggio's monumental and chaotic depiction of that day, the blood, the tiny bodies, the mothers' shrieking, helpless grief. It is not a Holly Jolly Christmas kind of scene.

Those who were looking for a sentimental Christmas are bound to be disappointed. Gary tells us, "This is not a story about a sweet little baby who was born to cheer everybody up. This is a story about a confrontation with the powers of darkness. It is this struggle for which Jesus was born, and the shadow of a cross lies over the manger. Herod is alive today, ever walking the earth in a new form. So we as Christians have to ever be ready to confront him in the name of Jesus. The little baby born in a manger is the Lord, Victor, Christ come to save."

I can hear Basil murmuring a low-key "Amen" from time to time. I know Gary asked him not to, but the old habit's been returning lately; he can't keep it in. I like it. I feel like Amening myself.

We move into the Eucharistic prayers. It's about midnight, and around the room people are yawning, and we're hungry. We sing the appointed Megalynarion to a very hollow-chant, cavelike melody. For the opening, the men take the melody and the women sing the ison, on a single dark note:

> O my soul, magnify her who is more honorable
> and who is more glorious than the heavenly host.

We switch back for the rest, rising from a murmur to a high, forte note on *cave.*

> A mystery I behold, which is strange and wondrous.
> The cave is heaven, and the Virgin is the throne of the
>   cherubim.
> In the confines of the manger is laid the infinite Christ our
>   God,
> Whom we praise and magnify.

About 12:30 we take communion, and as the liturgy concludes Gary processes around the interior of the church, holding aloft the icon of the feast. Unlike Western depictions of Christmas, which generally show Mary and Joseph kneeling upright by the manger, the central image of the Orthodox icon is a rocky cave, with Mary lying on the ground next to her swaddled son. She looks worn out; you could believe she just gave birth. Carl mentioned this when we had our information night a few weeks ago, giving it as evidence of Orthodoxy's earthiness and groundedness in body reality. As in many festal icons, lots of things are going on at the same time: in the lower-right corner, two women are shown washing the newborn baby. It's another realistic touch. Babies aren't born looking the way they do in the nursery window.

In the upper left angels are singing, and below them the Magi are hurrying to the scene. In the upper right an angel is speaking to two shepherds, who look scared out of their wits. Below them another shepherd sits on a rock, piping a tune on a reed, apparently accompanying the heavenly choir.

Joseph is not with the Holy Family in this icon; instead, he's sitting on a rock in the lower left, looking dejected, with his head resting on his left palm. An old shepherd is standing before him, leaning on a staff. This is Satan in disguise; he's trying to convince Joseph that this Virgin Birth stuff is a lot of malarkey. Mary, lying on her mat, has turned her face away from her baby and toward her husband. Her expression is consoling and kind.

Gary places the icon on a table in front of the altar, and we open up green booklets to sing some carols; no matter how Orthodox you get, there's no substitute for "Joy to the World." We sing that and "Hark the Herald Angels" and "O Come All Ye Faithful" and all the rest. The overhead lights are turned off, and we light candles, passing the flame back. In the darkness the streetlight splashes through the big window, leaving a mullioned swatch of white on the wall. The green exit signs glow as brightly as our candles, and I can see a diffuse green glow on the chest of the Jesus icon, about where a Sacred Heart would be. Megan and Sheila, on either side of me, lift candles while I hold open the little booklet; we sing not just classic carols but Ukrainian and Carpatho-Russian ones, too.

We sing the Romanian carol, the one about the apple tree blooming at the gate of heaven. Margo has redone the arrangement and it's much more interesting, but she has the men singing "Bum Brum" on some verses, and "Loo Loo" on others, and "Fum Fum" on yet others. This would be fine, except we haven't rehearsed it enough and we keep getting scrambled. The congregation doesn't seem to notice; by the third verse they're singing right along.

With a final rendition of "Silent Night," and Margo's fine voice soaring over all in a descant, we're through. The lights come up and the candles go out, and when Gary thanks the choir for our hard work Basil shouts, "Axios!" Several others join him in the sentiment. We close by lining up to kiss the cross, exchanging the greeting of the season: "Christ is born!" "Glorify him!"

We adjourn to the back room for some light refreshments provided by Smiling Jeanne and Frank. I run into Annette, with whom
I haven't chatted for a while. "What are you having for Christmas
dinner?" I ask. "Not goat, I hope."

"Oh, yes, goat," she says. "I've been getting it ready all day. My
son, Keith, works with a man who made a trip to Jamaica; he knows
that's where we're from. He brought him some goat meat back. So
Keith came home from work, and he said to me, 'Mama, what do
you think I have in this basket?' I said, 'What is it?' He goes, 'Mah-
ah-ah-ah-ah.'"

I ask how her health is; back at our Episcopal church, she had sat
on a picnic table one day after services and had it collapse under
her. That led to X rays, which providentially revealed an unsus-
pected tumor on her spine, followed by surgery and a lengthy con-
valescence. "I am lucky to even be walking, girl!" she says. "From a
wheelchair to a walker to a cane to this." She holds up her empty
hands; Annette is fully self-locomotive now, completely restored. I
think it's because she has such a hard head; the therapist told her
many other people would have given up. But Annette has another
explanation: "God is good, that's why I love him."

Saturday, January 6, 1996<br/>Holy Theophany

# Blessing of the Water

It sounds like the typical parent's lament: seems like only yesterday
that Jesus was a baby, but now he's a full-grown man. Two weeks
after Nativity is Theophany, when we commemorate Jesus' baptism
in the Jordan River. In the icon of the feast, John the Baptist (a.k.a.
John the Forerunner) is standing on the rocky shore stretching a
hand over Jesus' head. The river, in trick perspective, looks almost
vertical, a swirling waterfall curving from behind a hill and cascading down in corduroy stripes of gray. Jesus is floating atop the river,

standing on two crossed boards; these recall the broken gates of Hades in the icon of the Resurrection. Four serpents crane their heads up from under the boards, hissing in helpless frustration, while orange fish swim past wearing placid smiles. Farther downstream a tiny man and woman have turned their backs on Jesus and look at him resentfully over their shoulders. The man is labeled "Jordan," and he is pouring the river out of a pot, while the woman, "the Sea," is fleeing on a large fish. These illustrate the words of Psalm 114:3: "The sea looked and fled, the Jordan turned back."

*Theophany,* or Epiphany, means "revelation," and the significance of the feast is represented at the top of the icon: a radiant half-circle is broken off at the upper edge of the image, and a swordlike ray descends from it to Jesus' head, on which is overlaid a dove. The event of Theophany was the first revelation of the Trinity. John the Baptist heard the voice of the Father say, "This is my beloved son" (symbolized by the fragment of a circle; the reality of God extends beyond our comprehension), and he saw the Holy Spirit descend in the form of a dove. "It is not the day when Christ was born that should be called Epiphany, but the day when he was baptized," wrote St. John Chrysostom. Nativity disclosed the birth of a child, but Theophany revealed who that child was.

We are in deep winter now. The tree outside the high window is only a scribble of gray on a faded blue sky. David is the sole acolyte at today's Theophany service. We're considering sending Stephen to school next year instead of doing home-schooling; he's gone today to take a high school admission exam. He left the house frozen with tension, wearing an expression like he'd put his face in a pencil sharpener. Megan stands among the congregation wearing an assortment of clothes that, as usual, baffles me: a delicate blue princess-line dress, shrouded under a bulky maroon cotton turtleneck, and on top of that her boyfriend's military green windbreaker with numbers stenciled on the chest. An assortment of silver and beaded necklaces and many, many silver rings. Shoes that I can only describe as high-heeled sneakers, in glossy silver with broad domed toes. I feel like the aunts observing T. S. Eliot's cousin Nancy: "not quite sure how they felt about it, but they knew that it was modern."

On Theophany we bless the holy water that we will use for the rest of the year, and a plastic storage container the size of a foot-locker, full of water, is resting on a table near the sanctuary. Roman Catholics and Episcopalians keep their holy water in a font by the church door, dipping their fingers and making the sign of the cross when they enter. Orthodox don't, but we use the water throughout the year in many other ways, for example, sprinkling icons when they are blessed. The holy water represents baptism, and during the period between Theophany and Lent each year every Orthodox home is to be visited by the priest and sprinkled with the water, carrying our baptism home.

Also, members of the church will take home small jars of the water and use it throughout the year, to bless themselves or to sip. This was a startling idea to me at first; drinking holy water seemed akin to drinking perfume. But Orthodox keep a jar of the water near their icon corners and use it to bless themselves, sipping a little in time of illness or to accompany fervent intercession. Some take a little every day.

Dr. Pat's Sunday school students have decorated jars that we can buy to take home holy water, one dollar each, with proceeds going to the building fund. The jars sit on the table before the tub of water and on the floor, their former callings still recognizable under the decor: mayonnaise jars, instant coffee jars, a jug for orange drink. On the way in I selected a small honey jar with a yellow lid. A gold Christmas ribbon has been wound around it, and glued on the front is a photocopy of the icon, vividly colored in with markers. The Jordan is indigo blue, the desert rocks golden yellow. It's Theophany by Disney.

At the end of the Divine Liturgy we begin the service to bless the water with three readings from Isaiah. Gary then prays over the water, in the words of St. Sophronius, seventh-century patriarch of Jerusalem. This is only part of a vast, symphonic prayer:

> Today the grace of the Holy Spirit hath descended on the waters in the likeness of a dove.
> Today hath shone the sun that setteth not, and the world is lighted by the light of the Lord.

Today the moon shineth with the world in its radiating beams.

Today the shining stars adorn the universe with the splendor of their radiance.

Today the clouds from heaven moisten mankind with showers of justice.

Today the Uncreated accepteth of his own will the laying on of hands by his own creation.

Today the Prophet and Forerunner draweth nigh to the Master, and halteth with trembling when he witnesseth the condescension of God towards us.

Today the waters of the Jordan are changed to healing by the presence of the Lord.

Today the whole universe is watered by mystical streams.

Today the sins of mankind are blotted out by the waters of the Jordan.

. . . . . . . . . . . . . . . . . . . . . . . . . . . . . . . . . . . . . . . . . . . . . . . . . . . . .

Today the darkness of the world vanisheth with the appearance of our God.

Today the whole creation is lighted from on high.

Today is error annulled, and the coming of the Lord prepareth for us a way of salvation.

Today the celestials celebrate with the terrestrials, and the terrestrials commune with the celestials.

Today the assembly of noble and great-voiced Orthodoxy rejoiceth.

Today the Lord cometh to baptism to elevate mankind above.

Today the Unbowable boweth to his servant to deliver us from slavery.

Today we have bought the kingdom of heaven, for the kingdom of heaven hath no end.

. . . . . . . . . . . . . . . . . . . . . . . . . . . . . . . . . . . . . . . . . . . . . . . . . . . . .

Jordan turned back and the mountains shouted with joy at beholding God in the flesh. And the clouds gave voice, wondering at him that cometh, who is Light of Light, true God of true God, drowning in the Jordan the death of sin, the thorn of error, and bond of Hades, granting the world the baptism of salvation.

So also I, thine unworthy sinning servant, as I proclaim they great wonders, am encompassed by fear, crying reverent unto thee, and saying:

The directions call for this "in a louder voice":

> Great are thou, O Lord, and marvelous are thy works, and there is no word which is sufficient to hymn thy wonders.
> Great are thou, O Lord, and marvelous are thy works, and there is no word which is sufficient to hymn thy wonders.
> Great are thou, O Lord, and marvelous are thy works, and there is no word which is sufficient to hymn thy wonders.

Gary prays thus over the water several times, making the sign of the cross and then dipping his fingers in it. The choir sings the Theophany Troparion three times, and each time Gary dips the brass blessing cross into the water, then lifts it high. At last we file forward to pick up our jars, which Basil and Vince fill with kitchen ladles. As we bow to kiss the icon of the feast, Gary sprinkles our heads with the water, shaking droplets from a sprig of fir.

The emphasis on water seems prophetic, as a whole pile of frozen water is headed our way. As I head into the health club later this afternoon, the guy behind the desk tells me, "They're predicting two feet!" The snowstorm has been advancing on the radar for several days and is due to arrive tonight. The last I'd heard, yesterday, was three or four inches, but Baltimoreans are characteristically hopeful in anticipation of icy disaster. We get a little snow every year, a few storms bringing six inches or less. But this—this could be big time.

No one knows how big, but theories abound. A woman in the dressing room is telling a friend, "I just heard on the radio, eighteen inches!" The sky outside is graying, but the ground is still dry. I swim laps, looking out the big window and envisioning the snow banked up outside. On the way out I tease the counterman: "They still saying two feet?"

"Now it's three," he retorts. When I laugh, he smiles and asks, "What're you laughing for?"

"I won't be laughing later, right?" I say. In that case, I'd better laugh now.

# The Blizzard of '96

At three in the morning I wake to pray, and the light in my study is full and soft as spilled milk. The round moon is glinting off a fresh coat of snow, which looks to be about four inches deep. An old green gooseneck light is fixed above the garage door, and in the cone of cast light I can see a few swirling flakes. It's amazingly bright inside, nearly bright enough to read by.

At seven-thirty I wake again, and it's just as bright as it was at three—pretty dark, that is. The sky is choked with snow, bitter gray. The phone rings repeatedly, as parishioners call asking what to do. We'll have Divine Liturgy here, at our dining room table; Gary planned ahead and gathered everything needed last night. A few who live nearby will walk over—Dr. Pat and her girls, and Sheila. Michael intends to walk, though it's at least five miles. The idea distresses me; I imagine him succumbing to hypothermia, collapsing, and being lost in a drift for days.

We have some serious housecleaning to do and must begin one of several shovelings of the walk. Gary snaps on the television in search of weather news, but we are first greeted by a man smiling his face up till his eyes are little dots.

"A happy Jee-zus morning to you!" he says. Gary and I stare at the screen in dismay. "Now we're going to sing a little song, a little song that just tantalizes Satan. And it tells him he has no power. He just has no power! Hallelujah!"

"Wow," I say. A character like this prompts such a mix of emotions. I don't have any reason to question the sincerity of his commitment to Christ, and on the basis of that alone he'd have a better shot at heaven than the multitudes of more clever, more sophisticated unbelievers who appear on the small screen. But why can't Christians present our faith in better taste? Or is it my idea of good taste that is absurd? My under-the-mercy friend Terry occasionally scolds me for elitism, and I occasionally deserve it. I'm awash in self-chastisement, but over it all, when I look at the screen, I feel simply appalled.

"You know who that is, don't you?" Gary asks.

"No," I say, "except that it's False Teeth Man."

The figure on the screen clicks and mumbles through each cloying phrase: "Yes, Satan has no power! That's good news, isn't it? It sure is. That's good news."

"No wonder people think Christians are idiots," I say. "He's talking to us like we're six years old."

We begin vacuuming and straightening, and soon there's a knock at the door. Michael is standing there grinning, swaddled to the dimensions of the Pillsbury doughboy. He declines to come in but instead asks for a shovel, and he and David go to work on the front walk.

Before long Dr. Pat arrives with her daughters, Beth the ballerina and the twins, Cece and Krissy. Their family was assigned to bring refreshments today, so the twins have goodies in a backpack.

It's 9:30, time for liturgy, but where is Sheila? "She usually comes late," says Krissy. "She usually comes right before the Gospel." A phone call to Sheila's house reveals that she just left. The walk through the foot-high snow will take at least a half hour.

Almost immediately there's a knock on the door and it's Victor, Michael's boss, who braved the weather in his big green plumber's truck. "My grandmother calls that truck 'The Green Hornet,'" Michael says. "I guess that dates her." We send Victor back in search of Sheila, and before long we're all gathered in the front hall and ready for liturgy.

Gary stands at the dining room table to celebrate, facing the window; through the window I see Horace and Frances's house, obscured by nearly horizontal flying snow. We have three-part harmony, but it's hard on Dr. Pat and Michael as Gary steadily dips lower and lower and I'm not musically astute enough to lift the melody to a higher key. Megan stands near the stairs, joining in with her sweet soprano.

At last we conclude and then retire to the living room, where we sit around the fireplace, armed with the twins' cookies and nursing cups of coffee. It is wonderful to be gathered together on a morning like this. We make tentative plans to gather at Dr. Pat's for dinner—she has a pork roast, and Sheila can bring over a pot of chicken stew. But a lot more snow has to fall before sunset, and predictions now range up to thirty inches. More snow is due Tuesday, and then another storm will arrive by the weekend. This is deliriously awful news for locals, where such a blizzard exceeds the experience of nearly all, providing hardship stories to inflict on generations yet unborn.

It's a good thing we claimed the rushing Jordan yesterday and blessed it; now even frozen water is our friend. Such a reminder is timely. The snow is slanting up the window ledges and filling the upstairs balcony like a manger filled with hay. Across the street, the neighbors' illuminated plastic lawn Nativity set is gradually succumbing to the storm: Mary and Joseph kneel side by side, shoulder-deep in snow, smiling down at a smooth expanse of white. I know he's still under there, somewhere.

*Wednesday, January 24*
*Venerable Mother Xenia*

WEEK OF ZACCHEUS SUNDAY

# David's Icon and Jasper

"Sheila has small dogs and big cats," says David. "That's what I think." We step out of the dense morning fog into Sheila's narrow, crowded kitchen, posted with notes to her boarders regulating use. The kitchen has an earthy fragrance because she keeps a plastic container on the counter to collect scraps for the compost heap. The heap must be nearly reachable now under the slowly diminishing snow.

Onion, the white and gray Pekinese, sniffs at our ankles, and Sootsie, the muscular black cat, stretches out in greeting from a seat near the window. I haven't met Thomas, the orange cat; "He's pretty much this same shape," David says. But I have met Jasper, who comes toward us now barking her fretful, high-pitched cry. Poor Jasper is the sorriest-looking dog I've ever seen. She's dirty white, balding, and deaf; she limps and has a bulging eye—and that's only the outside. The pitch of her bark scrapes like fingernails. Jasper looks like an idea that just is not working out.

I am bringing David for his weekly art lesson. Over the last year and a half Sheila has guided David through charcoal sketching, pastels, painting in oils and acrylics, reverse drawing, and a self-portrait (a portrait, that is, of David as he would look if he were staring hard into a mirror). Now he's trying something new.

Last summer Sheila took an icon-painting course and came home with a stunningly beautiful Theotokos and Child. Vince commissioned a copy for his Hardworking Jeannie, and as Sheila begins the elaborate process of creating this new icon, David is going along for the ride. A couple of months have already been spent sawing the boards to size, then applying three or four coats of white gesso, a sheet of muslin cloth, another six or seven coats of gesso, and sanding, sanding, sanding. When the board was completely smooth and the edges slightly beveled, David laid over it a piece of carbon paper, then a sheet of tracing paper with an ink outline of the icon he was going to paint. Carefully he drew around the outline, transferring to the board an image of Christ the Ruler of All, or Pantocrator. I wanted to come earlier to view the progress, but Sheila warned me that there was really nothing yet to see. Now he has been painting at it for several weeks, and the day to view the work-in-progress has arrived.

Sheila appears on the narrow wooden steps and greets us with a beaming smile. We follow her upstairs into the dormered, white-painted room that serves as a studio. Little Meagan is already there, in her Oma's care while her mom, Liza, is at work. She is bustling with her collection of dolls and sings to them frequently.

On a table near the door is what appears to be a miniature version of a stage backdrop, showing an Arizona sky and distant pueblos. Turns out that's what it is.

"Dr. Pat's twins are making stage sets as part of their audition for School of the Arts," Sheila explains. This one is Cece's project, and

Sheila begins to set up the clay-covered, painted boxes and tiny figures that complete the southwestern scene.

"Oh, Cece, you didn't!" she exclaims. The wedge-shaped supports on the back of the backdrop have been glued to the wrong end, so the sky is below and the red dirt overhead. Sheila tears off one of the Styrofoam triangles.

"Uh-oh, ear," says alert Meagan.

"What? Oh, I guess it does look like an ear," says her Oma, looking at the detached white support in her hand.

Krissy's project is nearby; she's making a street scene of townhouses. "We've been looking in here to get an idea of how to treat bricks and windows," says Sheila, opening up a well-worn volume of paintings by American artist Red Grooms. Grooms's humor and whimsy have delighted me before, but I'd never stopped to think about the basic craftsmanship that also must go into his work. None of it would succeed if he didn't know how to make a brick look like a brick.

I've moved over to the other table, where David's icon awaits the day's work. It shows a few blocks of solid color, a sweep of red and one of dark blue, a band of the earthy red called bole, and another square of bole that will be the book in Jesus' hand. It looks like something you could knock off in a half hour.

"There are already at least fifteen layers of paint," Sheila says. "We're about a fourth of the way through." I know instantly that I could never paint an icon.

Meagan is trying to paint on the icon with a dry brush, but Sheila coaxes her away and gives her a baby doll. Meagan sings to it a fond "Happy Birthday." We return our attention to the icon.

"The paint is a very thin gouache, and you apply it with these tiny brushes—special extra-long brushes with a lot of give," Sheila goes on. She is holding a brush that appears to be made of a half-dozen eyelashes. "It's the closest you can come to writing; there's a lot of calligraphic brushwork. You want the smoothest finish possible, with no ridges to give it texture." Like a sheet of glass, like a window into heaven, I think.

Now that David has laid in the darkest colors, he will begin applying the second-to-darkest shades, then gradually will add lighter layers until the brightest colors are on top. In the process, of course, most of these carefully applied dark layers will be covered, remaining only as the edges of shadows. From darkness to light. "It's virtually a symbolic way of painting," Sheila says.

I didn't know it took such patience, such care. A son who can be patient with this at sixteen will be patient with me, I think, when I'm ninety.

I think about this sometimes. I come from a long-lived family; on my mother's side, they go on till a hundred. I'm afraid I'll have a lot of life left over after Gary goes home, and who will care for me then? What if I get dim and can no longer talk or talk wrong and stupidly? What if I don't make sense anymore?—me, for whom intelligence is so important, for whom bright conversation and words are the very meat and drink of life?

What if I drool? Wield a clumsy brush at an icon? What if I glue the supports on upside down? Who will fix it, break the ears off, give me a doll, care for me?

But of course, this is one of the reasons humans have children. When you have nothing left to give, they take you up. It's in the bones, this impulse to care, from Oma to little Meagan and Meagan to her baby doll. There is no financial investment I can make against the day that I am broken that could compare to my investment in my children. Someday I will draw heavily on that bank, on Megan's gentle good nature, Stephen's fierce devotion, and David's quiet patience.

On the way out David stops and pets wretched Jasper, scratches behind her ear. When I am Jasper, I think, I will not be alone.

---

# The Annual Meeting

Frank has come to the back door with a bag of ice, and he sets it on the porch next to a bag of IceMelt. It is a miniature Zen experience, a koan like one hand clapping. But there's no time for satori, because parishioners are beginning to pour in both front and back doors, bearing covered casserole dishes, salads, and baskets of rolls. The church's annual meeting has rolled around again.

This is the third annual meeting since Holy Cross was formed; three years ago this weekend Bishop Antoun chrismated the group of six families that was the Holy Cross starter set. Gary was ordained a deacon that Saturday and the next day was ordained a priest.

Everything was so new and strange. On that Sunday afternoon I remember waking from a nap to hear David noodling around on his keyboard. He was trying to pick out Russian Tone 1, which accompanies the Beatitudes. I could hear in the searching notes the emotion I was feeling—what is this strange and wonderful and baffling thing we've gotten ourselves into? He did a fair job of picking out the melody, then segued into the theme from *Star Wars*.

By the next annual meeting we had grown to twenty-five households. Most of them showed up, too, crowding into our home on a cold January night bringing chili and cake, joining in the house-blessing, and then staying for the hour or so of planning for the year ahead. One thing on the agenda: begin a building fund. A year later, at the second annual meeting, we were up to thirty-seven households, and the building fund stood at thirteen thousand dollars. Now our third year has passed. The building fund has tripled, and we've actually put down money on some land. Perhaps next year we'll have a little rented trailer there, beside the tiny creek.

It won't be too soon, because there's not enough room in my house for all these people. A steady stream pours in bearing potluck dishes, and I direct main dishes and salads to the dining room table and drinks to the sideboard. We'd phoned Frank and Jeanne this afternoon with a worried appeal: plenty of knives and spoons, cups and napkins; need forks, plates, ice, and soda. We didn't say "need desserts"; usually there's an overabundance of them at a potluck, but this time we're coming up short. Frank slips back out and returns with a heavy chocolate cake. Before long people are strewn around the kitchen, dining room, living room, hallway, and up the stairs with paper plates on their knees. The level of conversation is jovial and loud, but not nearly as loud as what can be heard by someone venturing up the stairs: all the teens have crammed into the attic and are shouting at one another over the stereo.

After dinner we gather as well as we can in the living room and stand in front of the icon corner. Gary explains that we are going to have our house-blessing now, and after a few preliminary prayers we will go through the whole house singing while he sprinkles the walls with holy water. For those Christians in other denominations who do house-blessings, it's usually a one-time event, setting aside the dwelling when the family first moves in. For Orthodox it's a yearly occurrence, to be done between Theophany and the feast of the Presentation of Christ in the Temple on February 2. This means a very busy few weeks for Orthodox priests, visiting every parishioner's home, blessing it, and often staying afterward for a meal or some fellowship. Three or four of these in a day can really wear a guy out, especially when coupled with food and wine.

Orthodox spring cleaning happens in January, because at the house-blessing the priest will see every corner of your house, including bathrooms. For us, it's the same thing from the other direction: the parishioners are going to see our house, including the bathrooms, so we've spent the whole day cleaning. As a result we have not always been in a good mood today, but we have accomplished most of what we set out to do. A couple of rooms were better off being preblessed and then having their doors securely closed.

After the initial prayers, Gary leads us through the house, sprinkling holy water on each wall in the sign of a cross. The boys and I follow, carrying a candle and the icon of the feast, the Theophany. We sing, to good old Russian Tone 1,

> When thou, O Lord, was baptized in the Jordan
> The worship of the Trinity was made manifest.
> For the voice of the Father bare witness to Thee,
> And called Thee his beloved son.
> And the Spirit, in the form of a dove,
> Confirmed the truthfulness of his word.
> O Christ our God who hath revealed Thyself,
> And hath enlightened the world, glory to Thee.

When we get to the end we start over again at the beginning. We don't segue into *Star Wars*.

When it's time for the meeting to begin we crowd into the living room as well as we can. Annette and Steve are on the sofa, M. David and Margo stand in the back, Greg and Andy sit on the worn red Oriental rug and pet Sparky simultaneously. This is the nearest that creature has yet been to dog heaven. Some bring dining room chairs into the hallway and scoot up to the living room door, looking sharply up the stairs every time the teens' whooping gets too loud.

After Gary makes his report on the overall state of the mission—it's growing, busy, and optimistic about buying land—Frank, the chair of the church council, stands to remind us that our whole purpose for being is to worship God. Anything else we do flows from that. Around the room, heads are nodding. Margo hands out her "Five-Year Plan" for developing Holy Cross's music ministry. She brings up an idea: that we record our simple small-choir version of the Divine Liturgy and offer the tape and a liturgy book as a resource to beginner choirs elsewhere. There are several magnificent big-choir versions available, but they're more intimidating than useful to new converts, as we well remember. If we can save the seed money for renting a recording studio, perhaps we can do this next summer.

We hear reports from Rose about the bookstore, from Andy about outreach, and from M. David about the men's fellowship. Frank presents the budget, and we vote to add a line for the men's fellowship, though currently it gets no funds. M. David holds up the budget handout, which is just a couple of dozen lines typed on a sheet of paper; it could fit on a three-by-five card, he says, and that's the kind of simplicity he hopes we maintain through the years.

Then come the elections. This is often a sensitive time for a church, but we're still so small there's no room for cliques and politicking. Nevertheless, the archdiocese requires there be at least two candidates to stand for every position. Vince is drafted to run against Frank, and Martha volunteers to run against Zenaida. Those four go stand in the kitchen for a few minutes, and Frank and Zenaida are elected unanimously.

As the evening winds up I'm reflecting on how easy this is; the psalm comes to mind, "Behold, how good and pleasant it is when brethren dwell in unity." Gary used to come home from Episcopal vestry meetings exhausted and sad. But here we have a tremendous advantage: all of us are here because we want to be, not because Our Family Has Always Sat in This Pew. There's the freshness and eagerness of a group with one mind, engaged on a common goal. The goal, as Frank reminded us, is not success or building a church, but worship. The group breaks up at 9:30, and people collect their casserole dishes and plates. We'll meet again in twelve hours and do what our calling is to do.

*Thursday, February 1*
*Saints Perpetua and Felicity*

WEEK OF ZACCHEUS SUNDAY

---

# Patron Saints and Martyrs

Upon chrismation, each new Orthodox claims a saint from the church's rich history as his or her own. Often the person will assume that saint's name and lay aside the birth name, entering new life in Christ with a new identity. This saint becomes that person's patron, a special intercessor and friend in high places.

Because the role of these saints is so often misunderstood, it's good to take a look at what saints are not. First, and most important, they are not dead. Life in Christ is eternal life, and they are merely on the other side of the veil, continuing that everlasting life that they began, as we do, on this side. This is why the interior of Orthodox churches are covered with icons; it makes visible the unseen reality that our worship is lifting us into heavenly realms, where we stand with the faithful of the centuries.

Lest this confidence in the saints' heavenly reality be pushed to an unhealthy extreme, it's important to note something else they are not: they are not deputy Gods. We don't ask them to perform supernatural feats under their own power, like superheroes with individual areas of expertise (this one finds lost keys, that one makes houses sell). We ask their prayers, just as we might ask the prayers of our friends here on earth, though we assume that standing in the unclouded presence of God gives special power to their intercessions. Unlike our friends on earth, the saints do not chat with us in return. Two-way conversation is not the goal.

Finally, the saints are not God's receptionists. We don't submit petitions to our favorite saints instead of praying to God; they don't stand between us and the Almighty, transcribing our requests and turning them in at an end-of-day meeting. We still bring our intercessions directly to the throne of the Father. But there is a place for uniting with fellow Christians in our prayers, and no reason to exclude from that the brothers and sisters who have gone on to stand before the throne.

Today is my patronal feast, the feast of Saints Perpetua and Felicity. Though the group of martyrs commemorated on this day also includes four men, it is for the two women that the day is named, with St. Perpetua in the lead. Contrary to popular belief, the Orthodox Church doesn't hesitate to honor women, even to honor them above companion men.

This awarding of honor is with good reason; Perpetua was an extraordinary woman. Her story is just one among thousands, but it is so marked by drama and courage that it offers a particularly good example of why Orthodox cherish our saints.

Perpetua was twenty-two years old, married to a man "of good position" (as *Butler's Lives of the Saints* tells us), and the mother of a baby boy. She was arrested during the persecution of 203 A.D. in the African city of Carthage, along with Saturninus and Secundus, the slave Revocatus, and another slave, Felicity, who was pregnant. Their instructor in the faith, Saturus, was not with them when they were arrested, but he hurried to the prison to turn himself in and joined them in awaiting execution.

This martyrdom has particular historical value because Perpetua wrote it down in her own hand, and her record leads up to the day before her death. Spurious martyrologies are easy to concoct, but the usually skeptical Butler's calls this "one of the greatest hagiographical treasures that have come down to us." The account was so esteemed by the African churches that St. Augustine had to warn the faithful not to place it on the same level with Scripture.

All of Perpetua's family except her father had become Christians, but he was adamantly opposed to her conversion. She was his favorite, and he no doubt feared—accurately, as it turned out—that her profession of faith would be her death warrant. The plight of this old man weaves through his daughter's story and adds much pathos. When Perpetua was first arrested, her father came to the prison in great distress, crying out, "Daughter, pity my white hairs! Pity your father if I am worthy to be called father by you, if I have preferred you to your brothers. Look on your mother, look upon your son who cannot live after you are gone. Lay aside your pride, do not ruin us all." Perpetua says he kissed her hands and cast himself at her feet, "and with tears called me by the name, not of 'daughter,' but of 'lady.' And I grieved for my father's sake, because he alone of all my kindred would not have joy at my martyrdom."

Soon after, the prisoners were summoned to be examined by Hilarian, the procurator. A great crowd gathered to hear the judgment, and from the midst of it stepped Perpetua's father, carrying her baby. "Drawing me down from the step he besought me, 'Have pity on your child.' Hilarian joined with my father and said, 'Spare your father's white hairs: spare the tender years of your child.'" Yet Perpetua still refused to offer a sacrifice to the emperors and declared she was a Christian with strong arguments for the faith. Her father remonstrated with her such that Hilarian commanded the old man be beaten away from her. "This I felt as much as if I myself had been struck, so greatly did I grieve to see my father thus treated in his old age."

Sentence was passed: the prisoners would be slain by wild beasts, as part of an entertainment offered for soldiers. "Joyfully we returned to our prison," Perpetua wrote. She asked for her baby to be brought to her for nursing, but now her father refused to surrender the child. "And God so ordered it that the child no longer required to suckle, nor did the milk in my breasts distress me."

Perpetua awaited martyrdom serenely and recorded several dreams and visions that reassured her. Her fellow prisoner Saturus wrote down a vision as well. He and the other prisoners were brought by angels to a garden, where they met friends who had been martyred shortly before. From there they came to a throne room, where a majestic figure sat surrounded by elders singing "Holy, holy, holy." Saturus wrote, "We kissed Him, and He passed His hand over our faces" (as in Rev. 7:17, "And God shall wipe away all tears from their eyes"). They exchanged the kiss of peace, "and the elders said to us, 'Go and play.'" Saturus told Perpetua, "You have all you desired," and she responded, "Thanks be to God that as I was merry in the flesh, so am I merrier here."

The remainder of the account was apparently composed by an eyewitness. Felicity began to fear that she would not be allowed to suffer with her companions, because even the brutal Romans balked at executing pregnant women. After all joined in prayer, Felicity delivered her daughter in prison, and the child was adopted by a Christian. A legend that does not appear in Butler's goes as follows: as Felicity cried out in the pain of labor the guards mocked her, saying that this pain was nothing compared to what she'd feel when the animals tore her apart. Felicity responded, "Now I bear my own pain, but on that day another will bear the suffering in me."

Finally the day of the games arrived, and Perpetua walked into the amphitheater singing a triumphal hymn, "abashing with the high spirit in her eyes the gaze of all." The guards tried to compel the prisoners to put on the robes of devotees of Saturn and Ceres, but Perpetua protested so forcefully that they relented. The men in the company were swiftly killed by leopards and bears.

Felicity and Perpetua were exposed to a wild cow, which tossed them both but did not kill them. Perpetua sat up, pinned her hair, then went over to lift Felicity to her feet. Not till then did Perpetua seem to awaken from a trance and ask when they would be taken to fight. She didn't believe the event had already taken place until shown her own torn clothing.

The crowd once again clamored to see the two women killed. They exchanged the kiss of peace, then were slain by gladiators. Perpetua's executioner was nervous and, at the first blow, only wounded her so that she cried out in pain. The second and fatal blow she herself guided to her throat. Butler's concludes, "Perhaps so great a woman . . . could not else have been slain except she willed it."

How little our age requires of us. There is no way to know if any of us would be capable of such heroism, but surely in every era courage unto death is a gift of God, and if such trials came again he would once again give sufficient grace to overcome them. It is the style with which Perpetua did all this that perhaps we couldn't match, and the image she leaves behind is a vivid one: courageous, bold, a powerful debater, with "high spirit in her eyes." Yet she was tender as well: a nursing mother, a loving daughter, and "merry." Perhaps "so great a woman" could be formed only by so great a faith and revealed only by so great a challenge. How many others like her, I wonder, are lost to history but not lost to God—and whom we will one day see gathered in that company Saturus envisioned around the throne?

Perpetua, and the many woman saints like her through the ages, stands as the best refutation of accusations that the Christian faith is oppressive, antiwoman, and inherently sexist. If that were so, women like this would not have been remembered and honored by the Church for century after century. If that were so, women like this would not have been moved to devote their lives and their deaths to the faith. Liturgical churches have always honored female saints, taking their names and putting their images near the altar, setting them on an equal footing with male saints; in Orthodoxy we even call some saints, women as well as men, "Equal to the Apostles."

Perpetua is a stunning figure, but she is not my patron saint. I chose the more humble Felicity, who suffered as much as Perpetua did but didn't have the wit or education to put it into deathless prose. Her voicelessness is an example to me, a reminder of all the voiceless and forgotten saints who surround the throne, many whose names are known only to God. The crowd is so broad and includes so many types of faithful, both humble and great, that it gives me room to hope I might stand there one day myself.

*Friday, February 2*
*Presentation of Our Lord in the Temple*

WEEK OF ZACCHEUS SUNDAY

# Megan Gets a Nose Ring

The feast of the Presentation of Our Lord in the Temple is also known as the "Meeting of our Lord," and as my car plunges through blinding snow at midnight in the far Virginia hills, I'm thinking I'd really rather this not be the night I meet the Lord. The flakes are flying at the windshield with percussive force, mesmerizing and unceasing; Rod the Reporter says they remind him of the "jump to hyperspace" moment in *Star Wars*. In good weather, we'd be home in Baltimore in a little more than an hour. But I can't see thirty feet in front of me, and the speedometer is hovering around thirty-five miles per hour. It's cold, dark, and scary.

Mary and Joseph brought the infant Jesus to the temple on this day, to offer the customary sacrifice, and were met by an aged man, Simeon. Luke's Gospel explains that Simeon had received a promise that he would not die until he saw the Messiah, and when he encountered the young mother and her husband in the temple he lifted the baby from her arms. Simeon prayed, and we sing his words each week at Vespers:

> Lord, now lettest thou thy servant depart in peace,
> According to thy word,
> For mine eyes have seen thy salvation
> Which thou hast prepared before the face of all people.
> A light to lighten the Gentiles,
> And the glory of thy people Israel.

We don't sing what happened next. The couple marveled at these words, and Simeon blessed them. Then he said to Mary, "Behold, this child is set for the fall and rising of many in Israel, and for a sign that is spoken against (and a sword will pierce through your own soul also), that thoughts out of many hearts may be revealed."

Rod and I have been out to Megan's college, at Connie's request, to speak to the student body about the joys of journalism. I had been urgently looking forward to this because I so wanted to see my daughter. Megan has become a sign that is spoken against, and she probably has it coming. My heart is not pierced with a sword, but her nose is pierced with a ring.

A week ago Gary and I and the boys were sitting around the kitchen table at dinner when Megan phoned. After the phone had been passed around and everyone had done some chatting, it came back to me. Megan hesitated, then said, "Mom, I have something to tell you, and you're going to be mad."

"Okay," I replied, prepared, after nearly nineteen years, for anything. "Go ahead."

"I had my nose pierced," she said in a small voice.

"You had your nose pierced," I repeated, evenly.

Across the table I could see Gary's face, always ruddy, rise up in flames. "She *what*? She *what*?" he demanded. It wasn't that he hadn't heard me.

"I just want to keep it in till the end of summer," Megan was hastening to add. "The guy at the shop who put it in said I have up to a year, and it will still heal up. It didn't hurt or anything. It was only fourteen dollars. I'm taking real good care of it. It won't get infected. I just want to wear it through the summer."

"Uh-huh," I said, noncommittally. Across the table, Gary was putting on his wall-of-stone expression. "She's *not* coming into the house with that thing in. She can't come home with that. I won't allow it," he was saying. "You tell her she can't come in the house like that." Despite his I'm-the-Dad-here voice, there was a measure of uncertainty in his expression. Gary is quick with an ultimatum, then quick to wonder if he made the right decision, and an episode like this precedes several roller-coaster days for him. There's a reason Megan chose to tell me first.

I was thinking how precious that little nose was the day she was born, and now she'd gone and put a spike through it. Would it really heal? A year seems an awfully long time to tempt fate. Maybe that's just what the nose-ring man tells skittish customers in order to facilitate the sale. If he's wrong, it's a disaster. You can't wear your hair in a different style to hide your nose. It will always be there, right in the middle of the front of your face, plain as . . . well.

"Honey, you know I'm disappointed," I said. "You know that most of the time I like to let you kids make your own decisions about how you look and dress, but I think this crosses a line. I'm going to have to think about this."

"She's *not* coming home," Gary muttered.

"Do you think the college will allow you to keep it?" I asked, suddenly hopeful. It's a small Catholic college and fairly conservative. Students aren't allowed to wear blue jeans to class. Surely a nose ring isn't in the dress code.

"Everybody seems so accepting," Megan said. "I'm sure it will be okay."

I didn't know what else to say, so I said, "Hmmm."

Late that night I sent out a short message on e-mail: "Megan got a nose ring. What should I do?" I filled the address box with fifty names, then went back and deleted people I didn't want to deal with yet: members of Holy Cross and the cousin who lives near my mother-in-law. One hurdle at a time.

The range of advice I received was bewildering and echoed my own confusion. A sizable, and youthful, contingent, felt I should ignore it. Let her rebel in these inconsequential ways. It's her nose. Major in the majors. Others (outraged older daddies, mostly) felt that I, as originator of the nose in question, should threaten to repossess it with a cleaver.

Some suggestions were subtle. Use reverse psychology, Chris said: have everybody tell her it looks "nice." Rod thought I should break the news to her that it's passé, only mall-rat teenyboppers do this now. Marvin reminded me that in Genesis Abraham's servant gives Rebekah a nose ring. Slip some decongestant in her orange juice, said Nick. Terry thought that we could add a chain and lead her around. Mark advised that a friend of his in a Christian rock band has a nipple ring, "if that makes you feel any better." That made me feel, oh, a *lot* better.

The main response from parents my age was fairly consistent: what does it mean? Does it imply other behavior, drugs, defiance, dangerous friendships? Is this something to worry about? What does a nose ring signify, anyway?

While I knew Meg well enough not to worry about other negative behaviors, I still wondered what it was supposed to mean. Actions have meanings, and a previous generation could consult guidebooks about the message intended by various kinds of flowers or by the way a woman carried her fan. I know nothing about the language of rings. As Dan wrote, "I suppose a ring in the nose is only inches away from a ring in the ear. 'What's the big deal?' my brain says. But my stomach won't buy it."

Extraneous piercings came after my time. I know what long hair means; I still like long hair on men, a lasting memento of my own youthful rebellion. I walked into David's room the other day, where he was doing homework, and took in the scene: golden hair past his shoulders, wire-rimmed glasses, smudgy goatee and mustache; guitars strewn on the floor and Bob Dylan on the stereo. It was like going back in time. And I wondered, once again, why it seems Gen X has no native culture of their own; they're suckers for boomer marketers, who repackage our nostalgia as current hiptitude. It's amazing this snow job is so successful; when I was David's age, I sure wasn't listening to my mom's Frank Sinatra records. Gen X, it seems to me, has an aimlessness that makes them patsies for whatever my busy-beaver generation cooks up.

But while long hair looks like part of my tribal costume, rings just confuse me. Ten years ago, at an annual conference, I met a friend I hadn't seen since the previous summer. In the meantime he'd gotten his left ear pierced, then not typical behavior for an insurance adjuster with kids and a dog and a station wagon. "I did it as a joke, for a party," he explained, "then decided to keep it."

"Why?" I asked.

"Because women think it's sexy," he said, with a small blush.

"You're *kidding!*" I burst out, laughing. And immediately I felt bad. Had I hurt his feelings? It was awfully insensitive. Would an apology just make it worse? I fretted over this all afternoon and finally went up to him at dinner.

"I just wanted to say, I'm sorry about what I said this afternoon," I faltered.

"Oh, not at all!" he said jovially. "When you said, 'I'll just bet they do!,' I figured you agreed!"

So that day I learned a lesson about the durability of vanity and the power of selective listening. And that, whatever rings meant, I didn't get it.

What to Do About the Nose Ring loomed large around our house for a few days, and I was genuinely perplexed. With teens you never know how hard to push. Though a nose ring was loathsome to me, I was torn between letting her have a few months with it and demanding immediate removal. Permanent nose decor was not under consideration. But for the present term, I was unsure.

Then we were rescued by a deus ex machina device: the college decreed she must remove it. A pierced nose was not contemplated in the dress code. Megan would have to return to the piercing shop on the following Tuesday and have the spike removed. I was relieved to escape the problem so neatly.

When Rod and I arrived at the college on the Friday before that Tuesday, we found chairs set up in rows in the large meeting room and a few students milling around, but Megan wasn't there. I was braced to see the nose ring before the event began, so I phoned her from the lobby. She was in the dorm waiting for a call from boyfriend Michael, still away in the navy, and she sounded irritated.

I was anxious to get back on the road as soon as the event was over, since the snow was becoming steady, but she couldn't get over until the workshop was under way. Our visit would have to be brief.

Connie bustled in, and we spoke briefly of the ongoing romance between her son and my daughter; she calls me her PoCoMiL, for "Potential Co-Mother-in-Law." The hour struck, and she got us lined up in our chairs on the stage, myself and Rod and two producers of television shows. Rod spoke first on the rewards of being a reporter, then, in the middle of my spiel about opinion and essay pieces, Megan walked in. She wore her dad's old navy pea jacket and a sour expression. I suspect Michael had just gotten his ear bent. She stood far in the back of the room with her hands in her pockets. I could see the nose but not the ring.

Before us spread a sea of youthful faces, polite and mostly interested. Some were clearly dreaming of the journalistic life, and it was strange to think of ourselves as occupying a position of envy. We talked about job descriptions, grad schools, the nature of electronic media. Rod warned them that writing is a tough field and they shouldn't go into it unless it was a compulsion, the only thing in life they could imagine doing. One student raised his hand to inform us that a recent study indicated journalism was the lowest paying of all professions. We kept smiling.

"Everybody says you have to build up a file of clippings," one girl said. "But how do you get started? How do you get the first one?" Look for a publication that has plenty of ink and paper but needs text, I said; probably every community has a *Shopper News*. Write a local story and turn it in. Then take that clip and aim for the next step up—maybe the *Elite Shopper News*. Now you have two clips. Keep climbing that ladder, and eventually you're in the *New Yorker*. In theory, that is. In theory.

While one of the television producers was tackling a question in his field, Rod nudged me and passed a note. "Look at them, they're all so young! They're babies!" it read. I looked at him, with his open, unlined face and no hint of gray in his glossy dark hair. Baby.

My baby was in the back of the room, and as the workshop wound up I hastened back to see her. She was pouting, but on her, pouting looks cute, a low-wattage version of "You're beautiful when you're angry." Yes, there was a big gold knot on the outside of her nose.

"It looks like a zit," I said. This is what one of my e-mail buddies had suggested.

"No, it doesn't," she said. "Zits are red."

I looked at her closer. It didn't look like a zit, it just looked like something in the wrong place, like a false eyelash worn across the chin. The part I didn't expect was the oversized gold clip on the inside, fixing the ornament in place. It protruded a little, unattractively.

"That clip looks like a golden booger," I said tactfully.

Megan made a face. "That's only because you're short. Nobody else can see it. Everybody else looks at my nose from the top."

We linked arms and strolled toward the refreshment table. Rod and I had arrived too late for dinner, so I tossed down handfuls of cheese and vegetables from the closest tray. Megan chattered and gradually brightened; it's hard for her to stay down. Time was flying, but I didn't want to leave, even though the storm outside was worsening by the minute.

Finally I collected Rod from conversation with one of the lovelier babies, the girl who had asked how to get her first clipping. "I just have to write," she was saying earnestly. "I just have to." I looked at her and saw myself, years ago. Yup, she's a goner.

It took some pushing and shoving to get my car up the hill and off the campus, and from there my whole attention was focused on not stopping, not ever, not even for stoplights, because I didn't know if I could get going again. I learned to drive in South Carolina, and the physics of snow escapes me, especially when hills are involved. Since my northward transplantation a couple of unhappy experiences had taught me that it's possible to drift unwillingly into the soft stuff, come to a halt, and be unable to go again without major assistance. Though the snow was presently only four or five inches deep, it was accumulating fast, and I had a hundred miles to go in the night. I could end up stopped anywhere along there with only Rod, a Louisiana boy, for help.

In light of my no-brakes policy, it was fortunate that the streets were nearly deserted. We paused to pick up a late dinner of grease-burgers, and as I swung onto the interstate ramp I could see the golden arches click off in my rearview mirror.

Mile after mile we pushed through the white-spattered night. It is good to be up late talking in the dark. I hadn't seen Rod since he moved to Florida last summer, and there was much to catch up on. But it was troubling not to be able to see very far, and there were no lines visible on the road and no way to identify the shoulder. The headlights blew the snow up into an opaque white curtain a few feet in front of the car. I even tried flipping off the headlights, to see if that improved visibility. No such luck.

Then, suddenly, we were sliding. The nose of the long station wagon swung left, slowly, inexorably. I couldn't tell what lane we were in or which one we were heading toward or if we were in a lane at all. The car continued to turn until it was broadside to the highway but still hurtling forward. I was thinking, calmly, "This is how it happens." I was worried about Rod, who had the kind of nervousness you get when you're not the one driving. I was hoping that we wouldn't turn over or that if there was going to be a disaster it would happen fast for his sake.

Still swinging around, the nose of the car completed its half-circle and came to rest pointing back the way we'd come. Now I carefully put on the brakes. And took a deep breath.

Nothing more to be done. Carefully, I aimed toward where I thought the right shoulder was and pulled forward. Backed up, turned, and pointed the car east again. Still no sign of where the lanes were, and still the snow came pounding down. Carefully, I stepped on the gas. We were rolling once again, and I hadn't met the Lord.

After a brief silence Rod said, "You handled that very well."

"I'm always good in an emergency," I said. "I'll get the shakes later." I thought, this was the easy part. I can handle skidding in the snow. What I don't know how to handle is a nose ring.

# 7

## PREPARING FOR LENT

*Saturday, February 10*
*Holy Martyr Haralambos*

---

## Greg's Ordination

The boys don't like wearing jackets and ties, and usually they don't have to; on Sundays they're our only acolytes, and the best thing to fit under the stiff golden robes is a flat-collared knit shirt. But today we are going to see Greg be ordained a subdeacon, and they'll be sitting in the congregation where a lot of strangers, plus a bishop, can see them. Into the oxford-cloth shirts, ties, and stiff long-forgotten jackets they went.

It's a time travel trick, because wearing these outfits magically turns them from kids into small, fresh-squeezed grownups. Probably not the kind of grownups they'd like to be; not hip grownups. In fact, David is wearing the jacket to a suit Gary's parents gave Gary when he graduated from seminary. My in-laws insisted he needed a suit, but privately we rolled our eyes. He was never going to wear a suit; we were always going to be blue jeans types. The last thing a Father Cool happenin'-now priest of the seventies needed was a suit.

The tan corduroy suit was sturdy; it outlasted our resistance, outlasted Gary's constant wearing, outlasted his youthful waistline, and now is set to outlast a second generation of Mathewes-Green scoffing. It's even outlasted my hiptitude. Now I look at my son in this jacket, so fine and tall, and think, with oblivious irony, "Cool." I invite Greg to admire the boys' dapper style.

"In the immortal words of Z. Z. Top," Greg begins, then pauses. "How does that go?"

I hazard a guess: "'Every woman crazy 'bout a sharp-dressed man'?"

"That's it," he says, then sighs. Greg is nervous today. He's clad in Gary's black cassock and is sitting at our kitchen table, but in a few minutes we have to get in the car for the more than two-hour drive to St. Philip Church in Pennsylvania, where he will be ordained. "Yes, I'm supposed to be sharp today," he says in a worried voice.

The trip north is uneventful; I sit in the back, behind Greg, with Stephen in the middle and David behind his dad. We take turns asking one another questions from "Trivial Pursuit" cards, but we lose confidence in the game when it insists that the Marine Hymn is "Anchors Aweigh." We toss around snatches of dialogue from Monty Python movies, and Stephen recounts a dream: "I was with Megan, and she said, 'I got a tattoo.' I thought, 'Here we go again.'" The boys are eager to show off to Greg their current favorite rock groups, and they sing along with the car stereo in the apparent belief that the groups would be just a little bit better if their own voices were blended in.

Greg is the kids' idea of a hip adult. Recently they were invited to spend a Sunday afternoon with Vince and Hardworking Jeannie's teenage daughters, girls they really enjoy hanging around. But when the invitation to stay for dinner with the girls was placed alongside the news that Greg and his girlfriend, Tracey, were coming to our house, the boys instantly opted for home.

We zip along the interstate under a gray afternoon sky. Greg is worried, in part, because none of us has a clear idea of what's going to happen today. There will be a regular Saturday evening Vespers service, and at some point Greg will be ordained a subdeacon, but he doesn't know exactly how or when. Episcopal special services, in contrast, were extensively drilled and rehearsed. "My friend Father Joseph said, 'You don't know, it might even be in the elevator,'" Greg says; he smiles, but he doesn't look much consoled. "If it gets to where Bishop Antoun is saying, 'All right, let's all go have some coffee now,' I'll ask, 'Did I miss something?'"

We pull up in the parking lot of the church with some breathing room before Vespers, and I go off to buy a disposable camera. Not just for pictures of the ordination but for pictures of the building, to add to our wish-list collection. When I return some of the Holy Cross contingent have arrived, but the choir members and others are still missing. So is Tracey, who was coming down from a trip farther north. This is not helping Greg's composure; he's sure that when she arrives she'll be rattled and upset. He keeps checking the parking lot anxiously.

I come up with my steno pad. "Any words for posterity?" I ask Greg.

"I regret that I have but one life to give for my church," he says, then barks a short laugh.

Into the church proper, which is a simple, square, white-painted room with an elaborate motif painted on the arch above the altar. From a large cross in the center flow grapevines with leaves and fruit, set with two dozen icons in medallions. The church has no pews, but there are chairs set up in rows, and Basil and Frank are sitting side by side in the back.

"You still writing that book?" Basil asks as I come up, still scribbling notes.

"This is the last chapter," I say.

We look around the place, a little enviously. "How do you like it?" I ask.

"I'm gonna take all these chairs and throw 'em out in the middle of the street," Basil says pleasantly, "but other than that I got no complaints."

Frank says, "I counted, they have forty-three parking spaces, with two handicapped. And, hey, isn't there a dome on top of the building? But it isn't open in here." Orthodox church domes are usually open on the inside, with an icon of Christ the Pantocrator directly overhead. This dome must be an ornament, not structurally integrated, which strikes us as second-best. "But hey, if they want to give it to us like this, I'll take it!" Frank adds.

Tracey sails in at eight minutes to six, looking not a bit rattled; Greg catches her eye and heaves a sigh of relief. Margo and M. David, Carolyn, Zenaida, and Michael come in a few minutes later and stand near St. Philip's choir. Tom and Rose are here with baby Nicole, as are Smiling Jeanne, Doris, Steve, and Andy. It's a nice-sized delegation from our church family; though most of us didn't know Greg a year ago, he's one of us now, and we're here for him.

As the familiar Vespers service begins I take time to study the icons strewn along the vine that runs across the face of the arch. Even from the back of the church I can recognize most of them. St. Mary of Egypt, of course, is distinctive with her tattered robe and sun-weathered complexion. Moses the Black, from Ethiopia, is opposite her. There's Peter the Aleut, Patrick of Ireland, Cyprian of Carthage, and Vladimir of Kiev. Two Nicholases: Jolly Old St. Nicholas of Myra and Nicholas of Japan, who's Steve's patron saint. On the lower right the curve of vine links Perpetua with Felicity.

There are other strong women here. Catherine of Alexandria, who consistently defeated pagan philosophers in debate, until the frustrated emperor had her tortured to death. There's Thekla, "Equal to the Apostles," who was a companion of the apostle Paul and one of the earliest martyrs. She founded a monastery for women in Syria that has been continuously occupied from the first century to this day.

There's one woman on the arch I can't identify, and I send Stephen to scout closer, but he comes back unsuccessful. "Every time I read it it just looks like 'St. Tuna,'" he says. I check and discover St. Nina of Georgia, another "Equal to the Apostles."

The array is so varied—black, white, Asian, old and young, male and female, queens and slaves—that one might think it was chosen by a clenched-jaw subcommittee for multiculturalism. But no, this is merely Orthodoxy, a faith that, after all, spreads around the world and through two thousand years. With such a range, variety would be hard to avoid.

The Vespers service moves along. While Gary and St. Philip's pastor, Father Boniface, serve at the altar, Greg stands near Bishop Antoun. Bishop Antoun is a hearty, gregarious man, and he looks relaxed as ever; Greg looks somber and still somewhat nervous. He looks, too, like my husband; they're about the same size, enough so that a borrowed cassock fits nicely, and they have the same dark hair. The most obvious distinguishing characteristic is that my husband's beard has gone white, while Greg's is still dark. Give him time. Bishop Antoun ordained Gary just three years ago, and standing in the back here I could squint and see that scene again, time traveling in my own story.

The choir is chanting through the appointed verses for this evening, then a woman's voice rings out with these words:

I was entrusted with a sinless and living land, but I sowed the ground with sin and reaped with a sickle the ears of slothfulness; in thick sheaves I garnered my actions, but winnowed them not on the threshing floor of repentance. But I beg Thee, my God, the pre-eternal husbandman, with the wind of Thy loving-kindness winnow the chaff of my works, and grant to my soul the wheat of forgiveness; shut me in Thy heavenly storehouse and save me.

I remember this. I noticed this verse at Vespers last year, on this very night, the Saturday before Meatfare Sunday. It was M. David singing then, his voice falling through the night with golden weight, and I was thinking about how frivolous and shallow I am and how patient God is with me.

Patience is a very good trait for God to have, because a year later I'm not sure I've learned all that much. Turning years are his work; he turns them in his hand like a glass globe, seeing everything at once. I plod in place, in a circle, looking down and marking footprints in the dust. A year later, I see familiar footprints. They're mine.

We're poised at a moment in time now, as Greg awaits his ordination with tumbling emotion, just as we were poised three years ago. Over that peak and down the slope and around the circle we'll rush again, again, and again, Lent to Pascha, Pentecost to Nativity, ordinations and baptisms, meals and music. Someday we'll have our first wedding at Holy Cross. Someday we'll have our first funeral. It might be for our own dear Yia Yia, Lillian. It might be, for all I know, for me.

Time travel is an illusion; walking in this way, day by day, step by step, dust to dust, is the only kind of traveling we know how to do. Somewhere in the midst of one circle we each find a door out, an exit from time, an entrance to something else, to the timelessness we always inhabit but never can quite see. We don't know what that will be like. The iconographer hints in the only language available: behind each saint the background is a sheet of gold.

The lowermost tips of the grapevine painted on the arch rest at nearly floor level. From there the vines with their disks of gold ascend, bringing the icons to eye level, and the saints join us as naturally as the familiar faces in the pews. Then the vines climb farther and the icons ascend, clearing the heads of the congregation. They bend above the altar, still rising, and reach to meet in the middle.

In the center over the altar the grapevines meet their source in the largest disk of all. It is simple, with a field of green, and purple stylized flowers. In the center of the disk is a cross. This is where everything begins.

# EPILOGUE

## Joining the Dance

And then what happened?

As I've circulated chapters from this book among friends over the last few months, the most frequent question I've heard has been, "What happened next?" Did you buy the land? How is Lillian doing? Are Greg and Tracey still dating? Did Megan's nose heal up all right? Did Margo ever get pregnant? Is Carolyn still painting icons?

Jesus said that the Holy Spirit is like the wind; you can't see it, but you can hear it passing by. I picture a field of grain rippling in the sun. All you can see is grain, not wind, but the way the grain dances shows where the wind has been. You can't see the Holy Spirit, but you can see people; you can see the path the Spirit takes as it ripples through their lives. Some of us may like pure theory, theology, or philosophy, but all of us like stories. It's where we see the Spirit best.

At Holy Cross Mission, the stories went on after my year of recording them came to a close. Many are the times I said, "I wish I was still writing the book!" For example, in early May my husband took a contingent of church members on a one-day pilgrimage to Chicago to see the weeping icons at St. George Church and St. Nicholas Church. After a long and spiritually intense day, the weary crew returned to O'Hare Airport for a night flight home.

Then a thunderstorm hit. It roiled overhead for hours, delaying all flights, blacking out electricity in the building. I was supposed to pick Gary up at midnight, but when I called to confirm the arrival time I waited on hold for forty-five minutes before giving up. I drove out to the airport to find Smiling Jeanne's daughter waiting at the curb in her van. When no pilgrims emerged from the terminal, we ventured inside and were told that the flight arrival had been pushed back to 2:00 A.M.

Shortly after 1:00 A.M. my phone rang; the flight was canceled entirely, and O'Hare was shut down. The travelers would arrive the next morning. In the airport the Holy Cross pilgrims located a chapel and offered Compline, then went to sleep at one of the departure gates, their heads under the banks of chairs to dim the soon-coming morning light.

Lillian was along for all of this, and when I arrived at the airport the next morning she looked chipper and sturdy as ever. "She was an angel," Gary said. "She never complained once. She did better than the rest of us." Yes, her health is fine. And of the many lessons Gary learned on his pilgrimage, one of the most memorable was: never go out of town without a toothbrush.

On the night of Greg's ordination something happened that isn't recorded in that last chapter: Carolyn and Zenaida noticed that many of the women at St. Philip Church were wearing head coverings. It's a custom we'd heard about but hadn't much encountered, and these two found it intriguing. "I will if you will," they promised each other, and the next morning both came to Sunday worship wearing scarves. Since Dr. Pat already wore a scarf all the time, that made three in the choir, which Gary took to calling "the babushka corner."

The custom spread through the congregation, as we found that wearing a headcovering felt appropriate and respectful, and helped focus our attention in worship. We tried different alternatives, struggling to reinvent the wheel, discovering that a pretty silk scarf is useless because the slippery fabric won't stay put, that hats plopped on top of your head fall off when you prostrate. Lillian got busy with her crochet needles and began fashioning for each woman a round doily-shaped cap. Now I see them scattered across the congregation, a large one lapping over Hardworking Jeannie's dark hair like the petal-cup of a flower, a small one clipped to the top of Debra's head with a perky orange silk daisy. There are slightly different sizes and hues for each woman, a blessing of Lillian's love on each head.

Yes, we've continued to attract new members, like Debra, a doctoral candidate at Johns Hopkins University and a cradle Greek rediscovering her faith. There's a new crop of people in chrismation class, including Debra's ex-boyfriend, Mitchell, who followed her here and ended up staying on, and Steve's wife, Mimi, who needed an extra six months to embrace Orthodoxy. With Mimi joining Holy Cross, there's an opening for another eager husband–reluctant wife team to take their place; sure enough, a couple filling that bill has arrived on schedule.

Ina and Mark moved here from Connecticut, bringing two sons who already knew how to acolyte, much to my tired boys' relief. Familiar faces return: Cheri and Gary, two early Holy Crossers, have returned to our congregation following his medical residency in Ohio. And some have moved on: Jonathan and Barbara to Florida, Don and Jan and baby Peter downstate, led on by their jobs.

The most significant departure has been Michael's; a few months ago he announced he'd decided to seek his vocation as a monk at Holy Cross Monastery, where the Mathewes-Greens go for confession. It was an emotional scene during the Paschal feast, as Basil stood to confer his blessing on Michael with tears and hugs and noisy acclamations. A couple of months later Michael is fitting in well at the monastery, enjoying the round of prayer and work, though Father Abbott Joseph made him trim his beard a bit.

Megan's nose is once again perfect, and she's still dating Michael, though he's now in Guam. As a teenager-in-love I would have hated the idea of a long-distance courtship; as a mom, I don't think it's such a bad idea. Carolyn is still painting icons; the one she showed us newly begun at the icon class in March, and placed completed on the altar in August, is on the cover of this book. Basil has gone from being the Baze-man to being the Iceberg. "Ask me how cool I am," he tells the teens, so he can supply the jaunty answer, "I'm so cool I'm frozen." David and Stephen are finishing up another year of home-schooling and looking to begin their third next fall. Rose and Tom's baby, Nicole, is robust and beautiful. We wrapped up a great year of Sunday school with a class on Russian folk dancing; Stephanie, who came to present the session from a local Russian church, brought music and costumes and led children in the dance. Gradually it all became so inviting that the grown-ups started joining in.

Not all stories turn out the way we might have hoped. Margo is still not pregnant. Greg and Tracey broke up. And, to our surprise and disappointment, we didn't buy the land.

One day in early spring our land planner and realty lawyer sat down at the dining room table with me and Gary and unfurled their plats and plans. Bad news. The parcel of land had serious problems affecting our hopes, not least of which was the county's requirements for easements on all four sides due to the streets on south and west, a neighbor's house on the north, and that strip of mud along the east officially recognized as a wetland. Once the required footage was deducted from the four-acre lot, the space in the middle remaining was too small to build a church. Reluctantly, we canceled the contract. It is a beautiful piece of land, and it still wears a "For Sale" sign.

Back to the search. Our realtor saw to it that fax paper spilled out of our machine in generous helpings, twenty pages at a time, as we prowled for empty lots, used churches, vacant buildings far and wide. One day Gary saw two churches for sale, each priced at over a million dollars, each constructed in the obvious, flat style of the last few decades. Finding something both attractive and affordable seemed impossible.

Then, with the third, he fell in love. A few miles from the airport he found a little stone church, circa 1912, with a worship space that's whitewashed and gracious and feels just the right size. The church proper is dwarfed by a hefty square tower that's, charmingly, far too short. It's a three-tiered affair that looks like it's been pressed down by a giant thumb and is set to spring into the air, launching its pointed slate cap like a toy. The structure was originally built as a Methodist church (Good Shepherd Methodist, I'll wager, based on the large stained glass window in front), but has been Baptist and Episcopal, and now houses a Pentecostal Korean congregation. All along the arch that sets off the altar area are taped up Korean characters in fluorescent orange, with a big (and to me, cryptic) numeral 14 at the top. Gary could just imagine taking down the orange characters and replacing them with icons. It would be the latest transformation of a church that has accommodated many flavors of Christian believers for nearly a century.

The price is right, the location is wonderful, the parking is nonexistent, we'll have to use the next-door neighbor's basement for Sunday school, and the bell in the chubby tower still rings. Previous congregations who have dwelt here, including the Koreans, have gone on to bigger things; this is encouraging, compared with those white elephants we've looked at that were being unloaded by congregations that died out. We don't expect to outgrow it; there will be plenty of room—once we take the pews out.

This morning at coffee hour Gary passed around photos of the church and a typed-up prayer he'd drafted the night before. "Take this home and pray it every day," he said. "You don't have to use exactly these words, but I want us all to have the same intention. This is an important decision, and we all should be seeking the same thing."

"Can we pray right now?" Margo called out.

Everyone stood and reached out to hold hands. "Miss Lillian, where do you think you're going?" Gary asked; she was headed toward the kitchen with a stack of dishes, as usual. Lillian ducked her head amiably and moved to join the end of the line. We bowed our heads and prayed.

"O Lord our God, hear our prayer: we your servants come before you asking your guidance and blessing as we proceed in establishing a new home for Holy Cross Mission. We pray that all we do in this process be according to your will. Indeed we pray that you would block and close any doors where your will is not found. And open wide those that lead to the upbuilding of your Kingdom. Be our only leader and guide, blessing that which is right, preventing that which is wrong. Finally, we thank you for our being called together as a mission family, for the ministries in this body, and most especially for our redemption through the Holy Cross of Jesus Christ: through the intercession of the Theotokos and of all the saints.

For you are holy, O our God, and to you we ascribe glory: to the Father, to the Son, and to the Holy Spirit, now and ever, and unto ages of ages. Amen."

We broke hands to cross ourselves, and I looked across the room at these faces I've come to love so well. We are at the doorstep of the next part of our adventure. We always will be.

The Holy Spirit is rippling through our lives in these stories and will continue to do so, long after this book is closed. The stories don't end, not even when our lives end; we're part of a story of Orthodoxy that's been going on for two thousand years.

But it isn't a story that's hidden or confined. The liturgy, the feasts, the fasts, the cycle of the year, and the stories of God's people are going on right now, in Orthodox churches in big cities and small towns across the nation. It's all there, already under way, open for all to see. Nor is the story restricted to current participants; it's open for anyone to join. After all, the Holy Spirit is rippling through your life, too. The important thing, with a story, is to listen.

As I listened to Stephanie describing the Russian dances, I grew more and more interested; gradually it seemed more and more possible that I could join in, too. Suddenly, to my surprise, I got up and danced.

# POSTSCRIPT

---

# Blue Sky

In the spirit of the Hobbits' "second breakfast" I can offer a second epilogue, on this the tenth anniversary of my beginning to keep the journal that became *Facing East.* On February 11, 1995, I grabbed a notepad and ballpoint and went over to the ReVisions building before the Vespers service began so I could make notes while the guys set up for the service. Basil was pointing and giving orders, while Frank and Jay pushed furniture around. My husband, Gary, was there to help too, and before long Rose came in with photocopied bulletins and three loaves of prosphora bread.

That's how the storytelling began, and it ran for a year and then ceased when it hit the back cover of the book. But though the telling stopped, the story went on, and now it's strange to look back at our little start-up band. As we bustled about the old schoolroom on that February afternoon we couldn't foresee all the ways the years were going to turn and deepen us. We could not see how they would hurtle us into an unseen future that would bring changes and challenges, ordinations and weddings, births and deaths.

When I began making notes that night I had decided to follow the trail of a year in our church. I didn't have much idea what I was going to do with it after that. I didn't have a book agent, and the whole world of publishing seemed pretty daunting. It was already September by the time I addressed a fat manila envelope to Harper-SanFrancisco and stuck it in a mailbox. Then, very quickly it seemed, the book was finished, out of my hands and into the world.

A lot of surprising things happened after that. The most surprising, to me, was that many of the people who bought this book were already Orthodox. Why would they want to read it? I wondered. Don't they already know all this? I found out that, in many cases, they didn't. They'd grown up in a church where the liturgy was in a language they didn't understand, and even if they were native-born Greeks or Russians, the archaic form used in the liturgy was to them like Chaucer's English would be to us. Converts like me were helping cradle Orthodox rediscover their own heritage. Many times people raised in the Orthodox faith came to visit Holy Cross and stood in worship, their eyes streaming with tears, as they comprehended the beauty of the liturgy for the first time.

Many people also wrote to tell me that *Facing East* was their first step in becoming Orthodox. That was pretty much my goal, to write a "first step" kind of book. When my husband was eager to be chrismated and I was confused and balky, I was handed many wonderful books about Orthodoxy that were too far over my head. *The Ladder of Divine Ascent* and *The Philokalia* were like grand staircases that were missing the first few steps. Once I became Orthodox I wanted to help people in my situation, by writing a book that would provide just those bottom steps.

I was able to write a "beginner's" book because Orthodoxy was still so new to me that I could see a sharp contrast between it and the Christianity I'd known before. I wouldn't be able to write this book today. I've gotten too used to things on this side of the divide, and the elements that used to be startling no longer stand out.

On the other hand, the very fact that I was a neophyte meant that it wasn't the book a more mature Orthodox could write. I am endlessly grateful to the priests and monks who kindly trudged through the original manuscript and offered their comments and guidance. I'm grateful for their forbearance in allowing my convert's exuberance to bloom unrestrained.

What happened next? That's what people are always asking me. Well, we grew. The church building we were praying about at the end of the previous epilogue is the one we ended up buying. In 1997 we moved in (you can read this part of the story in my subsequent book, *At the Corner of East and Now*), and the first thing we did was throw out all the pews, which made Basil happy. We sanded the floors and put down Oriental rugs, and then began making it as beautiful as we could. A mahogany iconostasis was set up, and gradually filled with Carolyn's icons. We have a silver Gospel book, a gold Epistle book, and an "unsleeping lamp" that hangs over the altar in memory of Gary's father and my own. We have a silver font for baptizing babies, but we still use the horse trough for adults. Some women of the church sewed a flouncy white skirt to hang around it and gussy it up, but you have to admit it's still a horse trough in the middle of a church.

The most daring addition to the church interior is a liturgical chandelier. This is an imposing brass construction composed of many slender, twining arms set with dozens of electric candles. It's big. It hangs from a rafter by a single loop, filling the very center of the worship space, to represent Christ the Light who dwells in our midst. It arrived from Greece in an impossibly heavy box, in the form of a couple of hundred shiny pieces of brass and no instructions. The guys did find a sheet of paper with some Greek writing on it, but they concluded that it was a bill of lading. They threw a rope over the rafter and began sticking pieces together, and eventually succeeded in assembling a light fixture of awe-inspiring proportions.

Now, on great feast days, the tallest person in the church seizes it by the bottom and gives it a mighty swing. Around and around the massive thing goes, scattering light on the walls in little shards, the kind of effect that later inventors would attempt with a disco ball. The effect is impressive, but also a little alarming. The rafter creaks, and people step lightly out of the way. You can only imagine what this was like before electricity, when the process would include flying drops of hot wax.

This little stone church is getting stuffed with every loving addition we can manage, but it can't hold many more people. On a typical Sunday morning we have more than a hundred worshippers, and that's about all it can comfortably hold. As I stand on the choir risers at the back I can barely see the altar for all the dads holding babies on their shoulders; about 40 percent of the congregation is under the age of eighteen. We have a fair complement of worshippers just over that age, as our new Subdeacon, Robert, continues to bring in more college students. He leads outreach groups at the Naval Academy and at St. John's College, both nearby in Annapolis. St. John's is a "Great Books" college, where the students have a musing, philosophical bent and generally look like absent-minded hippies. The Naval Academy is different. You can usually tell the students from the two schools apart.

There wouldn't be room for these new members if we hadn't sent some old Holy Crossers out into the world. Margo and Musical David have been living in Europe for several years now, their family expanded by the addition of a long-awaited son, Dietrich. Subdeacon Gregory is now Father Gregory, pastor of a church near Pittsburgh, accompanied by his lovely khouria, Jeannie.

On a typical Sunday the church is as full as it can comfortably be, and while we gladly go up to uncomfortable levels for major feasts and weddings, there's talk of starting a new mission to the south. The stone-walled church can't be expanded, and moving to a larger building is not desirable; why get fatter when you can reproduce? Orthodoxy works best when a priest knows his parishioners well and can give them personal spiritual direction and visit in their homes a few times each year. A "mega church" wouldn't do. It's better to start another congregation and launch a new community on its way.

Soon after I finished writing *Facing East* we acquired a second Subdeacon Gregory, one my kids called "Subdeacon Sting" due to his resemblance to the rock star. He ended up going to seminary and being ordained (becoming yet another Father Gregory), then coming back to the area to found a new mission north of the city. Some old-time Holy Crossers who live closer to him began attending up there. Basil was tonsured "the Reader Basil" and now booms out the Epistle each Sunday at Four Evangelists Mission. Father Gregory also asked our son Stephen to come be his choir director, so he and Jocelyn make the long trip each week, though we miss them very much at Holy Cross.

Yes, Stephen got married last summer, at the age of twenty-two; his bride, Jocelyn, is a graphic designer. All our children married young, I'm proud to say. Gary and I must have made marriage look inviting. Megan married Dave when she was twenty-three, and our David surprised everyone by marrying Marcella when he was just nineteen. Gary and I are enjoying the romance of an empty nest again.

But just as there are marriages and babies and new members of Holy Cross to baptize, there have been losses as well. Our first funeral, after seven years together as a parish, was for Doris; a few years later we lost Mary's husband, John, and last year during Bright Week we buried Annette. We were taken by surprise when one of our founding members, Jonathan, died of a heart attack. When I was writing this book he was using a wheelchair, due to multiple sclerosis, but a few years later he began to experience a healing. Jonathan began to walk again, and the first time he came up, leaning on a cane, to receive communion standing, I saw it through a haze of tears. His death was the first among the little band of founders of Holy Cross, the nineteen original converts who started the parish so long ago.

Lillian, our Yia Yia, is still with us, however. She is ninety-five now, living in a nursing home near the church and teaching the other residents how to crochet. When I see her, I think of a comment my grandfather made in his nineties: "Old age has passed me by." Old age forgot to take Yia Yia away, and I hope he continues to misplace her on his list. She is a treasure to us.

But not everyone is passed by, not even those who haven't reached old age. Last October I stood on a cold and windy afternoon as a casket was lowered into a red-dirt grave. We were burying Jay, the young Father who helped Frank and Basil set up the church on the first day I began this diary. He was only forty-nine. Jay had always had a heart condition, and he and Heidi had prepared for this possibility, but how can you really prepare for it?

Jay's funeral drew the biggest crowd we've ever had at Holy Cross. The nave was packed to capacity, another crowd filled the parish hall beneath, and those who couldn't fit into the building at all were grouped outside on the lawn. At the graveside Heidi stood with Jared, William, Lydia, and Greta, hugged by all her weeping friends in turn.

I stood near Megan, holding the hand of my little grand-daughter, Hannah; of my five grandchildren, she's the only girl. I was looking at the vast, hard blue sky overhead and the tops of the tall leafless trees tossing in the wind. When I was in high school a friend of mine wrote a poem that had this line: "The sky like a wild blue rose opens and breezes rush out."

Just when you think life is going to be cozy, something like this happens—a blue electric jolt, the black jagged trees dancing, a red pit in the earth. God isn't our pet and he isn't our pal, and when our lives are swept up into his, anything can happen. He never promises us safety. He only promises himself.

As I reread *Facing East* I worry that I've projected a happy-little-family image of our church, and although that's not false, neither is it best. We are extraordinarily blessed at Holy Cross; I've never been in a more joyous and vibrant church, and I give all the earthly credit to my husband's God-directed leadership. But even in a less functional church, in an inharmonious community or unhappy family, God is still fully present and still supplying all things needful to each person who seeks his face. It's not a comfortable earthly life that we are looking for but a transformed life in him, one that extends beyond the grave.

At the graveside I hold Hannah's little hand tightly. It's cold, and I can feel the bones of her fingers, so small and smooth, in my own. My fingers get more knobby and bent every year. I once had a tiny, pretty hand like Hannah's, but now the thin, wrinkled skin can't conceal the orderly bones lined up beneath. Bones are the signature we leave behind when we dive under the blanket of earth and strip down to nothing. Nobody has a choice about this dive into noth-ing. We can only choose who we're going with.

# APPENDIX

## The Divine Liturgy of St. John Chrysostom: An Outline

### *Preparation and Gathering*

1. "Blessed is the Kingdom . . . "
2. Litany of Peace
3. Psalms and prayers

### *Service of the Word*

1. Little Entrance (procession with Gospel book to altar)
2. Hymns, Trisagion ("Holy God")
3. Psalm Verses
4. Epistle reading
5. Alleluia with psalm verses
6. Holy Gospel
7. Sermon (sometimes given at conclusion of liturgy)
8. Litany of Fervent Supplication; Litany for Catechumens (used only when catechumens are present)

### *Service of the Eucharist*

1. Cherubic Hymn and Great Entrance (procession with prepared elements through the congregation and to altar)

2. Litany, Kiss of Peace, Nicene Creed
3. Holy Anaphora (prayer of consecration): Thanksgiving to
   the Father
   Memorial of (the work of) the Son
   Epiclesis (invocation) of the Holy Spirit
4. Litany, Lord's Prayer, Prayer with Heads Bowed
5. "Breaking of the Bread," precommunion prayers
6. Holy Communion

### Postcommunion and Dismissal

1. Postcommunion hymn and Thanksgiving Prayer
2. Prayer Behind the Ambo (at the icon of Christ)
3. Blessing and Dismissal

The people come forward to venerate the blessing cross and receive antidoron (blessed, noneucharistic bread).

# GLOSSARY

*Akathist.* Service to a saint or Christ, but usually to the Theotokos, consisting of a hymn of twenty-four stanzas, often sung within Compline.

*Aposticha.* Short hymns interspersed with psalm verses sung at Vespers and daily Matins.

*Artoklasia.* Service on special occasions, usually at Vespers of a feast, in which five loaves of bread, wheat, wine, and oil are blessed; the people are then anointed with the blessed oil. The term is also applied to the loaves of bread used in this service.

*Axios.* Greek for "He is worthy," proclaimed by an ordaining bishop, to which the congregation responds with the same words.

*Bridegroom Matins.* The early morning services of the first days of Great (Holy) Week, each with its own themes, but also highlighting the image of Christ as Bridegroom, most notably in the troparion (hymn): "Behold, the Bridegroom comes at midnight. . . ." Often these services are served the evening before, "in anticipation."

*Cherubic Hymn.* Hymn sung before and at the conclusion of the Great Entrance; normally the hymn "Let us who mystically represent the cherubim . . . "

*Chotki.* See Prayer rope.

*Chrismands.* Persons about to receive the Mystery (Sacrament) of Holy Chrismation, anointing with the Holy Chrism (oil) consecrated by a bishop.

*Chrismation.* The mystery (sacrament), usually celebrated in conjunction with holy baptism, whereby the Holy Spirit is imparted to the believer through anointing with chrism, oil consecrated by a bishop.

*Communion on the spoon.* Method of communing in Orthodoxy; the priest places a portion of the Sacred Body and Blood in the mouth of the person, having removed it from the chalice with a small spoon.

*Compline.* The prayer service offered at bedtime.

*Divine Liturgy.* The eucharistic mystery (sacrament) served every Sunday and feast day, at which the local community gathers to take part in the heavenly worship of the Holy Trinity and to receive the "Body and Blood of our Lord, God, and Savior Jesus Christ."

*Dormition Fast.* The two-week fast preparatory to the Feast of the Dormition (or Falling-Asleep) of the Theotokos (August 15); one of four such fasts in the liturgical year, the others being the Nativity Fast (forty days) prior to Christmas, Great Lent, and the Apostles' Fast (length varies according to date of Pentecost) prior to Feast of Sts. Peter and Paul (June 29).

*Dunamis.* Greek word, meaning "with strength," used by the deacon to exhort the people before the third and final verse of the Trisagion Hymn ("Holy God").

*Epiklesis.* In the Divine Liturgy, the central act of consecration of the bread and wine to become the Body and Blood of Christ, invoking the Holy Spirit to make the change.

*Epistle.* Any of the New Testament writings, other than the Gospel, read at the Divine Liturgy according to the Church's cycle of readings known as the lectionary.

*Epitaphion.* Large cloth showing an icon of the dead Christ, held in his mother's arms, and usually surrounded by St. John, St. Nicodemus, and St. Joseph of Arimathea, on which is inscribed the troparion (hymn), "The Noble Joseph, taking down Thy most pure Body from the Tree, did wrap it in clean linen with sweet spices, and he laid it in a new tomb."

*Epitrachelion.* The stole of priesthood.

*Eulogetaria.* Two types of hymns having the refrain "Blessed art Thou, O Lord, teach me thy statutes," one for the departed, the other sung at Sunday Matins, with a resurrectional theme.

*Forgiveness Vespers.* The service during which the season of Great Lent begins. At the chanting of the psalm verses (prokeimenon), the priest changes his vestments from bright to somber colors and the musical tones shift to a minor key. Concluding the service is the rite of mutual forgiveness, in which believers ask for and grant forgiveness to one another for any sins committed during the previous year.

*Hieromonk.* A monk who is also a priest.

*Holy Unction.* One of the mysteries, or sacraments, of the church "for the healing of soul and body," and preparatory for participating in the most solemn services of Holy Week, including the receiving of Holy Communion on Great And Holy Thursday and on Pascha (Easter); usually served publicly on Great (Holy) Wednesday; those anointed with the consecrated (olive) oil must be prepared as for receiving Holy Communion, through prayer, fasting, and confession; the service includes seven Epistles and seven Gospels, followed by prayers.

*Jibby.* Arabic name for the full-sleeved, loose-fitting formal black cassock (robe).

*Kneeling Vespers.* Vespers of Pentecost Sunday, characterized by several lengthy prayers accompanied by the first kneeling allowed since Holy Week.

*Kontakion.* Second principal (short) hymn of the day.

*Lazarus Saturday.* Day before Palm Sunday, on which is commemorated Christ's raising of Lazarus from the dead, thus revealing Christ's mastery over death and foreshadowing his own Resurrection.

*Litia.* Procession with troparia and prayers, often followed by the Artoklasia service.

*Metania.* The profound bow accompanied by crossing oneself and touching the floor with an open hand.

*Omophorion.* Wide, outer stole worn by a bishop; also used to signify the episcopal office, as in "I am under the omophorion of Metropolitan Philip."

*Pantocrator.* Icon of Christ as "Ruler of All," often found on dome interiors over the central nave of an Orthodox church building.

*Pascha* (Greek, from Hebrew *Pesach,* or Passover). The Christian feast celebrating deliverance from bondage to death, evil, and sin, effected by the death, descent into Hades, and resurrection of Jesus Christ; in the West called Easter.

*Phelonion.* Large, capelike outer vestment worn by priests.

*Phos Hilaron.* The ancient lamp-lighting hymn of Vespers, "Gladsome Light."

*Prayer of St. Ephrem the Syrian.* The most characteristic of Orthodox Lenten Prayers, it is prayed many times privately and during services throughout Great Lent and is accompanied by bows and prostrations.

*Prayer rope* (in Russian: chotki). A circular, usually woolen, chord of knots, often one hundred, used to mark repetition of the Jesus Prayer.

*Prayer with Heads Bowed.* Prayer of supplication made while bowing toward the icon of Christ

*Prosphora.* The prayerfully made yeast bread from which a special portion (the "Lamb") is taken to be consecrated in the Divine Liturgy to be the Body of Christ. Other portions signify the Virgin

Mary, certain orders of saints and martyrs, and the living and the dead who are to be remembered before God. The remainder of the bread, called antidoron, is distributed to the faithful, and in some churches to non-Orthodox as well, as fellowship bread.

*Song of St. Simeon.* "Lord, now lettest thou Thy servant depart in peace" (Luke 2:29–32): canticle sung toward the close of Vespers.

*Staretz.* Person, usually a monk, who is sought out for spiritual fatherhood because of his sanctity and gift of guidance.

*Stichera* (pl.). Verses, usually short, sung between verses of certain psalms, notably at Vespers and Matins, that pertain to the feast or saint(s) being honored.

*Theotokos.* The single most common and most important title ascribed to the Virgin Mary. Often translated as "Mother of God," but more accurately "Birth-Giver of God," the title was given official status by the Third Ecumenical Council (Ephesus) as signifying the divine nature (as well as the human nature) of the Son she bore.

*Trisagion Hymn.* The "thrice-holy hymn" sung solemnly during the Divine Liturgy and at other services: "Holy God, Holy Mighty, Holy Immortal, have mercy on us."

*Troparion.* Generic name for several types of hymns; most often the first principal hymn of the day, called the apolytikion.

*Vespers.* The ancient evening service of the Orthodox Church, commemorating Christ as the true light, as the sun sets and the lamps are lit; also the service marking the beginning of the day, since the liturgical day starts at sunset.

*Virgin Glykophilousa.* Icon of the Theotokos in which Mother and Child are shown with faces touching in affection; often called "Sweet-Kissing Jesus."

*Virgin Hodegetria.* Icon of the Theotokos in which she is shown gesturing toward her Son Jesus; often called "She who shows the way."

*Xerophagy.* The mode of fasting that restricts food to "dry-eating": usually vegetables, raw or cooked, but without oil.

DATE DUE

DEMCO 38-297